Perfect
Happiness

SCEPTRE

Perfect Happiness

RACHEL BILLINGTON

SCEPTRE

First published in 1996 by Hodder and Stoughton
A division of Hodder Headline PLC
A Sceptre book

British Library Cataloguing in Publication Data

Billington, Rachel
    Perfect happiness
    1.English fiction – 20th century
    I.Title
    823.9'14[F]

    ISBN 0 340 67512 8

Typeset by Palimpsest Book Production Limited,
Polmont, Stirlingshire
Printed and bound in Great Britain by
Mackays of Chatham PLC, Chatham, Kent

Hodder and Stoughton
A division of Hodder Headline PLC
338 Euston Road
London NW1 3BH

For Kevin

Emma Knightley, handsome, clever and rich, with a husband whose affection for her was only equalled by her affection for him, had passed upward of a year of marriage in what may be described as perfect happiness; certainly this is how she described it to herself as she sat at her writing desk from which she had an excellent view of her father, Mr Woodhouse, taking a turn round the shrubbery on the arm of her beloved Mr Knightley.

Emma smiled as she watched them, smiled and repressed a sigh as she saw the tender way in which Mr Knightley – she would never bring herself to call him George – put his upright, manly self between the cool autumnal breeze and the frail figure of her father. Since she, herself, usually performed this daily office for her father – Mr Knightley often being occupied in the mornings when her father felt the air most conducive to good health – seldom did she have the opportunity of seeing her parent as he appeared at a distance to the objective eye.

His walking was tentative, it could not be denied, but then he had never been quick, or never since she could remember him. It was possible – Emma considered the idea from the heights of her still new stature as a wife – that his sense of himself as an invalid had stemmed from the early death of Mrs Woodhouse, causing him to distrust health.

If that were the cause – and, by his affectionate accounts of his wife, she had possessed all the vivacity, intellectual vigour and good health that any woman could wish for – then it was understandable that her adoring husband's temperament should receive a severe shock at her unexpected death; that he would never be the same, but always fearful, not just for himself, but for his daughters (Emma had an elder sister, Isabella), their husbands, Isabella's five children (soon to be six), his friends, acquaintances and, in short, the whole world, small as it was, that he inhabited.

For Mr Woodhouse, a draught from a not properly closed window was as dangerous as a wind chased from Petersburg over the snowy wastes of Siberia; a sneeze from relation or friend caused as much consternation as the plague spots in a Turkoman port; a boot only slightly damp from a walk across mown grass excited his terror to such an extent that the wearer – usually Emma, who was his nearest and dearest, although not of an especially active, energetic disposition – must submit to a hot mustard bath and constant enquiries as to her temperature.

All this Emma had known since she was a child and such was her love for her father, so fond was she of him, that she had thought of it as illustrating the kindness of his heart rather than as any weakness of character. But that had been before her marriage.

Making no more pretence to write her letter – it was to be a note to mark the birthday of her eldest nephew, Henry, who was with his family, in London – she once again contemplated the two figures so closely adjoined in the pathway. They had now turned and were directly facing her, although they were seen some way off and the sunlight in their faces would have precluded them from any view of Emma.

Ah, indeed! thought Emma, it is the contrast that makes me uneasy. But this was too dangerous a way of thinking and must be quelled instantly. Yet, as is often the case, this little acknowledgement of unease led on to a much graver one for, as she watched her father with the same fond eyes that had put him first all her life; that had, indeed, insisted that she could never leave his side and thus brought her husband from his home at Donwell Abbey into her home of Hartfield, she found herself wondering how long he, Mr Woodhouse, an avowed invalid, would live.

It was a terrible thought for a daughter to have about her father, so terrible, so utterly filled with vice that she disowned it at once, clanged shut the door into her heart that had revealed such grimacing horror, and, in a moment, was smiling once more into the sunny garden and thinking, with all contentment, how wonderful it was that her strong Mr Knightley, so much outdoors with his farm business, such a powerful walker that it needed all her wiles to persuade him into using the carriage, should yet so comfortably subdue his step to fit her father's. He did it, she knew, not only out of his love for her or even out of his respect for his father-in-law but because he truly loved her father. He had told her so; and Mr Knightley never lied.

Emma dropped her eyes to her paper, now adorned with blobs of ink resembling some fantastic beast. Another thought, as misshapen as the ink, appeared irrepressible in her mind. Why was it that the more patient, kind, understanding, candid, Mr Knightley showed himself to her father, the more uneasy, restless and unsympathetic she herself became? Why, in the face of such goodness, was she tempted to become bad?

Scrumpling the paper with a frown, Emma stood up briskly; she would go and meet the two people she loved most in the world and join their pleasure in each other's company with her own delight in theirs. She was on the point of summoning her maid to bring shawl and hat when the girl herself appeared, holding a letter which had that moment been brought to the door.

Seeing at once it was from the very household, that of her sister, to whom she should have been writing, Emma sat back down on her seat again and broke the seal to the envelope. First, however, she noted with satisfaction that Mr Knightley and her father had turned their backs to her and were started on their second turn round the shrubbery. News from his eldest daughter, whether good, bad or of no real account, was equally capable of arousing Mr Woodhouse's fears – as if change itself was threat – so Emma was in the habit of first apprising herself of such information as Henry's little successes at school or baby Emma's new tooth; and then gradually passing it on to her father.

For her, to the contrary, news from outside the house of Hartfield where her days passed so quietly, was always exciting and as eagerly read as a romance. Emma, whose fertile imagination had become very active, as if to compensate for an uneventful life, seldom admitted herself disappointed with even the dullest material. On this occasion, however, she had no need to use any exceptional powers, and, as she read, her mobile face expressed consternation, shock and something most like disbelief. Her youthfully clear skin changed from pink to pale to pink and finally – as tears started in her eyes – to a pallor from which all colour had drained. Indeed, it almost looked as if she must faint, so shocking to her were the contents of the letter.

But Emma was no weakling and soon she had wiped her eye with her little embroidered kerchief and, with a more resolute expression, picked up the letter once more.

My dearest Emma, I take up a pen to write to you as soon as I could free myself from my poor little Emma – who is feverish and needs the nursing of her mama. I feel it my duty to tell you the sad news as soon as possible – in part because you will be sure to hear it from those unhappy people at Randalls and it will be easier for all of you if you have it already and can be preparing to give comfort where it most surely will be needed.

You may wonder why it is I and not my dear John writing to you or to Mr Knightley – but John has been away some days now and when the letter came from Mr Churchill I felt obliged to open a missive that was obviously delivered in urgency. You will, of course, convey everything – this letter whole – to your Mr Knightley for he is such a man as will always help in a case like this.

But I must come to the point of what I have to tell or my little dear will call me away. In short, Jane Fairfax – or Mrs Churchill as she has been for nearly a year now – gave birth to a baby boy, five days gone now and – although the baby is strong and healthy and called Frank – after his father – the mother – poor Jane – contracted a high fever which, barely twenty-four hours later, took her away. I understand she has been delicate, even sickly, since her marriage and – perhaps, you will know the circumstances of this better than I – rather before. But it has nevertheless come as a completely unlooked-for shock to the Churchill family.

Mr Churchill wrote that Frank Churchill is almost out of his mind; that, indeed, is the reason for writing to me who knows him so little. Mr Churchill hopes – through me – to contact the Campbells who treated Jane so long as a daughter. He feels that they may be the best people to influence his son into a greater calmness. But they – as always at this time of year – are with their daughter, Mrs Dixon, in Ireland. Poor old man, he was intending to avoid laying the burden of Frank on the Westons when Mrs Weston is likely to be soon herself – indisposed – nor did he wish to cause more grief than was necessary to our dear old friends, Miss Bates and Mrs Bates. The loss of their beloved niece, their granddaughter is enough—

At this point, Emma put down the dreadful letter, although it still had another page or two to run. She was struck, not by the easy emotion of surprised horror, as on her first reading, but by a deeper sense of what this would mean to her particular circle of friends.

Frank Churchill, although brought up by his uncle whose name he took, was her own dear Mrs Weston's son-in-law; Mrs Weston who before she married Frank's widowed father had been first Emma's governess and then her closest friend. Mr and Mrs Weston both worshipped Frank as if his imperfections – of which she, Emma, knew more than most – were virtues. Jane Fairfax – a true daughter of Highbury, although brought up by the Campbells since the age of nine – was the centre of joy and happiness in the little Bates' household which had nothing much else of comfort. Mrs Bates was old and infirm, they lived in a narrow house in Highbury which, for reasons Emma had never understood, they had continued to inhabit, even after Jane had married the inheritor of a large fortune.

At least the Westons had each other, a new young family since Mrs Weston was expecting again; for the Bates, however, Jane was everything – and now they had nothing.

Emma was aroused by this depressing picture of the Bates's future – which would surely affect her father deeply since Mrs Bates and Miss Bates dined at their table more than once in a fortnight – by a tear dropping from her eye on to the letter so that it reduced the word Frank to a small lake.

Frank she would not think of. She had been glad that he and Jane had spent their time between London and

Yorkshire, only once visiting the Westons at Randalls and then for but a day. She would not enter into Frank's suffering. That was beyond her.

With a stern expression on her still pale face, Emma looked up and saw her husband but a few feet away, staring at her intently. The sun had come round and now he could see her through the glass of the window and his face showed all the loving anxiety of a man who sees that his wife is sad but cannot that very instant, as he would like, take her in his arms and smooth out the trouble with caresses.

Oh how Emma loved him in that moment, as she saw, fully revealed, his love for her! And how conscious was she, too, of the peacefulness that this terrible letter had come to rupture. How quiet they had been together! How good to each other! Gone now were the shades of restlessness. Tragedy had restored calm in her breast.

2 ∫

Mr Knightley was ever deliberate in his behaviour. For him were written the lines by Mr Lovelace: 'I could not love thee, dear, so much, lov'd I not honour more.' He took Mr Woodhouse on his third turn about the shrubbery with as much attention as if he were not aching to be beside his Emma, holding her pretty smooth hand and asking her, with all devotion, 'What is it, my dearest, that has made you so troubled?'

Indeed, it took a full half-hour for Mr Knightley to complete the final turn in the shrubbery and settle Mr Woodhouse in his favourite chair in the drawing-room, with the book he most preferred falling asleep over; only then did Knightley allow himself to come to his wife and ask her that question.

By that time Emma had endeavoured to calm herself by taking up her sewing in the cosy little parlour they had made upstairs all for themselves; the moment Knightley held her little hands clasped in his big strong ones and looked so closely into her face that she could see every beloved line and wrinkle and the little greying at his temples, she burst out weeping – 'It is too bad! Too terrible!'

'Oh, my dearest' – gravely. 'What can such a passion mean? Not Isabella? The children?'

'No! No! It is not that.' Emma took the letter from her bosom and gave it over, somewhat damp and crumpled.

'A letter – Ah – So you were reading it when I saw you through the window?'

'Yes. Yes,' cried Emma impatiently, even in her sorrow noticing how Mr Knightley had delayed coming to her. 'Read it and see if it is not a dreadful thing.'

Hesitating no longer – for he had only waited till her tears had ceased to fall and now he could see she was more herself – Mr Knightley took the letter to the window where he stood quietly reading.

Emma found that the very sight of her husband taking command of this terrible news had made her heart beat less excitedly. He would make everything easy – or as easy as anything could be in such circumstances. She had perfect reliance on him.

'My dear, this is sad news indeed.'

'So young!' cried Emma; as she spoke she pictured Jane Fairfax, her colourless clear skin always like mother of pearl and so unlike her own rosy-cheeked health. She pictured Jane's slender fingers flying over the keys of the pianoforte with an execution that none could match in Highbury and certainly far exceeded any talent that she, Emma, could boast of. Jane had always excelled in everything, education, elegance, even – now she had gone for ever Emma could admit it – beauty.

'Her life has not found the happiness she deserved.'

'Deserved?' Emma looked up suddenly. 'Does one deserve happiness?'

'Goodness. Virtue. Does it not deserve happiness?'

This was a more philosophical approach than Emma had expected from Mr Knightley and she found herself crying out with a voice that shocked her by its petulance, 'Oh, sir, I believe Jane Fairfax was made for tragedy. And now she brings her own tragedy to break our peaceful lives!'

'Oh, Emma! Emma!' Knightley came back to her immediately and held her so close that she could feel his warmth. 'Nothing will break. It is a tragedy indeed; but such things must happen and let us not forget the baby is alive and well. In their sorrow, her relations – Mr and Mrs Weston, Mrs Bates, Miss Bates – will have a baby to dote on; there has been a death, certainly, but a birth also.'

'Oh, you are so good!' This was the Mr Knightley Emma loved, who could put everything to rights, tell her how to think and behave. 'I had almost forgot the baby, little Frank. Of course a healthy boy will go at least some way to softening the loss of the mother.'

Mr Knightley found himself near smiling at the eagerness with which Emma snatched at the chance of a mitigation of general unhappiness. It was in her nature, part of her youthfulness, for she was nearly seventeen years younger than him. While he understood that tragedies occurred and were borne with as well as possible, if not forgot, day by day, absorbed into other happier states until their outlines were blurred, she must take up one position or another, see either tragedy or joy, sorrow or delight. It was a decisiveness in her which he both admired her for and feared. Yet if the image of the baby made her more able to sustain this news, made her stronger for her father, for her dear friend Mrs Weston and the Bates's, all of whom would certainly rely on her for sympathy and comfort, then his mention of the Churchill son and heir had been a happy choice.

'We cannot rejoice,' said Mr Knightley, 'the circumstances are too sad for that; but we can, at least, allow that our mourning must finish – and that there is a future to which the Churchill family can look forward.'

'A second Frank Churchill.' Emma spoke and paused; although she looked up at her husband, he, too, said nothing. His face was calm, serious, even stern. 'We must pity Frank Churchill,' said Emma, casting her eyes down to her fingers, twined about with her handkerchief.

'We must. His devotion to his wife was the best thing about him.' There was another silence during which Emma tried not to recall certain improprieties in the past with regard to her association with Frank Churchill – but failed. Blessed with the gift of seeing herself in a good light whenever possible, she was also in possession of an excellent memory which sometimes put obstacles in the way of the smooth operation of the first blessing. There had been a time when she had thought herself close to Frank, when he had made her think so.

'We will not be able to avoid sharing in Mr Frank Churchill's distress, I have no doubt,' added Mr Knightley in a clipped tone quite unlike that he had used before. 'I think I am right in saying that Mr Churchill's letter was written out of a deep concern over his son's behaviour. That poor old man has had much to put up with. But we need not concern ourselves with such things immediately. I must ride to Donwell where I have business; every day I miss old William Larkins more; on the way back I will call in on the Westons and the Bates to see if they have yet heard the news. You, meanwhile, dearest Emma,' here he bent and stroked her hair, smoothing lovingly the escaping curls, 'you must compose yourself – as best you can – for no purpose will be served by your father discovering this too early. Let him be in peace a little longer and I will return to you before dinner.'

Mr Knightley was gone; no further kiss or caress. This was the man Emma had chosen to love, the best man in the world, one she had known all her life and had always looked up to her as the arbiter of everything good – everything good in her. To please him had always been her pleasure, for when she went against him as being a spoilt and headstrong girl and prone to taking her own way

– as she had sometimes done – it had invariably turned out for the worst. Marriage to him was a safe harbour. Now, as he had ordained, she would compose herself, take up her sewing, and prepare to face her father when he woke so that he should not guess a thing.

But human nature is not so easily ruled. Emma had scarcely put more than three not very regular stitches into her cambric when she threw down the little square and jumped to her feet. 'It is impossible to sit here when such things have happened which so concern those we love!' she thought to herself incoherently. 'It is all very well for Knightley to leap on his horse and gallop off to Donwell but how can he expect me to sit here quietly? I would have to be made of stone to behave in such a way!'

With such thoughts racing and her heart starting up again with as much vigour as Knightley's horse's hoofs beat the ground, Emma rang for her maid and then for Mr Woodhouse's servant. From one she ordered her coat and hat and commanded her company on the walk into town; to the other she was more specific: 'Inform your master – if he should awake – that I have gone to Ford's to buy a new ribbon for my cap; and that I have taken Merry with me; and that I shall return directly!'

'Yes, ma'am.'

'That will not alarm dear papa a scrap,' thought Emma with satisfaction as she speedily tied the surprisingly new ribbon on her bonnet and did up the buttons of her jacket. 'The very triviality of my errand will set his mind at ease; for he can think of me as a silly girl who must haste to shop when the new stuff is in. He will await my return anxiously, certainly, but not with the sense that anything is especially wrong.'

'Now, Merry!' she said out loud, for the girl was dull and stood with her hands dangling. 'Carry an umbrella with you because it looks as if the sun is not so securely outside of the clouds as it was this morning.'

So mistress and maid set out briskly from Hartfield, down the driveway which was bordered by high chestnuts, and on to the land which led to the inhabited part of Highbury. Indeed, a spectator who did not know the sad circumstances of her visit – for Emma was resolved to see her dear old friends, the Bates's – mother and daughter – might have taken her bright face, in which the rosy colour was fully restored, and elastic step as indication of a light heart and a cheerful disposition.

Such a spectator, however, would have had to admit his mistake when he overheard the large sighs emitted by the young lady, accompanied by such doleful words as, 'In truth, this is a sad mission I am on, Merry, and one in which only a strong sense of duty encourages me forward.'

'Yes, ma'am,' agreed Merry, attempting to make her own looks suitably echo her mistress's sentiments, although her imagination, such as it was, was much taken by thoughts of the ribbons in Ford's shop.

3 ʃ

A strong autumnal wind, only partially revealed in the Hartfield shrubbery, made Emma's arrival in the centre of town an occasion of relief.

Although she had never endured a day's illness – apart from the usual childish ailments – Mr Woodhouse's acute fears for his daughter's safety had inevitably limited her taste for exercise. It would be a cruel heart that made a father suffer for too great boldness; so Emma had grown up to believe even the short walk to Ford's – a small general draper but the centre of much activity – quite long enough. She always arrived with a sense of achievement, a little out of breath, her senses heightened enough to make it pleasurable.

On this occasion she arrived with a great deal more reason for glowing cheeks and beating heart; for not only was there the possibility of meeting those who were undergoing all the pain of recent bereavement, but she could also no longer disguise from herself that she was acting in direct opposition to Mr Knightley's most carefully stated wishes. Oh, if she had only stayed to think a little longer! She had acted improperly – hastily – foolishly!

What if – horrible thought – Mr Woodhouse heard the news from some other source – quite likely in a place as small as Highbury – and she was away from home! She could hardly bear to contemplate how he might react. And then – more inevitable still – for had Knightley not said that he would, himself, visit the Westons and the Bates's – was the chance that she would come face to face with her husband. This fear which, once they had entered town, made Emma turn every time she heard a horse's hoof on the cobbles, threw her into such confusion that she stood with her hand on the knob to the door of Ford's shop, without finding the power to turn it. Oh, that she could fly back to Hartfield and be safely in her chair with her needlework in her lap and her father in the room below her!

'Miss Woodhouse. Good morning to you. I may dare to guess you have walked in on such a blustery day on an errand of mercy.'

Emma turned to the respectful nods of a middle-aged man who had come upon her unawares; he was a man better known at Hartfield than almost any other, Mr Perry – Mr Woodhouse's doctor.

'Oh, Mr Perry. I—' Emma, confused, could hardly speak.

'Perhaps you are resting a moment, preparing yourself before you go to Miss Bates. They have taken it very ill, very ill indeed. You will not see poor Mrs Bates, I make certain. I have just come from her. She will not leave her room, her bed. I am in some fear for her. But a visitor – such as you – at this time – will be felt an honour, a consolation. You may see neither of the ladies but the walk you have made – the blustery weather – not waiting for a carriage – they will be honoured. Their spirits, so low, still must be sensible of such attention from such a one as you.'

As Mr Perry made the speech – he who was not usually so loquacious but, perhaps felt that the gravity of the situation deserved many words – Emma tried to order her thoughts. It seemed that the doctor was commending her for her action. In her distress at risking her father's death (he would talk of it so) and crossing her husband – above all, she hated to displease Mr Knightley – Emma had almost forgotten the tragedy which had caused her to take her walk. But Mr Perry's lingering words brought it before her again and a ready tear started in her eye. Perhaps it had not been so wrong to come, after all, whatever Knightley might think.

With Merry behind, still casting unrequited looks at Ford's window, and Mr Perry at her side, Emma proceeded with more tranquillity to the Bates's place of abode. At their door Mr Perry bowed and left and Emma was about to knock when she was addressed by another male voice.

'Miss Woodhouse! You are here before me!'

Blushing with vexation, Emma turned once more to see the Reverend Mr Elton close behind. There was a time when she had thought of this man, still young, good-looking, as fit company for her evenings, but that had led to a misinterpretation that still caused her pain and, since his marriage to a Miss Augusta Hawkins and hers to Mr Knightley, there had been avoidance on both sides. Yet here he was, confidently hailing her.

'Good morning, Mr Elton,' she said quietly, with a distinct frown.

'You are going in?'

Emma decided that needed no answer. Why else would she have her foot on the doorstep?

'It is appropriate on these occasions that the representative of Christ in our midst should do whatever he may to alleviate suffering. Suffering in such a case is heavy. Our human condition makes it so. Our passions lead us into the temptation of temporal attachment which only true spirituality can counter. I shall go up and do what I may but I am not sanguine. Mrs Bates has not attended church for more than a year.'

'Mrs Bates is old,' defended Emma, driven to speech.

'Miss Bates has not such an excuse.'

'Miss Bates cannot leave Mrs Bates.'

'Do not think that their absence from my church shall forfeit their right to any comfort I may afford them. I am not so harsh. However, there are those who think well enough of my Sunday testaments to copy them down. Such words can, I am assured, be a consolation in times of distress.'

Again Emma was silent. She was struck by the worsening of the arrogance in Mr Elton's manner which she put down to the vulgar influence of Mrs Elton. They had both been prone to make a great fuss of Jane Fairfax before her marriage and departure from Highbury. Yet she could see no trace of unhappiness in his behaviour, only pomposity and self-satisfaction. It struck her further that her last wish in the world would be to visit poor old Miss Bates in the company of Mr Elton, representative of Christ on earth or not.

'Please do me the favour of conveying my condolences to Mrs Bates and Miss Bates, Mr Elton. As you say, you are more fitted – more practised – for such a task. I shall visit them at a later date – when your spiritual comforting has soothed the grief following the loss of such an altogether virtuous, dutiful and beloved granddaughter and niece!'

With such ringing words, Emma flashed on her heel and started so fast down the road that Merry had to run to catch her up. Mr Elton was left standing, feeling vaguely put down, although not quite certain why. Assuming a face of deepest sympathy – which in his case meant contorting his smooth cheerful face as if he were sucking a cough drop – he slowly raised the knocker and brought it down with one solemn gong as if God himself had come to call on the two sorrowing ladies. They, unlike Mrs Knightley, had no way of avoiding him.

Emma, meanwhile, was still flying along although the wind, now against her, made progress difficult. 'If I hurry,' she was thinking to herself, 'I may be back well before Knightley and, though of course I shall tell him I have been out – for if I did not, dear papa would – he will not be so cross when he sees me safely back and papa comfortable and no harm done. He may even commend me for my sensibility, if not my good sense.'

Unluckily for such sanguine hopes, Emma did not allow, in her haste, for the danger of over-strained ankles, a nervous lack of proper attention and a deep, partly hidden, rut in the lane. One moment she was up, the strings of her bonnet stretched out behind her in the wind, like the tail of a kite, and the next minute, she was down, sitting heavily in the dirt. She sprang to her feet at once but the twinge in her ankle was so sharp that even Merry's strong arm was not enough to support her forward.

'Oh, Merry, and we are so near home!' cried Emma, her anger with the way things had turned out greater than any pain. 'We have nothing else to do but to summon James to bring the carriage.'

'Yes, ma'am. But should I leave you here on your own, ma'am?' asked the girl doubtfully.

This was a dilemma indeed; but soon solved as the sound of horse's hoofs was heard coming from the direction of Randalls in which house Mr and Mrs Weston lived. With a mixture of relief and anxiety, Emma knew it could be no one but Knightley on his way back from his visit. It was clear that he had not gone into town at all. Oh, what foolishness had led her to this moment! When all her energies should have led her to help others, now she herself would need the helping!

4

'You have had a fortunate escape,' pronounced Mr Knightley later that evening as he and Emma prepared themselves for sleep. 'You are young; Mr Perry makes certain your ankle is only slightly twisted. It will recover in a day or two. But, tell me, why did you feel such urgency in visiting the Bates? If you had wanted to pay a visit, then Mrs Weston would have been more natural an object as your far greater friend.'

How to explain? Emma could not – because she did not know the reason herself. She remembered feeling stifled in her little parlour. Why else? She scarcely wanted to think further – with all turning out so much less badly than she had feared.

Mr Woodhouse, quite to his daughter's astonishment, had accepted the death of Mrs Churchill with an equanimity bordering on hard-heartedness. 'She was of sickly disposition,' was his immediate judgement. 'I remember her, pale as a ghost, liable to every infection. Such women should not get married. I have said so often enough. Or – if I have not said so – I have thought so. You, Emma, my dear, are of quite a different constitution; besides, you have not been brought up as she was, cooped up in a little room, with the worst of everything, draughts, without fresh air—'

Here Emma had intervened to protest that from the age of nine, when she had been removed from the Bates's,

Jane had been very well looked after in Colonel Campbell's household. But Mr Woodhouse had allowed no such fact to intervene between the consolation that perceiving Mrs Churchill in perfect sickness and his daughter in perfect health afforded him. 'You, Emma, have not only had the benefit of Perry since you were a child but also the tender care of poor Miss Taylor – before her marriage to Mr Weston – and now the attentions of our dear Mr Knightley. On your account – even though you will walk when you should take out the carriage – I am sanguine. Curb your fondness for an open window and—'

'Papa!' Emma would have defended herself against such a heinous accusation but discretion taught her otherwise. 'You may order James and the carriage for me whenever you please, papa,' this said meekly; and then dinner had been announced and all else forgotten in Mr Woodhouse's anxiety at Cook's over-liberal use of butter.

'So, Emma, why did you dash off to Highbury?' Mr Knightley, his good, kind face turned towards her on the pillow of their bed, waited for an answer to his unanswerable question.

'Oh, do you not remember our walking by the sea at Weymouth!' It was not an answer but it acted as a diversion, whether Emma meant it to be such.

Knightley's features softened. 'Those two weeks were the happiest of my life.'

'But now – here – don't you some times feel confin'd?'

'Confin'd? – Oh, no. I am too occupied' – this said kindly, without reproach. 'Dearest Emma,' his strong fingers reached out to touch her cheeks, her brow, her soft mouth, now quivering a little with emotion. 'How could I feel confin'd in any way that I should not enjoy when I am with you? I am your captive – I never thought to be so blessed as I am – your love still fills me with wonder. Oh, my dear, dear Emma, I wonder if you realise—'

Here he stopped quite abruptly, as if he must not say too much; but he had already said enough to content Emma and for her to accept his kisses with a sweet mix of modesty and eagerness.

It was perhaps reprehensible that in their happiness neither let the tragic news of their friend's death so recently received darken the end of the day. Yet, just before they slept, Mr Knightley murmured a few words which showed that the sad event was not forgotten – in one part of his mind, at least.

'You called him the child of good fortune,' were his words, only half heard by the sleepy Emma, only half understood.

Yet the next morning when the sun, coming through the light curtains, woke her, she remembered them at once; they rang in her ears. 'The child of good fortune' was how she had described Frank Churchill in those days when they were close. Frank had subsequently written it in a letter to Mrs Weston which Mr Knightley had read. He had not liked it then; how sadly it sounded now!

Emma put out her hand to feel the space beside her in the bed; cold, as always. Knightley left so early that she was still in too deep a sleep to hear him go. Lazily, Emma sat up and rang for Merry. How was her foot? she wondered, moving it gingerly under the bedclothes. Hardly a twinge. She was the child of good fortune.

'I will wear my sprigged muslin with the blue shawl,' began Emma and then thought again of the day ahead. Today she must not be so cheerful, for Knightley had suggested that she see poor unhappy Mrs Weston. 'No, Merry, I have changed my mind. The plain green and the white shawl.' That would show respect, without being too drab on such a bright morning.

The maid went, returned, while Emma sat on the side of the bed, idly turning between her hands the cap she had just taken from her head. What was it about that ordinary nightcap, white frilled muslin, which suddenly brought Jane Fairfax before Emma, with all her seriousness, her charms, her elegance? Perhaps it was the delicacy, the pallor of the material, but suddenly Emma was cast into a passion of weeping. 'Oh, Jane, Jane – how can you have passed like this! Oh! Oh! I never behaved to you as a friend! I never truly liked you! And now it is all over! All too late!'

Merry, coming in to see her mistress so distraught, was ready to call Mr Perry in another moment. But as fast as the passion had risen, it had abated. Cold water splashed on the face was accompanied by good resolutions. 'Jane Churchill is gone but there are others left behind. To them I shall be the best friend that ever breathed.'

Fortified by the sense of virtue in prospect, Emma descended to breakfast with her father in her usual cheerful manner so he could not suspect that, just fifteen minutes before, she was sobbing as if her heart would break. He was glad to see her looking bright for he had news for her that she would not like.

'My dear, 'tis a sad business when husband and wife must be separated – and for such a place as London. But Mr Knightley would be off—'

'Papa, what is it you have to tell me? I assure you I am strong this morning.'

'Personally, I do not believe anything is worth the journey to London – and you, my dear, have managed your life without it very well – would you not say?'

'Yes, papa' – in agreement but with mounting impatience. 'Are you trying to inform me that Knightley has left for London?'

'It is true, against my advice, an hour ago. He did not wish to disturb you from your sleep after such a day as yesterday.'

'And when will he return?'

'Not today, I think.'

'But London is only sixteen miles and he is a quick rider with a good horse. I assume he has not walked?' Emma attempted an injection of playfulness, although her heart had sunk at the news. No Knightley for a whole day! Perhaps more – and just when her spirits needed his calming presence.

'It is on Mr Weston's behalf he is gone. That is why I could not object more strongly. Poor Mrs Weston in her condition – Mr Weston could not think of leaving her himself. So I could not object too far, indeed I could not, although they say a sharp sun in the morning means rain before gloaming—'

'But why has he gone, papa?' asked Emma who had certain suspicions.

'I have already told you. He has gone to search for Mr Weston's son – his natural son, Mr Churchill, and send him back to Yorkshire, where he should be. It is all most unfortunate. And we are the sufferers – you and I – such a disturbance – so early – and not knowing when he will return. I don't know how you will bear it—'

Mr Woodhouse's ignorance of his daughter's strong will went unnoticed by Emma who soothed her father with a solicitude practised over many years. But as soon as he was comfortable and, finding she had no appetite for breakfast, she removed herself to her little parlour – despised as 'stifling' the day before but now seen as a haven of solitude and peace.

Here she could think of Knightley's mission in all its strangeness – as it seemed to her; for of all men Knightley had least respect or affection for Mr Churchill, yet here he was setting out as his saviour – from whatever evils even Emma's fertile imagination could not imagine. But there would be evils where Frank was concerned, she was sure of that. He had proved himself, to her, a liar and a hypocrite.

She believed that it was only Jane – clever, beautiful, fragile Jane – who could have kept him straight. Now his suffering must be great indeed! His temptation to fall away from the proper path, proportionately greater. He had no strength of character, she was sure of that too, but would, at all times, choose the easiest path. Oh, if Mr Knightley could only find him in time! Before – before . . .

Emma could not quite complete her thoughts as they whirled through her agitated mind; but she was so far from attending to the ordinary domestic sounds of the house that Merry had to knock twice before her mistress bade her enter.

'Mrs Weston is downstairs, ma'am.'

Mrs Weston here! And she had neither finished dressing nor interviewed Sterne, the cook, about last evening's stale apple pie which she had promised herself to do before anything. Yet Mrs Weston must not be kept waiting a second more than was necessary.

'Oh, my dear! My dear!' Both ladies were in tears as soon as they met and clasped each other close.

'Now, we must not cry.' Mrs Weston recovered first. 'It is too tragic for that. I said to Mr Weston, no fainting, no hysterics, no crying, just arrangements. But arrangements, I believe, are the very worst of it.' Despite her own advice, Mrs Weston was forced to put her handkerchief to her eye again. 'He is so overcome, poor man, so utterly distraught.'

'Tell me,' said Emma when her friend had recovered a little, 'where is Mr Frank Churchill gone?'

'That is why I have come. I thought it wrong to take Mr Knightley from you without explaining the circumstances. But, to answer your question, we hardly know where poor Frank is, except that he is reported seen in London. Mr Knightley plans to stay with his brother and find out what he can from there.'

'Is Mr Churchill not in his own house in London?'

'That is shut up, for poor Jane had wanted the baby to be born in Yorkshire and she had prevailed on Frank to be with her. Oh, Emma, you can imagine how Mr Weston feels – to be a grandfather for the first time in such tragic circumstances. It is no wonder he is incapable.'

At this, Emma saw the truth of the case. Mr Weston, a kind-hearted man but not of strong disposition, had passed on his responsibility to one he knew possessed the virtues he himself lacked. It was not all out of consideration for his wife's condition, as Mr Knightley had kindly let it be thought. Emma's heart swelled in pride at being the wife of such a man as Knightley who would take so much trouble over a man he truly disliked. It was for love of her that he had done it – and out of duty, of course. His sense of duty was ever strong.

'He will find him, be assured. But then what will follow? Frank will never stay content with old Mr Churchill and the baby – indeed, what of the baby? Who will look after the baby?'

This aspect of the case had not much presented itself to Emma so far; but now, reminded, in part, by her friend's own condition, she thought of it with dismay.

It was clear from Mrs Weston's heavy sigh that she had much considered little Frank Churchill's fate. 'Dear Emma, we will not talk of that yet. It is too soon. The baby will stay in Yorkshire with his nurse. But, as you can imagine, it would be my greatest joy if my dear Mr Weston's grandchild could join our own little nursery. But time must pass. The baby is not yet a week old.'

At the thought of the poor, motherless baby who had not much of a father at present either, both ladies had to clasp each other again, and weep a little more.

This time Emma recovered first for she, after all, had no intimate knowledge of babies and therefore somewhat less vivid a picture of little Frank's abandoned state and the motherly caresses he was foregoing. 'I am so glad Mr Knightley has gone. I shall bear his absence with patience. Perhaps, if he is still not returned, tomorrow, we shall dine together.'

'Oh! And I have quite forgot to ask about your ankle!'

'It is nothing. I was on my way back from—' but here Emma paused and a flush crossed her cheeks, because she did not wish to pronounce the word 'Bates'.

'The Bates's!' Mrs Weston had too many anxieties to try and fathom the blush. 'They were so grateful for your message. Their misery is acute. But we must not talk of them now or we shall find ourselves in tears again and my little Anna will wonder what has become of me.'

'Yes. You must go. But I shall call the carriage.'

'No, Emma. It is too short a distance.'

'Not in your condition. And look, papa foretold right – the sun is turned to black cloud.'

'It is but half a mile. I will be back before James can bring round the horses.'

'I will not be denied.'

In such heartfelt arguments – very usual at Hartfield – the visit, with all its drama and unhappiness, ended. Mrs Weston prevailed – but only because James could not be found. The two friends parted, although not before promising to speak as soon as there was any news or, indeed, if there were no news.

Emma, pleasantly conscious of having provided the best of husbands to soften the Westons' unhappiness, went to the kitchen. There she gave Sterne a hearty lecture on the over-use of soft apples and the under-use of bottled plums which was received in silence, giving Emma some hope, if not certainty, that her advice would be followed.

From there, she proceeded to her father, determined to devote the rest of the day to him, for she could not but value the calmness of her family condition when she compared it to what Mr Knightley must face in London. At least he would stay with John and Isabella and bring back news of them.

So Emma's day passed quietly. Night fell without the return of Mr Knightley and Emma went upstairs to her bedroom without the usual comfort of a devoted husband. They had not been parted in the year of their marriage and solitude felt strange, the room full of shadows, the bed bigger and cool.

She went to sleep, eventually, however, and might have slept on till morning – Emma was as heavy a sleeper as any young and healthy person – had not a sharp noise outside her window wakened her, thereby, incidentally, proving well-founded Mr Woodhouse's suspicions that she pushed up the casement even on cool nights.

Perhaps Emma's sleep had not been so sound that night because she was over by the curtains remarkably quickly and peering out into the garden. A moon, bright enough, though made crazy by a gauzy film of clouds, illuminated the well-known paths and shrubs. Nothing else was visible; nothing at all, although Emma had such faith in her ears that she sat until her feet were quite cold.

The cloud thickened under her gaze so that the moon hardly shed more light than a taper. She was just turning to return to her bed when, out of the corner of her eye, she thought she saw a figure. But it was too quick, too shadowy, for certainty and then the sky was entirely black and the garden too.

Giving up her watch – if it were the Highbury turkey thief come back, then he was clever to come in Mr Knightley's absence – she hurried back to bed and pulled the clothes right over her head. Morning would be soon enough for any further investigations.

5

The next morning, the weather was cold, blustery and wet, as if winter were trying to shorten the golden charms of autumn. At midday a message was brought for Emma from Mr Knightley. He informed her in a short note that he would be remaining in London at least another couple of days since he would take the opportunity to do some business, long overdue.

The tone was warm but not containing enough of either regret or information for his abandoned wife; he only mentioned Frank Churchill as far as to say that he had not yet found him – which was hardly kind to Emma's excitable curiosity – and made no inquiry about the injured ankle. (The ankle was perfectly recovered but he was not to know that.) 'It will be luck if we are not all to be murdered in our beds,' thought Emma, remembering afresh her adventure of the night before. It was vexing, too, that she had no one with whom to share such a story since she did not dare arouse her father's ready fears. In truth, daylight had lessened her belief in the existence of a shadowy figure but that did not alter her sense of grievance that 'business' should keep Mr Knightley from her. If she had been given even a whiff of the gaming dens or dark alleys where Mr Knightley was forced to go in his search for the tragic widower, then, at least, she would have something to make the day less dull.

But dull it had to be; no intercourse with anybody beyond her father and no prospect of it if the weather continued so bad.

'You are inattentive, my dear,' commented Mr Woodhouse as he sat with his daughter over a game of backgammon. They had finished dinner and there were several long hours to be filled before tea and bed.

Emma frowned, quite startled; she presumed on her father's thinking her perfect and this 'inattention' was as near criticism as she had ever heard him make. It forced her to realise how much she had come to rely on Knightley for the entertainment and well-being of her father.

'You are not feeling unwell, I hope, my dear?' continued Mr Woodhouse, with rising anxiety.

'No. No. I am in very good health, papa,' Emma spoke warmly, a flush of guilt across her face. 'I was merely distracted by the thought of Knightley – where he may be, as we sit so comfortably here.'

'Where he is?' cried Mr Woodhouse, voice rising, 'But surely we know where he is. He is – with poor dear Isabella and Mr John Knightley. He is with your sister and his brother. There can be no reason there for you to be unsettled, I trust?'

The question at the end of his sentence convinced Emma that the matter was serious and a bowl of the gruel Mr Woodhouse found the most beneficial drink in the world, and everybody else the most disgusting, must be ordered at once. She was just outside the room, having felt a restless need to give the order in person, when a small commotion occurred and Mr Weston, coat-tails flapping, was blown in through the front door. This was a welcome diversion, indeed. But he met Emma's smiling countenance with a frown quite unusual for one usually so easy and good-humoured.

'My dear Mrs Knightley, Emma. I cannot stay. I must return at once. Poor Mrs Weston is not well – hardly ill at all, she would say – but I insist she stay quiet – her condition – the news—'

'Is there any news?' whispered Emma, hoping to avoid her father's hearing. 'Mr Knightley has told me none.'

'Nothing further. It is just the slightest cold – no fever – but, under the circumstances, I shall keep her inside – such a wind blowing, such rain. You would not wish to visit, I make certain – but do not do so – tranquillity, the company of baby Anna – Mrs Weston is a practical woman.'

Emma had never seen Mr Weston so talkative in such a depressed manner and began to wonder if his protestations concealed greater illness than he described; however a close examination proved that Mrs Weston had nothing worse than a slight cold but that her husband was increasing her ill-health by the sum of his own general anxieties. It was natural enough and doubtless the rest would do Mrs Weston good. Yet, as Emma bid him good-night and watched the draught caused by his departure eddy round the hallway, before daring to open the door to the room where her father sat, she thought – with a selfishness she could not control – that now one more of her small circle was taken from her and tomorrow would be as tedious as today.

In this gloomy mood, the rest of the evening and the long night – without moonlight, without lurking apparitions – and with only the gusting wind to keep her company, passed by for Emma.

But she was young, her depression not deep and, in the morning, when the day was a little brighter, if not blue, Emma's spirits rose; and with good spirits came resolve.

'I believe it is my duty to visit the poor Bates's, this morning, papa. I shall take James and the carriage for the horses need the exercise and they can put up at the Crown.'

Thus Mrs Knightley arrived this time in Highbury with some style, not blown about and panting but pampered and looked after as a young married lady in her station should be. This time her visit felt as it should and she was in good humour as the Bates's servant showed her into their living-room which, she was glad to see, had no other visitors.

A few moments passed, long enough for Emma to look round the room and notice something very peculiar in the corner. It was, in fact, a very large object, very large indeed, entirely draped by black cretonne. The effect was so strange as to be sinister and Emma's curiosity could not be resisted for long. Rising quietly, she went over to the source and raised a corner of the cloth. It was in this attitude that Miss Bates, entering quietly, found her.

'Oh, Mrs Knightley – you have discovered it – poor Jane's pianoforte – Oh how can I pronounce her name!' Sinking down into the chair nearest the door, Miss Bates was overcome by sobs and could say no more.

Dropping the cloth as if it had dangerous properties, Emma hurried back to the sofa on which she had been sitting before. Her mind, previously so clear, clouded with confusion at the sight of Miss Bates' grief. To her shame, she had not envisaged such a scene – the poor lady's red and swollen face, her hair in a tangle, her handkerchief reduced to a soggy mess – worst of all, the lack of words. Miss Bates without words was like a tree without leaves. Visits to the Bates's house were always accompanied by a running patter of goodwill, a commentary on every moment, that which was important finding equal place with the trivial. Miss Bates was, normally, a babbling brook of words, a stream of words, and now she was merely water.

If such thoughts did Emma little credit, then it must be

remembered that this was her first experience of a serious loss. Her mother had died when she was too young to remember and, since then, her circle had only expanded with the arrival of healthy nieces and nephews. Health was a constant preoccupation in the Woodhouse household but its black demon, death, never discussed.

So Emma was unprepared for this degree of misery and correspondingly overcome. 'Oh, Miss Bates – I am so sorry – dear—' But she found she could not pronounce the name, 'Jane', and she, too, fell silent. Now, she found herself almost wishing for another visitor. Even Mr Elton, previously so despised, might be of some help in such things, as he had pointed out.

'I am ashamed,' muttered Miss Bates, rising. And, before Emma could protest that she would leave her in peace, she had gone, murmuring, however, on her way out, 'I shall return, composed. Please wait.'

So Emma must sit longer and look further at the black object in the corner which had now taken on for her the form of a coffin – although it would have had to be a very large body indeed, quite twice the size of Jane who was so elegant, so slender. Trying to divert her thoughts from such morbid fancies, Emma pictured Jane at the pianoforte on the first occasion she had seen it – Frank Churchill so attentive, she, Jane (their engagement still being a secret), in a state of nerves that at first precluded her playing. Oh, their union had started in secrecy and ended in tragedy!

A good ten minutes passed before Miss Bates returned; but she was quite calm, hair smooth, voice low. 'It was seeing you – her good friend – but we will not talk of her or I will fail again.'

'Dear Miss Bates. I would not cause you unhappiness—'

'No. No. Sensible of the honour—' Normally such a beginning would be a forerunner to a litany of such grateful sentences, but not today. An almost businesslike look came over Miss Bates' face. 'You may know Mrs Bates is feverish in bed—'

'Yes. I—'

'It is the pianoforte that distresses her particularly – its arrival – the donor – poor Jane. The night before last, Mrs Bates was in this room, very late – she would touch it, hang over it – I could not stop her – when she imagined she saw a face at the window—'

'At the window!' exclaimed Emma.

'It is imaginings – her fever – but the piano preys on her mind. I had thought by covering it – but it does no good. She thinks someone wishes to steal it. She will talk of nothing else . . . Oh what will I do, Mrs Knightley? She did not sleep all night. It was pianoforte all night long!'

The appeal in Miss Bates' reddened eyes was a challenge to Emma's vigour and good sense. Here was something practical in which she could help. 'We must remove it altogether!' she said decisively.

'You think, remove it – of course – but where to? It is, I suppose, Mr Frank Churchill's but he—' Her voice ended despairingly.

'It can be a temporary removal,' said Emma. 'Mr Churchill will not object when he hears the circumstances. I shall make arrangements and let you know. It will be safer and better for poor Mrs Bates.'

'You are so good – although I shall miss it, as the best reminder of my dear . . .'

Here Emma rose hurriedly before Miss Bates should be overcome by her tears once more and she, herself, felt a swelling in her throat and a pricking in her eyes. 'Tell your mother, the piano will go to Hartfield.'

'Oh, Hartfield! Well, in that case – an honour indeed—'

Emma left them with all the speed that sympathy and politeness allowed and it was only when she was safely back in the carriage on the way to Hartfield that she wondered whether she had not been too hasty in offering a home to Jane Fairfax's pianoforte. The more she thought about it, the more she recognised that she did not want it where she spent her every day. It would recall too much in the past – her foolish intimacy with Frank and her less than charitable feelings for Jane – which she would far rather forget. Besides, Jane had always been so much a superior player to her that it would take away the pleasure from her own efforts. No! The pianoforte should not come to Hartfield. But where, then?

Now that she had promised Miss Bates, she must find it a home and a suitable one. Doubtless the Eltons would snatch at such a prize; but that the vulgar Mrs Augusta Elton should take it – and cover it with shawls fringed and over-fringed – she could not countenance; the Westons at Randalls were obvious in one way as Mr Weston was Frank's father but their house was not big and, under the present circumstances of Mrs Weston's delicate condition, she was certain it would not be received as a good idea.

What possibilities were now left? Few, indeed; for Mrs Bates must be assured that it would be safe from her imagined burglar. At this point it struck Emma with a start that Mrs Bates' 'burglar' had been seen the very same night as her apparition had slunk behind a shrubbery. Such a coincidence could not be overlooked; perhaps there were truly cause for alarm! Now there was even more reason to look forward to a message announcing Knightley's return.

But Emma arrived back at Hartfield to find no such message. As the day progressed into evening and once more the backgammon was resorted to, with – and there was some excuse – even less concentration from Emma than the night before, despite all her best efforts, Emma felt more and more the lack of an equal companion in whom she could confide the troubles of the day.

Two troubles in one day! – burglar and pianoforte; it was

as many as she had to solve in a year and now she was on her own with no one to help her.

Emma spent a disturbed and wakeful night during which the rain and wind, gusting about the house once more, seemed to echo the turbulence in her mind. With no excuse of unexplained noise, she rose from her bed and went to the window. The effect that met her eyes was spectacular. Jagged clouds, silver edged by the light of the moon, beamed, raced by in continuous sequence. Now and again, a gap appeared between them and then the brilliant orb, as full as it could be, shone more radiantly than any light. Then the garden appeared as if a stage, fully lit, almost glaringly lit; nothing could be hid. But as far as Emma could see, there was nothing to be hid, nothing to see but the wildly shaking shrubs and trees which flung their leaves out like pennies to the poor.

'To the poor!' Emma exclaimed out loud. That was the answer to the fate of the pianoforte. It should go to Mr and Mrs Robert Martin. They were a musical family but despite being in farming, unable to afford anything but a very inferior instrument; they would be truly grateful to borrow a better. She would go on the morrow and visit Harriet Martin whom she had a somewhat guilty apprehension of not visiting as much as she should lately. Harriet would be grateful, Mrs Bates' fears calmed and she, Emma, would have something to fill her day.

Quite sleepy now, Emma returned to her bed and knew nothing further till morning.

6

Emma's inclusion of the Martins among those she thought of as poor hardly did justice to that family's situation. It was true that Mr Robert Martin was a farmer who did not own land but rented Abbey-Mill from Mr Knightley; but he was a gentleman-farmer. Moreover, although but five and twenty years of age, he had been in sole charge of the farm for several years, since the decease of his father, and was full of energy and good sense. He was supported in his work by his mother and two sisters and now by his wife, Harriet, whom he had married just a month before Emma married Mr Knightley. The Martin household was not rich but it lacked in none of the essentials: a good old house, in a lovely setting, abundant food and fuel; and it rejoiced in those riches that many, with far more pounds to their name, could not boast of: health, happiness and loving kindness. It was to visit this fortunate household that Emma took out her carriage for the second morning running. 'Dear Harriet,' she thought to herself, 'I have neglected her sadly. How pleased she will be to see me!'

The knowledge of the joy she was soon to confer occupied Emma at the start of the short journey but as she entered the valley in which the farm lay, and peered from the window at the pastures on either side, her mind turned to other thoughts. It was impossible not to be conscious that these were her husband's lands – his own house, Donwell Abbey, just beyond a coppice and, although on rising land, hidden from view. Donwell should have been her home; and yet now it stood empty. These were unpleasant thoughts, for she knew how Knightley loved his home and what a sacrifice he made so that her father should be kept happy. It was a relief when the carriage stopped and they had arrived at the path to Abbey-Mill.

Emma stepped out, trying as much as possible to avoid the patches of water in the broad gravel path and looked around her. The wind had entirely died with the coming of the day and the sun had just broken through in a sky that had been smoothly grey. A neat espalier of apple trees, evidence enough of Mr Martin's efficient husbandry, led up to the front door and was now touched with gold. At intervals, rosy apples still hung on the trees, looking more like baubles for decoration than anything nature could produce. Emma imagined that it was a whim of Harriet's to let them hang there, rather than bring them in as the Martins would be used to do. She was lingering there, almost against her will admiring the ancient beauty and serenity of the place – different, of course, to the modern elegance of Hartfield, but perhaps expressing more of the true nature of the English countryside – when Harriet herself burst out of the door.

'Mrs Knightley! I am so happy to see you! We are all so happy to see you!'

'And I am happy to be here' – feeling this was indeed so, for Harriet's pretty, fair face was wreathed in smiles and, peeping behind her, was Elizabeth Martin, and her sister, equally welcoming, and even a glimpse, she fancied, of Mrs Martin not far behind.

'But, come in, Mrs Knightley, or the damp will get through to your shoes and Mr Woodhouse would never forgive me!' Harriet laughed merrily.

This playful reference to the master of Hartfield did not

totally please Emma but her earlier gratification and the pleasant impression of the scene, carried her into the house with good humour intact. Harriet had always been a silly girl.

Soon the party was gathered in the best parlour and a cheerful servant despatched to fetch chocolate for Mrs Knightley – 'after such a journey with the paths so unsteady from the rain.' At first the talk was all about the weather. 'I do declare the wind kept me awake the whole night long!' from Harriet, yellow curls bobbing round her fresh complexion. 'I am quite done up!'

'My brother has said two limes came down in the avenue at Donwell,' from Elizabeth Martin, with gravity.

'Limes are never long-lived but a favourite in so many gardens,' from Mrs Martin with much good sense. 'It is the lightness of the leaves that attracts, I believe.'

'They are my favourites, in particular,' said Emma, surprised that such a homely body as Mrs Martin should notice such things as the colour of the leaves. 'And that avenue is very dear to Mr Knightley. I am sure he will wish to consider replacing the trees when he returns to Hartfield.'

'Returns!' exclaimed Harriet. 'He is away then!' The idea seemed to fill her with amazement and she turned a look of pity towards Emma.

'On business,' said Emma briskly. She had forgotten the simple affection that she allowed Harriet to feel for her. 'Men in his position must go to London on occasions.'

'Indeed, indeed,' commented Mrs Martin and all three Martins fell silent as if newly impressed by the grandeur of their visitor. Or, possibly, made anxious by her silent frowns and the way she looked with eager, darting glances about the room. Was there something amiss? wondered Mrs Martin, and yet Mr Knightley came there often enough and sat there over his tea – like a man who felt himself as near at home as he could be when away.

Elizabeth was naturally of quiet disposition and therefore did not speak, but even Harriet, who was agog to raise the subject of her condition – so obvious, she felt, that Mrs Knightley must notice it and, yet, perhaps not, for she had always been plump – could not break the silence. There was, too, other news, which she desired to share, news of great importance to the Martins – but there seemed no way for that either, with Mrs Knightley alternately gazing eagerly about the room or bent over her chocolate.

The truth was that Emma, usually so sprightly with words, was searching without success for an introduction to the subject of Jane Fairfax's pianoforte. She had noted to her satisfaction that there was no instrument in the parlour and, although she had a memory of a small instrument being played in an outer room, she felt assured of a need and a space to fill. If only the matter could be handled directly, without mention of poor Mrs Churchill! For that, in such company, was a conversation which – except in the most formal of terms, and she did not believe it would remain formal with Harriet taking part – she would rather avoid. Frank Churchill was a name that between her and Mrs Robert Martin held few respectable memories. However, she was resolved on her plan and must start anyhow.

'You do not have a piano in this room, I see?'

As if it were a cue she waited for, Harriet sprang to her feet. 'Oh, such a coincidence that you should mention it! Perhaps if you are not too tired you would come to see it! It is not yet fully unpacked but we can inspect a corner. Of course, as you know too well, I am a hardly adequate performer but Elizabeth Martin plays so very lively an air—'

Seeing Mrs Knightley's bewildered air and that Harriet might run on for ever without properly explaining herself, Mrs Martin intervened. 'We have just received delivery of a new pianoforte. You may not know but Mrs Martin's

father has recently died and there has been a sum of
money . . .' Now her voice, too, died for Emma's face
expressed anything but satisfaction at this news. Harriet's
birth, not sanctified by her father's marriage to her mother,
was perhaps not the subject for parlour conversation and
silence might have fallen again, had not Emma resolved
to talk herself, with all politeness, out of the house. Her
mission had failed. Her visit must end.

'This room has fine proportions,' she said – and 'The
light comes in very prettily from that southerly window,
not too bright but bright enough' – and 'My father sends
his regards; he always hears about Donwell and Abbey-Mill
with interest' – this not true, but it would serve.

Eventually Emma was out of the house and standing
once more in its pleasant surroundings – behind her the
lush pastures on either side of the river that encircled the
house, before her the start of the Donwell home farm which
led up to the gardens and the Abbey itself.

The sun still shone, the air was mild, and Emma felt
disinclined to mount her carriage which had waited all this
time, with the faithful James, in the lane. But she said her
goodbyes amiably enough and even allowed Harriet to tell
her the reason for her added dimples and glowing health.
'I congratulate you, Harriet, you and Mr Martin can look
forward to a happy future.'

But the moment she was inside the carriage, she gave
directions to James which caused that faithful servant,
accustomed to only the most settled and practised destinations, to assume an expression which said very clearly,
without the necessity for words, 'I have already stood for
half an hour in the damp. My horses will not like the wet,
uneven going; my wheels will not like the mud and the
jolting – one may even come off – and I will not like missing
my usual place by the kitchen stove with a hot cup of soup
in my hand.'

But Emma was peremptory. Her humour, already discomposed, had not improved as Harriet's telling of her
own happy news was followed by a questioning, if humbly
questioning, look in her blue eyes. She had not asked but,
like James, Emma knew exactly what she wanted to say:
'And when will you be looking forward to a happy event,
Mrs Knightley?' It was intolerable that such a question,
even with only a humble look, should be made to her by
such a person!

In truth, there was not a person in the world that Mrs
Knightley allowed to raise the subject. Even when her
own Mrs Weston had made a scarcely more than sidelong
reference – 'You will not be so free for long, my dear
Emma' – she had been received with a pursed mouth
and a frown. Any references Mr Knightley made could
scarcely be received with such a show of reluctance, but
she tolerated without encouraging; he was too restrained
a man to press her. Emma was conscious, however, that a
man of nine and thirty must be looking for a family before
he was too old to enjoy the company of small children; but
he was an active, young-looking man and the idea did not
weigh on her too heavily.

It was stranger, perhaps, that Emma, in her perfect love
for her husband, did not desire a child to complete their
happiness. Yet she had for so long thought of herself as
unlikely to marry, for so long thought of Isabella's children
as Knightley's heirs, that there was some excuse. Besides,
although she enjoyed the company of her sister's two oldest
boys, there were times when she found the ever-increasing
nephews and nieces somewhat overwhelming. She had
seen them change her lively sister into a mother permanently vexed and worried so that she sometimes seemed as
old and anxious as their father. It was a wonder her health
had not given way under the strain of it, and indeed John
Knightley – a bad-tempered, ironic sort of man, although

adored by his wife – was little support. Isabella had lost her looks, her temper and, thought Emma, as cruel as any loving sister, her intelligence.

There was a better model now for Emma to see: Mrs Weston was happy and calm, with one daughter and another to come – or rather had been happy until the news of Jane Fairfax. And now there was that tragedy to add to the many good reasons why motherhood should not be regarded as the crown of life. Let Harriet Martin's proud smiles turn to sympathetic, pathetic patronage – she, Emma, could not yet regret that she was still at liberty, unfettered by the joys of bringing new life into the world!

Such thoughts were interrupted by James, announcing in lugubrious tones, 'I can go no further; the road is quite washed away.'

'Then I shall descend,' said Emma, putting her hand on the door handle.

7 ∫

Emma had known Donwell Abbey and its grounds since she was a child; and yet hardly knew it at all. This was due to her family circumstances for, since Mr Woodhouse seldom ventured out, Mr Knightley had been the visitor rather than the visited. Yet, in the world, she was known properly as Mrs Knightley, mistress of Donwell. It was an odd situation, leading to melancholy, and Emma mused on it as she wandered up the lime tree avenue. Indeed, there were two trees down, lying across each other, like fallen comrades in battle – as her romantic sadness led her to imagine.

'One knocked the other over, I'll be bound!'

A deep voice caused her to put her hand to her heart.

'I startled you, my apologies, Mrs Knightley; I had thought you saw me coming.'

'Mr Martin! I am not a deer to be so easily startled. But I was mourning for these two lost soldiers.'

'Soldiers, you say, ma'am. Fighting at each other then. Look, how one has pushed the other flat and now lies on top of him.'

'I thought it for comfort in dying,' Emma smiled and found that the sight and sound of this hearty man had quite dissipated her gothic mood. 'I have come from your Abbey-Mill.'

'And saw Mrs Martin?' A soft look came into the manly face which, for some reason she did not care to identify, made her uncomfortable.

'Yes – and Mrs Martin and the two Miss Martins. You have a veritable household of good women there.'

'I have; and know it. I am a fortunate man. But I must not keep you talking. Your boots are wet through already.'

'I wished to see the worst the storm had done,' Emma replied, thinking she should have a reason for her visit.

'For the same purpose I am here. I understand Mr Knightley will be back tonight.'

'You do. Ah!' Emma could hardly hide her surprise for she did not know such a thing.

'Let me hand you back to your carriage.'

But Emma's enjoyment in Mr Martin's company had gone with the news that he was kept better informed about Mr Knightley's whereabouts than that gentleman's wife. She did not allow for the fact that she had been out all morning and a message might have come in her absence. Her open, friendly tone changed for a haughty sharpness. 'No! I shall continue up to the house now I have got so far. My feet cannot be wetter than they already are and I am quite warm.'

'Then let me accompany you – show you the quickest, cleanest way.'

'You may direct me; but I will go alone; the best service you can render me is to cheer poor James and see that he meets me at the house.'

Alone, Emma went as quickly as the waterlogged and slippery ground allowed; she was conscious that it was only wilfulness that had led her on to this extra walk. Nevertheless, it was pleasant to see the many wings of the house – in comfortably antique but not always homogeneous styles – come into view. Knightley loved this place; he would be pleased by her curiosity, Emma reassured herself. Now she felt herself foolish in not allowing Mr Martin to accompany her for he, doubtless, held a key and could have let her inside. She must merely stare, admire, imagine. She would walk round the main part of the house, note every feature and then return to wait for the carriage that must follow the long way round by road.

Emma was carrying out her own prescription, eyes noting each window, each door, the angle of the roof, the stone steps that led up to a longer window, when her attention was attracted by something moving behind the glass. She came closer. It was a man's figure; but such was the play of the light that she could see no more than that. She came closer still. Whatever Emma's faults, lack of courage was not one of them; besides, she assumed it must be the caretaker who lived, as she knew, in a cottage adjoining. But he was old, grey, short, and this was a tall figure, even though shadowy.

'Oh, Miss Woodhouse! Miss Woodhouse!' Who was that calling the name she had not heard for so long and in tones of such anguish? Emma pressed closer to the glass and saw – but how could it be? – Frank Churchill's face, handsome still but oh so pale and distraught.

'Miss Woodhouse – I beg you – I plead with you – for the sake of your friendship with my dear wife, Jane – Ah, Jane . . .' he broke down and moved further inward so Emma could scarcely perceive him, although she thought she heard sobs – wild unfettered sobs such as she expected to hear from no man.

'Mr Churchill,' her own voice faint, for the surprise was great and her position, pressed flat against the window for a better view, most strange and difficult. 'Mr Churchill' – a little firmer.

And now he flitted back, tears streaming from his eyes; an arm beckoned her. 'If you please – follow—'

She followed; she outside the house, he inside, until they

both came face to face in a little side door, half covered by ivy but the top fitted with a single pane of glass; she had no further time to wonder for the door was open in a second and Frank, a frenzied hand claw-like clutching at her, had drawn her in.

'Oh, even to see you – her friend!' he began at once, standing so close that Emma could see his reddened eye and unshaven cheek. 'My Jane – oh there will never be such a one again – her beauty, her virtue, everything that was good and sweet and noble – but you know all this – Oh, Miss Woodhouse—' Here his face came closer still and she smelled the alcohol on his breath.

'Mrs Knightley. I am Mrs Knightley.' Why did she insist on this so firmly? What would a name matter to a person in such extreme depths of despair as this man? Nevertheless, she felt it must be said and the saying made her stronger. 'Why are you here, Mr Churchill? In Mr Knightley's house? How have you come through this door? Mr Knightley is in London looking for you.'

'Knightley. Knightley,' repeated Frank, as if the name meant nothing to him, indeed, Emma reflected – for her shock was fading and she was beginning to find the use of her mind again – it probably did not. Frank's nature had always been of the sort that lived only in the moment and forgot what had gone before. And yet this wildness, this wreckage, that she saw in front of her, was pitiful and no one could ever doubt that he had dearly loved poor Jane Fairfax.

'You cannot understand – no one who has not lost – Ah the agony – the misery . . .' Here he broke off to weep again.

'You must not give way to these feelings, Mr Churchill, you have a child—'

'A child!' – interrupting her in a mad cry. 'A murderer! – My Jane' – an eager, frenzied pulling at her sleeve. 'You remember the whiteness of her skin – we talked of it – I said it too colourless – you praised it – Ah, now she has the pallor of death . . .' Here he fell back and seemed to swoon against the wall.

Emma became further alarmed. She must run to James and together they would get him to the carriage and take him – but where? Not to Hartfield; she could not do that to Mr Woodhouse. To his own father at Randalls? That would be the right place. But how could she take him there when poor Mrs Weston was indisposed and so near her time? If only Mr Knightley were back!

But he was not. Perhaps – to the Martins! This was the most practical way forward – Mr Robert Martin, a strong man – and yet Emma hesitated. And, while she was silent, deliberating, Mr Churchill, as if divining her thoughts – or maybe he had heard the carriage crunching the gravel under its wheels as it arrived in front of the house – suddenly lifted his head and fixed Emma with his crazed eyes—

'I must be gone – do not come after me—'

'But, Mr Churchill – you are not well! You must be looked after!'

'No! No! Jane – I feel closer to you here—'

'But this is Mr Knightley's house—'

'At night I can go out to Highbury, to her room – see the pianoforte I bought her – where she played. I watch, I stand, I see her again – Ah! Oh!' – how his sobs were groans – 'you cannot know the reason for my despair! Would that I were dead – dead! Ah, such a word – dead – I would join her who I only caused to suffer, although I loved her. Oh, how I loved! Her last words – Frank, why, why? I can hear them still – shall hear them for ever—'

'Please, Mr Churchill, you must calm yourself and come with me. It is not all over – there is the child—'

'No! No! I can hear no more!' And he was gone, back

into the dark recesses of the great old house. In a moment, the silence was total, as if the ranting figure had been an hallucination. But just as Emma was about to turn and re-enter the garden, he was there again, hissing in a horrible wheedling tone, 'Do not tell a soul of my whereabouts for the river runs deep and fast around the house and if the fox is chased from his lair he must take to the water—' and then he had gone again.

Far too agitated to consider that a fox takes to the water because its excellent ability as a swimmer makes it a sure way to evade capture, Emma pictured, with horror, Mr Churchill's drowned body carried along the swollen river; it was too awful to contemplate. She stepped out hastily into the still sunlit garden and, feeling the fresh air on her burning face, let out her breath with a gasp near a sob. What could she do? The first move was ordained: she must go and find the carriage; that much she could do, though her legs shook ever so much. But what then?

If Emma was considering driving to the Abbey-Mill and seeking out Mr Robert Martin, one look at James's grave face reminded her that poor Mr Woodhouse, by this late hour in the morning, would have consigned the carriage to a ditch and herself to the grave; she could not delay her return for the sake of Frank Churchill.

Mr Woodhouse was so out of sorts when the carriage turned into the drive at Hatfield that he had had his chair turned round from its accustomed place at the fire so that he might face the window.

'My dear Emma,' he cried querulously, as she – face still pale and legs a-tremble from her terrible experience – entered the room. 'My dear, you see I have had to move my chair. I sit now between such draughts that I cannot bear to think how they will make me suffer in the future. The least I can expect is a cold and you know how colds lie on my chest. I should not be surprised if I were not in my bed by the evening.'

'Oh, papa!' Emma crouched by him, glad that her tremulous state could be put down to anxiety over his health. 'Let me bring you a rug directly. It is only that I walked too far!'

This was a mistake.

'Walked too far!' an exclamation of horror. 'You took the carriage. I made sure that James was with you and James is the most practical of men. I told myself once if not a thousand times, "James is a practical man; if she is with James, she will not take harm." James has had the carriage over without anyone taking harm – you remember the occasion? Foul weather, foul weather— ?'

'Dear papa. Indeed James was with me. You were right to feel confident of my safety.'

'Walking? You say, walking?'

'The day is so fine,' began Emma, blushing despite all her efforts, 'I called in on the Martins—'

'The Martins? You walked with the Martins?'

'Yes, that is—' She had walked to the garden gate with Mrs Harriet Martin; she had seen the fallen limes in the company of Mr Robert Martin.

'Yes, papa' – more firmly.

'Well – you should have told me that at first; now I am quite at ease. Mr Knightley, I know, places as much confidence in Mr Robert Martin as I do in James. I do believe I could make use of a rug, just round my knees – if you would ring?' Mr Woodhouse, fears for his daughter at rest, was able to concentrate fully on his own health, an occupation which took up both his and Miss Woodhouse's attention for upward of an hour.

As soon as she could – under the pretext of seeing Cook to order especial cold-fighting delicacies – Emma escaped to her bedroom; there she lay across her bed and burst into tears. The relief was great, the comfort of giving in to her emotions so restorative that she rose not ten minutes later with fresh optimism: she was not Frank Churchill's keeper nor could she ever be; his talk of the river was bravado, a kind of play-acting of which she knew him to be master – nearer the stories she read under such titles as 'The Castle of Count Rudolpho' or 'The Midnight Bell'. Even Emma's buoyant youthfulness could not admit that Mr Churchill did not suffer – his gaunt face, the flaming eyes, stayed before her – but she managed to convince herself that his was not the kind of nature to do himself damage. His emotions were violent but not deep; he would rush to the river-bank, stand at the edge, stare at the rushing water, imagine himself, pale face upturned, strewn with weed, carried along by the current like a branch broken off a tree – but he would not cast himself in; the imagining would be enough for him.

So Emma convinced herself and, washing her face in cool water, descended again with far greater composure than most ladies might have shown in such a situation.

'There is a letter from London – from Mr Knightley,' Mr Woodhouse greeted her.

It was a reward for her calmness; Emma opened the letter eagerly and was immediately disappointed by its brevity.

'My dearest Emma – I will be here one more night but expect me on the morrow by dinner time – In haste, your ever loving—' and then there was a squiggle as if he had added something else, before 'Knightley' in his handsome, bold letters.

'He is coming?' Mr Woodhouse, anxiously.

'On the morrow.'

'And poor Isabella – the children – Mr John Knightley? They are in good health?'

'He does not refer to them.'

'Not refer to them! How not? Is it a concealment? Do you detect something amiss?'

'No, papa,' replied Emma as patiently as possible; but a long evening lay ahead and then another day. Her courage began to wane a little and, as if to mock her earlier calm, the unsolved problem of what to do with Jane's pianoforte, made more difficult now with Churchill's interest added, came into her mind. Clearly, it was her duty to report his presence. Oh, Mr Knightley, why have you not come?

8

The night passed – as all nights, however dreary, do – and Emma rose to find another bright day beyond the casement, although the wind had risen again. After breakfast, she retired to her upstairs parlour and sat over her sewing which had been sadly neglected during the last few days – a neglect to which the square of cambric was so accustomed that it had gradually transformed from a brilliant white to a shade of grey, as if to acknowledge its lack of importance and desirous of drawing less attention to itself. Emma, sober-faced but inexorably pretty, drew the thread through and, as often as it came, frowned and sighed; there was clearly much on her mind.

Outside the window, the arrival of a carriage in the driveway sent the gravel into a flurry. Emma knew Knightley was on horseback and was not of the changeable nature to alter his time of returning, but she ran eagerly all the same and peered through the glass. A lady descended from the carriage and entered the house, a glimpse of feathers and frills, of velveteen and veiling, was enough.

'Mrs Elton is downstairs, ma'am.' Mary's knock at the door was confirmation of her gloomy fate.

'The weather has kept us apart, dear Mrs Knightley, I do declare it!' Mrs Elton's declaration was made with all the enthusiasm of a loving friend.

'Mrs Elton! It has been too long indeed – but the weather must not be blamed. The weather is too ordinary a reason, too vulgar – using the word in its common meaning. We must find sickness, travel, friends, perhaps a small disaster—'

'A disaster?' repeated Mrs Elton, a little bewildered and unwilling to relinquish her role of warm goodwill. 'Dear Mrs Knightley, how I have missed your ready wit! I was saying so to Mr Elton this evening gone and by such a coincidence that confirms one's belief in the Almighty God, this very morning what should come but a letter from Mrs Serena Suckling.'

'A coincidence, Mrs Elton! I confess I do not follow you. But pray, be seated. Some refreshment perhaps?'

'Yes. You are too kind.' The settling of Mrs Elton with all her tails behind and her swathing in between and her rigging on top, took some time; but the coincidence was not forgot.

'Mrs Serena Suckling, my dearest sister,' she began as soon as a drink was in her hand, 'has writ that she is coming to visit my little house – my little doll's house, as I call it to her that lives in such a castle of a place. Maple Grove has twenty bedrooms, you know, and all of them freshly wallpapered within the year.'

'I am very glad that Mrs Suckling takes so much pleasure in wallpaper, though not, I suppose, as glad as those whose business it is to supply her with the paper – but I still cannot make out the coincidence.'

'My dear Mrs Knightley. We shall of course entertain Mr and Mrs Suckling to several dinners during their stay with us and that, in short, is why I must come at once to Mrs Knightley to ascertain when she and Mr Knightley and Mr Woodhouse are free of engagements. Hartfield must come first, I said to the *cara sposa* over breakfast – he was just out to visit poor Mrs Bates, but I will come to that later. Mrs

Knightley is in Highbury; I shall take the carriage at once, I said. Now, you see the coincidence – one evening I talk of not having the pleasure of seeing Mrs Knightley and the next morning I have urgent reason to pay her a visit.'

'A coincidence indeed,' agreed Emma, who saw she was supposed to feel complimented by this rigmarole when all she wished to do was avoid contact with the Vicarage as far as possible. This she achieved much of the time but it would be certain that a dinner with the great Sucklings could not be refused without causing offence. She did not, however, entirely lose hope since the Sucklings had been much promised over the last year and not yet found time in their busy schedule – 'so near to all the inducements of Bath', as Mrs Elton described it – to put in an appearance.

'I hope Mr and Mrs Suckling will not arrive too soon,' said Emma 'for Mr Knightley is away.'

'Away?' – a voice of astonishment.

'Business has called him to London.'

'London. You surprise me. I understood his business was in managing his estates and as a local magistrate.'

'Then you were misinformed.' There was a silence while Mrs Elton sipped her drink with a finger so genteelly raised as you could hang another cup on it. But good manners must not be entirely abandoned and Emma knew she carried the responsibility of a hostess, even if her guest was pushing and patronising and in no way to her taste. She cast about for a more convenient subject and remembered that Mrs Elton had made a mention of Mrs Bates. Perhaps she could find out how that old lady continued. But before she could get to that she must submit to Mrs Elton's recovering her aura of friendly goodwill and telling her much more about the Sucklings' visit than a positive admirer would have wished to know.

At last a conclusion was reached with words of honest satisfaction, 'They are so much above everybody here that

I must cast wide to keep them in spirits – save for yourself, of course, Mrs Knightley.'

Emma managed a gracious bow at this and did not give her visitor time to start again before asking, 'You spoke of Mrs Bates. Is she no better?'

'Better? No, far worse! When Mr Elton returned to me, he was quite shaken, quite pale. He was fond of her, of course, although she was very old, very deaf. I hardly conceived what he saw in her but he reminded me that she had been a vicar's wife—'

'Was! Was?' Emma interrupted her. 'She has not, not—'

'Not yet. But she is not expected to recover.'

'Whatever has occurred?'

'Poor old woman – After the tragedy of her dear grand-daughter's delivery she could not sleep at nights, so she was in the habit of getting out of bed and going to the parlour – you know their rooms are so small, so close together. In particular, she went to poor Mrs Churchill's pianoforte. She would sit there on the stool – in the cold, in her nightwear. Miss Bates told all this to Mr Elton and I had it from him. Oh! It hardly bears thinking about how people come down in the world. A vicar's wife to be so low!'

'But how did she get worse?' Emma dreaded to hear, but must – and yet she half guessed already what was to come.

'Last night she escaped poor Miss Bates again – she blames herself most dreadfully – and sat at her usual place by the pianoforte when a dreadful face appeared at the window—'

'Oh no!' The cry came from Emma's heart.

'That was really the finish very nearly. Her terror was so great that she had a stroke, fell – lost the use of limbs and speech—'

'If she could not speak, how can you tell she saw this – this apparition?' quavered Emma.

'She fell below the window, hand reaching upwards.'

'Perhaps she was looking for air?'

'No. No. I assure you.' Mrs Elton became a little irritable as someone whose story is doubted. 'She confided in Miss Bates a day or two earlier. This face had been at the window – a man's – violent – I do not know how we shall all sleep in our beds. The terror has been the death of her—'

'She is not dead,' objected Emma with desperation.

'She will not recover.'

'No! Poor Mrs Bates. Poor Mrs Bates. And yet, and yet the face is most likely to be in her imagination.'

'It is best you believe so, with Mr Knightley out of Hartfield.'

'Thank you. I am not afraid for myself. But I shall not tell my father. It is bad enough that he should know his dear friend, Mrs Bates, so ill, perhaps dying.'

'Assuredly dying.'

Now Emma was even more keen to see her visitor out through the front door and into her carriage. Her news was so terrible that she must be alone to face it fully: Mr Churchill had killed old Mrs Bates, killed his own wife's grandmother. As Mrs Elton returned to the theme of the Sucklings' visit, Emma's thoughts raced with hideous self-accusation. If she had told Mr Martin, Mr Churchill could have been taken away, and there would have been no ghastly face in the window. In worrying about the fate of a young man – however unhappy – hale and hearty in body, she had sacrificed the life of a poor old lady who had never done any harm to anybody and had, moreover, given her father many happy hours at the quadrille table.

'Oh!' Emma gasped and put her face in her hands.

'You are not well!' Mrs Elton interrupted herself in joyful anticipation of not a night passing without ten places on the table, to peer curiously at Miss Woodhouse.

'Yes. No.' Even in her state of nerves, Emma at once perceived that Mrs Elton did not link her cry and her pallor to poor Mrs Bates. She did not rate her sufficiently important for such a reaction, but attributed it to quite another cause – a cause that all Highbury perfectly knew was her dearest wish for herself.

'You are faint – I can see it – I understand.'

Emma, who had lifted her head to see the expression on her visitor's face – false concern, ill-concealed envy and absolute certainty – dropped it again. Mrs Elton thought Mrs Knightley was with child because it was what she herself most desired. Emma could almost wish that in this one case Mrs Elton's understanding – in her experience invariably wrong – had, for once, been right.

'No. I am perfectly in health – it is nothing.'

'I shall leave you.' Mrs Elton rose – her happy mission, thoughts of the Sucklings, turned to dust in her mouth. 'Do not see me out.' Her frills subsided and her feathers failed to flutter.

'I shall inform Mr Knightley of your invitation,' said Emma, for even a dinner with the people she least desired to meet in the world was a better prospect than what lay in her head. She must tell Knightley everything, however painful the telling – that was her only hope. He would put it in a better light for now she could see only black.

9

It was to be expected that Mr Knightley, after a separation from his youthful wife of several days, would be looking forward to the reunion.

Emma, of course, had particular reason to await his coming home with eager anticipation. From the moment the hall clock struck two, she was unable to sit still but was constantly moving from room to room, always making sure she had a good view of the front driveway. She had ordered Mr Knightley's favourite dinner of minced scallops followed by roast mutton and potatoes (he was never fond of elaboration) and put on the gown he favoured – a light muslin of a pale blue which he had confessed, at Emma asking why he stared so, put him in mind of the sky in spring.

Emma was prepared; the dinner was prepared; Mr Woodhouse was all happiness at the return of the only man who could have made the marriage of his daughter the opposite of a reason for mourning. There remained only for the hero to return and to make Hartfield a happier place.

At last, just half an hour before their usual time for sitting down, there was the unmistakable clatter of well-shod hoofs – not the creaking of boughs nor the banging of pots in the kitchen nor even the rattle of firearms in the grate – and Mr Knightley, mud-spattered and fresh-faced from his ride, came through the door.

'Oh, Knightley! Knightley!' Emma threw herself into his arms – so close that the spring sky became cloudy with brown spots – and burst into tears.

'Emma, my Emma. My dearest.' She was hugged. 'Now, now,' she was pushed away a little.

With tears and smiles Emma watched as his greatcoat was removed, his boots – 'Oh, I have missed you so!'

'Tears on your face – my dearest—'

'It has seemed so long.' Upstairs they went, without even giving Mr Woodhouse a chance to express his own relief at a safe escape from dangers unimaginable, and Emma stood as Knightley washed himself. 'I am so glad you are returned. It has seemed like weeks, not days.'

'Where is my independent Emma?' – smiling.

'Disappeared quite' – serious.

'But what if I were a sailor, gone far away – to the Indies or China – for months or even years?' – still smiling.

'I would never have married a sailor' – still serious, for all the while, through all the delight at his return, she was thinking of the moment when she must tell him about Frank Churchill; she looked forward to it with dread and yet longed for it, as a wounded soldier begs for the pain of the surgeon's knife. She felt, also, a barrier between them as long as she had not told him. He thought his warm reception only a demonstration of her affection but she must show him it sprang from another source as well. They were not in perfect understanding until she spoke and yet her father waited and dinner must be got through first.

'I had not thought I would be quite so missed,' Knightley tucked her arm in his to lead her down the stairs.

'You do not place enough emphasis on your importance at Hartfield – we are like sailor men without our Captain.'

Knightley looked pleased, even very pleased, at this

revival of Emma's more playful manner and so they greeted Mr Woodhouse and went into dinner.

The meal was long and tiresome to Emma who had to convince her father that such hearty splendours as she had produced for Mr Knightley would do him good rather than harm.

'The liver after such a ride as you have just taken – so shaken about – perhaps even twisted. Some light soup – gruel— ?'

'No, papa. Dearest papa!' interrupted Emma, who had been defending visitors against her father's kind frugality and obnoxious gruel from the moment she could speak. 'Mr Knightley's liver has the firmness of a mattress – the springing of a sofa – the strength of a stone wall—'

She broke off as the owner of such a liver began to laugh and confess that he had such an appetite that only a man who had been in London could build up.

'There!' said Emma, triumphantly, and signalled for more roast for the returned hero.

London was then discussed – or rather Mr Woodhouse, having failed to find fault with his son-in-law's constitution, inquired fearfully as to the health of that dear family in Brunswick Square. Knightley answered, firmly enough, but Emma, made more sensible by her own secret anxieties, noticed that there was something not quite like himself in his manner, as if he were holding himself under restraint. He bantered with her father but his face smiled only with the lips; there was a shadow, she made certain.

With all her preoccupations, Emma only now asked herself why Mr Knightley had stayed so long in London when, as she knew only too well, and he must have discovered, he could have found no trace of Mr Churchill – his reason for the visit – since Mr Churchill was hiding in his own house in Surrey, when not making faces at windows and scaring old ladies to death.

'Ah!' Emma gave a little unconscious groan.

'What is it, Emma?' – Knightley, anxious.

'It is the fat – you cannot roast without fat' – Mr Woodhouse, nearly exultant.

'No. No. I bit my tongue—'

'There! Did I not say such an excess was a danger—'

So the dinner carried on with only a little more interest for Emma when Knightley inquired how she had amused herself in his absence and she described her visit to Abbey-Mill Farm and how pleasant a scene she had found there. She knew his fondness both for Robert Martin and Harriet so that she expected her words would give him pleasure and indeed, almost for the first time, his face lit up.

'I am so pleased, Emma, that you have seen them for what they are – good people, good, honest people, and not as uncultivated as they may appear to those who do not know them as well as I do.'

Such commendation struck a note too far for Emma and, although she had fully intended to confess to her visit to Donwell as a prelude to the real confession later, she now felt disinclined. The Martins were farmers, whatever he might try to convince her otherwise, and Harriet hardly sensible at all. Dinner finished.

Afterwards there was backgammon where Mr Knightley took Emma's place so that she wondered at his patience, and she, more to give occupation to herself than to give pleasure, sat at the piano and played the sort of light easy airs that required no dedication. But even this lowered her spirits for she imagined Jane Fairfax's clever fingers flying over the keys and her pale face, ghostly face, staring into the distance.

At last, just as Emma felt she must scream or fly at her father for his gentle pleasure in his children's company, Mr Woodhouse rose and declared, 'You have kept me up much beyond my time' and the evening was at an end, or, rather, now the evening, the true purpose of the evening, might begin.

Emma's bedroom was large, a corner room with windows in either wall. In the middle stood the four-poster bed that had been constructed for their marriage. On the other wall a fire, burning low, illuminated a pretty mantel, two comfortable-looking chairs and a small dressing table.

Emma lay in bed and listened impatiently for Mr Knightley's quick brisk stride. At last it came; she sat up. 'There is something I have—' but he was distracted, stood staring down at the fire. She hesitated, 'You did not find Frank Churchill, I surmise?'

'Churchill!' – he started, as if the name was far from his thoughts, turned to her. 'No, no. At least, I am clear what he has done with himself—'

'Clear?' in tremulous voice. Could he know? It was impossible!

'As I would expect of such a man – he has fled—'

'Fled?'

'Fled abroad. He was always talking of it, apparently – the Grand Tour – such frippery as he would think to make him more fashionable-seeming – so he has taken the opportunity of his wife passing away to tear off on a trip—'

'But how do you know?'

'He left a note – Mr Churchill found it – not exactly a note, but making his intentions clear enough – Florence, Venice, Rome – leaving all the sorrowing behind him, father, child – My opinion of him was never high, as you know, but – still, I must not be so vehement – it is not my business.'

'Oh, Knightley,' Emma, feebly, 'do not stand there in the cold. Come to bed.'

Now he came to her, clasped her hands in his. 'Oh, Emma, my dearest child. How lovely you are. You know nothing of the evil in human nature – evil is perhaps too strong a word – the weakness – it is all weakness. Ah, and others suffer.'

Returning to the fire, he sat down heavily on one of the chairs and bowed his head, apparently in such despair that Emma, even in her own perturbation, was surprised. It seemed too much. Where was the strength – good sense – she was relying on? 'There is something else wrong?' she inquired eventually, timidly, almost reluctantly. But her love and woman's instinct told her it must be so.

'No. Yes. But I cannot tell you, although it concerns you.' He was up again and close. 'It is another's secret, not mine to tell you' – A groan, a look into Emma's frightened eyes. 'You must trust me, my dear. I am so much older than you and this is a burden I must bear on my own a little longer.'

'I am not a child.' But as Emma whispered this her mind raced into despair. For how could she tell the story of Frank Churchill now? It would be too cruel.

'I *will* get into bed. But be patient. Trust me.'

They lay in bed, close in body but both staring into the dark. 'Is it a business matter?' whispered Emma, after five long minutes had passed.

'Yes, Emma, a business matter, but not mine.' There was a pause. 'I must go back tomorrow. I meant to have one night and not tell you till the morning, but now I have said so much—'

'But not all—'

'It is not my secret – I repeat. Oh, I am so tired, yet it is such a comfort to see you, my dear – your face, your innocent enjoyment of my return. How people can lie, deceive those they are closest to – you would not believe it!'

'But, Knightley!' Emma threw her arms round her husband and might then have spoken but he held her carefully, like a child.

'Good, sweet Emma. I rode all this way to look on your

bright face – to give me strength to return to what I must deal with.'

The moment had gone. She could not speak. He could not, or would not, tell her his secret and she could not, or would not, tell him hers.

'Good-night, dearest Emma, I must sleep now.' A gentle hug and he had turned from her; soon the evenness of his breathing announced that he slept – even in such anxiety, he slept.

Emma, more anxious still or less tired, lay awake until the sky had lost its deepest hue and the evening star no longer shone. Feverish in her thoughts, she considered whether it was a change in her, not in him, that had made it impossible for her to speak out. As an unmarried girl she had always minded confronting him with her own differing views, but had never avoided any occasion. Often, she had thought herself in the right. They had been equal, she in high spirits, he in good sense. But now she was his wife. The foolish and spoilt young lady who had made so many mistakes in the year before her marriage, now bowed to Mr Knightley – as a wife. She was a wife! Never had the word seemed less happy. Knightley now assumed they were one – and yet – and yet – she could not think further. It was too much. Out there Frank Churchill waited, wild-eyed; at her side her husband lay – not very close, he had turned on his side away from her. She perceived that she must hold her secret, after all; if it were defiance, then it was a defiance forced upon her – an independence that she had not sought but which had chosen her. If her nature was not utterly set against such a course, if she found the strength to sustain the secrecy, then she must be glad of it.

Mr Knightley gave a snore and, by a barely perceptible inch, Emma moved further from his side.

At last the mists of Lethe came to close her eyes and she slept.

10

It seemed that every day was bright now – a last gilding of autumn before winter. The days of rain preceding, combined with the high winds, had washed down many of the leaves which lay on the dark ground like patterned Turkish rugs.

'This sun is most deceptive,' Mr Woodhouse told Emma. 'I hope Mr Knightley took his greatcoat.'

'I am sure he did, papa. Mr Knightley is never foolish in looking after his person.'

'For sure he is not a foolish man in any way. He is the only man I would have allowed you to marry, my dear, for just that reason. If he must dash up and down to London twice in a week, then he will have a reason, even if he does not share it with me. He is rational in all things.'

'I know, papa.'

'Although he is a little over-fond of red meat.'

To this Emma made no answer. A silence passed while Mr Woodhouse looked at the paper and Emma made up her mind. 'I must visit the poor Bates's this morning, papa. Mrs Bates is most unwell, most unwell—'

'Then that is a reason for not visiting. You are very likely to catch something.'

'I fear our old friend is suffering from a sickness too deep-grained to throw itself at others.'

Mr Woodhouse's objections were overcome eventually and Emma set off with James whose face showed even more clearly what he thought of his mistress's constant requirement of his services. 'To Highbury, ma'am?'

'To Donwell, James' – short and crisp.

If there had been anyone deserving of explanation, Emma would have spoken of a glove lost on her last visit. She would not, however, have described how she had got hold of the heavy old key that filled what space was left over in her little bag from a handkerchief in which two biscuits were wrapped and a couple of silver coins.

On arrival at Donwell, Emma leapt forward and handed a note to her driver. 'This is for Miss Bates. You may leave me here and deliver it to Highbury. Do not linger. The task I must execute for Mr Knightley will not take me long.'

Emma stood in solitude outside the fine old house. Her sleepless night had left her with an aching head and she drew in deep breaths of the cool autumnal air. It was purer here than anywhere, she thought, perhaps the propinquity to the river and open meadows giving a translucency more refreshing than the bush-shrouded environment of Hartfield. How Knightley must miss it!

Boldly she walked to the front door and put the key into the great lock. It turned easily and, in a moment, she was inside the darkness of the hall – for on this side the shutters were entirely closed.

'Mr Churchill! It is I – Mrs Knightley,' and then, in case his mind was further disordered, 'Miss Woodhouse!' But no sound came back to her – except the scuttle of mice chasing as far away as possible behind the wainscoting.

'Mr Churchill, I have no one with me! I wish only to be of aid to you!' Still no sound – not even a mouse this time. Emma walked further inside – into the large panelled room which – it seemed so long ago – they had visited on that strawberry-picking summer's day. Frank had arrived late, ill-humoured, having ridden from London; she had told him to eat to improve his temper – it had been in the days of their friendship – and he had returned to them recovered in spirits. It was only later she had discovered that the true reason for his reaction had been his meeting, on the way, with Jane Fairfax, who had refused to let him accompany her back to Highbury. They had quarrelled.

Ah – secrecy and deception – how it led to deeper and deeper waters. The echo of these thoughts, both exciting and frightening, stayed with Emma as she wandered through the shrouded empty rooms. It took an effort to remind herself that she was mistress of this house – as her husband was master – and not to feel as much of an intruder as Frank Churchill. Of him there was no sight; evidence of his presence recently, however, was presented to her when an old bird's nest falling down a chimney – she jumped much at the sudden sound and her heart clapped like a bell – led her to the grate. There she saw the remains of a fire, just such an inefficient, messy fire as she would expect Frank to make.

In expectation of James's return, she could look no longer; once more she stood out in the sunshine, although the cold of the uninhabited house had crept into her bones and she felt light but no warmth. Shivering and beating her hands, she set out to walk a bit. Her steps – how it led to deeper and deeper waters! – took her across the lawns through the shrubs, and towards the closest point in the loop of the wide river.

'You will not find me floating yet!'

'Ah!'

'I gave you a fright.'

'You are good at such things.' Anger helped Emma to recover her composure. 'Poor old Mrs Bates! Your wife's grandmother. What have you done there?!'

Emma stared at Frank's face – still unshaven, gaunt, and

now as sullen as a child's in front of a disapproving adult. Where was the handsome young man she had admired? 'You must come with me now before you do more harm to those you love – or those you should love. You can come with me to the Martins. They are good, kindly people.'

'Good, kindly people! Oh, Emma! I am a soul in torment and you talk of good, kindly people. What are such people to do with me? I, who am nearer the bottom of that river than you could ever understand – you who are happy, content – in perfect happiness – you who have a husband – a good man – Ah, I am doomed, utterly doomed—'

On these words Frank made a dash to the edge of the river so that Emma felt obliged to dash with him and grab his arm – although something told her that he would not jump or, if he would, he could swim – Yet his wife was dead . . .

'I feel your sadness, your suffering. But you will do no good living such a life as you do now – it merely encourages you in dangerous fancies—'

'Oh, Emma! Your kindness – I do not deserve—' He had flung himself violently into her arms, clung, sobbing.

'No. No!' Vainly, Emma tried to disengage herself but their position – on the very edge of the river, the bank slippery – made it difficult to be too energetic. 'Mr Knightley,' she began, as if waving a wand of good sense, and indeed Mr Churchill did at last loosen his grip so that she could remove herself with fervent agility.

'You have told him?' – that sullenness again. 'But why are you here without him?'

'I have not—'

'How can such a man as Mr Knightley understand me? A man without passions – an old man—'

'An honourable man!' – stung into angry retort.

'Ah, yes. Honourable.' In Frank's mouth the word became

an insult. 'It is easy to be honourable when the blood in your veins runs thin.'

'I will not listen.'

'No, do not! Why should you, Miss Woodhouse, Mrs Knightley! You are above such things. Your blood is as thin as his—'

'Mr Churchill!'

'Oh – I am sorry – I am mad – but you do not know— Do not go – I beg you – I am far worse— She was so often ill – out of sorts – forever wanting me to stay quiet – and then she would be ill— The pianoforte – we were happy when she played – but I could not sit there, day after day – the long dark nights in Yorkshire— Years I have had of it – first at the beck and call of one Mrs Churchill and then at another Mrs Churchill – is it surprising I wanted to be in London?'

'But you had a house in London.'

'She did not like it – my friends – my occupations – She wanted to be in Yorkshire, and me to be with her.'

'She loved you!'

'Love!' Groans. 'Love – if only love were the end of it – or even the most of it – I loved her – I will never love another.'

'If you loved her, you would want to be with her.'

'Ah, you make it sound so easy. Be my love ever so strong I could not give up my life for her – and she was obstinate too. She could have come to London, it would not have hurt her.'

'No.' A silence came to both of them. They stood at the water's edge and both thought that the harm that had come to Jane could not have been surpassed.

'Come with me,' said Emma, eventually, quietly.

'No. I will not. But I will not stay here. Do not worry, I shall go away further, much further.' He was quiet, too.

'Abroad?'

'You may think of me as you please, where you please. But remember, my faults arose out of too much passion, not too little. There are those—' Seeing Emma's expression he stopped himself. 'No, I will not speak of your husband again – I have apologised – I spoke out of madness – but you are not like him. Mrs Knightley – see, I call you by his name, with respect – you are a woman whose nature it is to feel deeply—'

'Mr Churchill, I will not listen to you further.' She walked a few steps, frowning, and yet there was a part of her which did want to hear these words; so false as they must be and coming from a man so unlikely to recognise the truth or be capable of telling it, yet they took hold of her. Mr Knightley and she were very different in temperament. Previously, she had seen his good sense as a welcome regulator to her impetuousness; but Frank Churchill's words showed it in a different light, and she remembered how Knightley had turned on his side the night before, slept evenly while she had lain awake.

'Here is your carriage – I will not see you again. Be content with Mr Knightley. It may be that people like you and I – so passionate – should find someone to look after them, as a parent, as a father. Goodbye, Emma!' He departed along the riverside, a slim, tattered figure, yet with something of the hangdog desperado exchanged for the old jauntiness.

Emma did not look further. Her hands and feet were very cold; but her cheeks were burning; she felt as if something momentous had come out of this meeting – to do with her, not him. But there was no time to examine what exactly it was. Hurrying on feet that felt numb, she reached her carriage and sank into the cushioned seat. The horses were whipped up and they started the journey back to Hartfield.

The news that awaited Emma on her arrival swept out all

ideas of her own condition. Mr Woodhouse was agitated enough to greet her in the hall.

'My dear. News! What sad news, indeed! Mr Weston has just called – I am surprised you did not cross him on the road. He was coming at Mrs Weston's most particular request so that we should know at once that Mrs Weston is much improved and, although keeping to the house a little longer, would most enjoy a visit – but you must think of yourself, my dear Emma – the infections—'

'But this is good news, papa' – taking off her bonnet and cloak, pinching her cheeks to take off the draining pallor.

'No. No. You do not understand me—'

'Come, papa. Let us enter the room.'

This was allowed but with Mr Woodhouse speaking all the way. 'Mr Weston had business in Highbury before he came – you were not there, I understand – and it was there he heard the bad news. Poor old Mrs Bates was taken away from us in the night!'

'Oh!' Emma sank into a chair.

'You are shocked. What a pity that you should be so shocked.'

'Papa – such an old friend!'

'Yes. Yes. I felt it deeply. When Mr Weston gave me the news, I could scarcely find words – I feared for myself – on my own – no one to support my spirits,' a dart of reproach to Emma, 'so I set to thinking—'

'Thinking, papa? That was brave in such a case—' Emma spoke almost at random, for this morning seemed to be determined to give her nothing but pain. Now she must find strength to cheer her father when she only felt weakness, or his spirits would give way. In this she underestimated Mr Woodhouse.

On the death of an old friend, a rational man, bent on not adding needlessly to the sum of human misery, may have two reactions: the first will lead him to the term 'a merciful release' and the second will find him dwelling, almost with exultation, on his own continued existence in this world. In his daughter's absence, Mr Woodhouse partook freely of both these consolations and was now made even happier at the prospect of sharing them with Emma.

'Mrs Bates was, I fear, no longer the Mrs Bates who played such a sharp hand at quadrille. Poor old lady – stone deaf – rational mind quite gone – blind—'

'Mrs Bates could see only too well,' Emma lifted her head.

'But she could not give a proper interpretation of the message of her eyes – hallucinations – it is the same as blindness, perhaps worse! It is a wonder she lived on so long. We must console ourselves, Emma – it is better that – in all, a merciful release!'

'Yes, dear papa' – for Mr Woodhouse seemed to expect approbation for his attitude. 'She was made very wretched at her granddaughter's passing away – although the child—'

'She had determined to leave us – we must not hold her back—'

'No, papa.'

The first point agreed, Mr Woodhouse proceeded with even more satisfaction to the second. 'You have noted that I am not overwhelmed?'

'I am very glad to see it, papa.'

'It is one of the peculiarities of the case that poor old Mrs Bates who has never had a day's illness in her life should be carried away while I – a martyr to my health – should be here. It must be put down, my dear – I must speak immodestly here – to strength of purpose, strength of will—'

Emma was about to point out that it could also be put down to a difference in age since Mrs Bates was a good fifteen years older than Mr Woodhouse. On reflection, however, she saw that Mr Woodhouse had for so long thought of himself as elderly and in need of care – perhaps ever since his wife left him – that he truly believed he was the elder. Besides, there was no reason to contradict any attitude that gave him comfort.

'Indeed, dear papa, you are an example to all in Highbury.'

'That is true; I cannot contradict it. Now, Emma, you must change your shoes which I perceive are wet to the ankles.'

'Ah, poor Miss Bates,' Emma spoke quickly. 'I cannot think of her without unhappiness.'

'Poor Miss Bates – poor Miss Bates.' Mr Woodhouse's face fell, then brightened. 'We shall invite her here. Mrs Goddard may come too,' he added, naming the respectable widow who ran a school for young ladies in Highbury. 'But poor Miss Bates we shall invite very often. Emma, you will see to it that Miss Bates sits down with us,' a sigh, 'Ah, change is hard to bear – but we must remember it was Mrs Bates' own wish. She is at peace.'

So Emma escaped from her father to her parlour and could find relief in tidying up after her morning's excursion; the key must be replaced in Mr Knightley's desk and the biscuits, still wrapped in her handkerchief, eaten for want of any other means of disposal. They must have had a strengthening effect for then she was able to look forward, with a measure of calm expectation, to the visit she would make to Mrs Weston on the morrow. Rational intercourse was the least she could expect and far more than she had heard all this troubled day. Her best consolation, however, lay in the knowledge that Frank Churchill would no longer haunt Donwell Abbey; and with this came the idea that the very best place for Jane's ill-fated pianoforte – even if it were a case of shutting the stable door after the horse had bolted – was at the Abbey.

11

'Mr Knightley is long away?' Mrs Weston sat in her accustomed chair, a lace bonnet tied neatly under her chin and her child, Anna, playing comfortably at her feet.

'The sight of you is such a comfort!' cried Emma, looking at her dear friend and erstwhile governess with a smile that brought a tear to her eye.

'So much emotion,' commented Mrs Weston, smiling. 'We all must lose our husbands to business – except that—' she hesitated as if to remodel her thought, 'you are young—'

'Not so young; not so young as Harriet Martin – beside her I bear immeasurable years.'

'Immeasurable years?'– a grave smile. 'Oh, Emma, it is not that. You are not comparing your situation – there is time.'

But although they were such good friends, the delicacy of her nature and the consciousness of her own good fortune in being shortly to produce a second child, when one had been more than she hoped for, made her incapable of inquiring whether it was Emma's own childless condition which was the cause of her unsettled mood.

'It is not that I care about Harriet,' said Emma, sensitive to what her dear friend was thinking. 'I do not need a child to make me satisfied with myself or my life. I will not object; but I do not mourn.'

'And Mr Knightley?' With all the goodness of her heart and her kindness towards her former charge, Mrs Weston could not resist the question. She did not add 'a man of his age' but the thought was clear on her face.

'What has made you happy and Mr Weston happy may not do the same for Mr Knightley and me!' Emma's voice was stiff; here was something near reproach when she had come for comfort. On her walk over to Randalls she had considered confiding the story of Frank Churchill's stay at Donwell but now that held no temptation.

'Mr Knightley returns today, perhaps?' After a pause Mrs Weston reverted to her first remark for she had something more to say on the subject, although she too was wondering whether it would be wise. Emma seemed such a child today, her usually bright face clouded, her hazel eyes dropped down. And yet a small warning to something that might, anyway, turn into nothing, could do no harm.

'Mr Weston has also been in town on business.'

'Ah. He saw Isabella?' Emma brightened.

'Indeed he saw Mrs John Knightley.'

'She is well?'

'Better than can be expected – in health – but—'

'But? Speak, Mrs Weston. I am all agitation. You are like a doctor who says his patient is quite well – except that his head is off his shoulders. There is so much that is morbid around us that my fears – and you know how little I am accustomed to groundless fears – are up and bristling as soldiers on a battlefield.'

'My "but" was because that is how Mr Weston spoke it to me. He also saw Mr Knightley who hinted there was an anxiety, a matter of business, as far as Mr Weston could understand it, about Mr John Knightley. He could get no more out of him. Doubtless you will know all on

Mr Knightley's return – I thought it kindly to prepare you a little.'

'Yes,' agreed Emma, trying to smile, for in truth she did not think it kindly of Mrs Weston to inform her that Mr Weston knew more about her family's situation than she did herself. She hid her agitation by bending down to play with little Anna who was a cheerful child and pleased enough to be bounced on this grand lady's knee.

'We will not talk any more of unpleasant things. Perhaps I was wrong—'

'We will not,' said Emma, bouncing the child till she screamed in delight and Mrs Weston quite gave herself up to motherly pride. There was no place after for any conversation of serious import.

Another day was to pass before Mr Knightley's return, giving Emma's ever-ingenious imagination time to create many an explanation for Mrs Weston's hinting. Mr John Knightley had never been much appreciated or fully understood by Emma: cold, irritable, ambitious, he lacked the upright openness of his elder brother and seemed to think that a clever phrase made up for a warm heart. Emma, for her sister's sake, had grown to like him – even to admire his flow of wit when in good spirits – but she had never been able to love him. In short, she was ready to believe that he had run off with an actress – except his nature seemed too cold for that – that he had quarrelled with the Lord Chief Justice (a creature Emma could not imagine but assumed very important to her brother-in-law) since he could quarrel with anyone, or even, this was an inspiration of the later reaches of the night, that he had revealed an earlier liaison which had produced a child, only now acknowledged – a Harriet Smith, perhaps, whose existence would cost poor Isabella all her happiness.

All these imaginings were, Emma admitted to herself eventually, merely the products of a complete lack of knowledge and would remain so until Mr Knightley should return. At last, on the second day, a note announced his arrival later that day. Spirits already raised, Emma set off for Highbury. Her father had remarked that morning how out of countenance she was looking; the walk and fresh air would do her good, for her vanity would not allow Mr Knightley to think that she could not sustain his absence without wilting.

It is a well-known truth that one preoccupation drives out another – or at very least, lessens its impact. This latest anxiety had pushed to the back of Emma's mind the situation of poor, doubly bereaved Miss Bates and her own guilty involvement for not revealing Mr Churchill's secret presence.

It was some days since Emma had paid Highbury any attention and she was surprised to see that all the ill dispositions she had suffered over the last week – the turmoils, trials and tribulations – had not altered its aspect of everyday cheerfulness and activity; the butcher still carried his tray, a tidy old woman travelled homewards with her full basket, two curs quarrelled over a dirty bone, and a string of dawdling children round the baker's little bow-window eyed the gingerbread until she approached, upon which they chased each other away with much laughter. In short, she might feel changed, enveloped, at times, in what felt like a black cloudiness, but Highbury was the same; for no reason at all, this was consoling and Emma found herself tripping along more lightly and with a smile at her lips.

'You smile. It is good to be young and free of care.' If there were one person to remove Emma's smile from her face it was Mrs Elton, who came out of Ford's just at the most inopportune moment – inopportune from the point of view of one, if not the other.

'I am glad to see you, ma'am,' continued Mrs Elton, who

today wore stripes which had the curious effect of making her look like a bolster before the cover were on. 'I fear I have a sad disappointment to impart. Most sad indeed.'

'I am sorry for that,' said Emma, 'the gay style of your dress had led me to hope that it indicated a cheerful heart.'

'I always try to be elegant for Mr Elton's sake – my position as his wife – even though our way of living is so humble at present – but I must tell you: Mrs Serena Suckling is unwell, most unwell.'

'Unwell! Mrs Suckling. Can this mean her visit may not take place?'

Mrs Elton bowed in assent, too overcome by melancholy to speak.

'Well,' began Emma, considering how she might combine politeness with truth, but the case seemed hopeless so instead she changed the subject. 'Have you visited poor Miss Bates?'

But Mrs Elton had no wish to exchange Mrs Serena Suckling's illness for Miss Bates' bereavement. The one gave grandeur to her view, the other diminished it. There was no help for it; Emma must stand and listen to Mrs Suckling's liability to heavy colds that might turn into coughs, to details of the remedies she found helpful, although in this case not helpful enough.

'We must do without her!' exclaimed Emma after five minutes, in a tone not at all grieving enough for Mrs Elton who seemed about to step aside and allow Emma to leave when she unluckily added, 'I will inform Mr Knightley when he returns tonight.'

'Returns tonight!' Mrs Elton, who had been pulling on her gloves, looked up, the tip of her beaky nose quivering as much as the tassel on her bonnet. 'My dear, Mr Knightley is returned. I saw him myself, just an hour back. I was visiting Abbey-Mill – I patronise Mrs Harriet Martin, you know –

when I saw him walking with Mr Martin. From my carriage window, I saw him approach the house as I left. Well!' Mrs Elton made no attempt to conceal her satisfaction in the knowledge that Mr Knightley, after several days' separation from his wife, preferred to visit the Martins before her and that Mrs Knightley did not know it. She left in joy; and left Emma hardly able to disguise her mortification.

Mr Knightley's step was one of the most typical things about him; it was the step of a man who did not doubt himself, who thought himself equal to the task ahead, who made his way in the world with the expectation of success. Firm, regular, unequivocal, it had been the beat to Emma's childhood, growing up, and to her marriage. She heard it unconsciously and only noticed it if the beat of the tread altered – as it did the afternoon Mr Knightley returned to Hartfield.

Emma had determined not to rush out to greet him so from where she sat in the parlour she could hear him cross the length of the hallway. His step was slow, dragging and hesitant. He entered the room.

'My dear!'

'You are back.' She would not smile too wide but looked up into his face; the colour whipped into his cheeks by his ride could not disguise an expression of languor and dejection such as she had never seen it wear before.

He came to her, kissed her, 'Oh, Emma, I have missed you more than you could guess.'

She hardened her heart, 'I might not believe it.'

He looked at her questioning.

'You did not come here straight. You preferred others to your wife' – trying to sound light, she merely succeeded in petulance.

'Ah, I see. My dear.' He sat down beside her on the sofa and took both her hands between his. 'You think if I had my choice, I would prefer to spend my time with Mr Robert Martin above the company of my wife?'

'Mrs Elton saw you there' – now a whine. How she disliked herself!

'Mrs Elton. Ah. Despite being Mrs Elton, she was right. I had business with Mr Martin.'

'That could not wait?'

'That could not wait.'

A silence followed which Mr Knightley seemed either unwilling, or too tired, to break and Emma too vexed. Where was the explanation she had a right to expect? She withdrew her hands from his and stood. 'I must dress for dinner. I will tell papa you are returned.'

'I shall follow shortly.'

But he did not, and when Emma returned with her father on her arm, he was slumped asleep where he sat. This was extraordinary, inexplicable! – or explicable only by illness. Both father and daughter stood in horror – Mr Knightley asleep at four o'clock in the afternoon was as if the cock were to crow at midday or the moon to rise before breakfast.

'Ah. My apologies.' Mr Knightley opened his eyes to see two faces staring down at him with – for perhaps the first time he could remember – exactly the same expression. He rose instantly. 'I am well, very well. Quite well.' He took Mr Woodhouse's arm and led him, as briskly as possible, to table. Emma followed, for Mr Woodhouse's fear must be quelled by reassuring chatter before it grew into a flood, but just before they sat Mr Knightley cast her a look, again untypical, an appeal – she was sure she read it right: 'Be patient, be kind, I will explain all as soon as we are alone.'

12

'My brother is bankrupt.'

'Bankrupt!' Emma sat at her little dressing-table and gazed, round-eyed, at her own reflection. Behind it, she could see the shadowy form of Mr Knightley who hunched against the four-poster. 'Bankrupt,' repeated Emma, for the word meant so little to her – indeed she hardly thought she had ever heard it spoken – that she had to try the sound to find if she knew the meaning. 'He has no money left?'

'Worse. He has creditors. Unpaid bills.'

Emma, still looking into the mirror, saw Knightley put his head in his hands. Should she go to him? First she must know more. 'Isabella? The children?'

'He has no money for them. He has less than no money. He has speculated unwisely – in grain initially and then in canals—'

'In canals!' interjected Emma, and a wild view of glassy water was accompanied by an image of Frank Churchill. How unimportant that secret seemed now.

'Canals in South America. He had used every penny and more, sure in success – but there were no canals and he is bankrupt!'

That word again. 'But he is a clever man!—'

'That is the trouble. It is his cleverness that has led him to believe that he could make money more readily by canals – by some fancy foreign scheme – than by steady application.'

'I cannot comprehend it. Your brother is a lawyer; he is a professional man. I know he has sometimes not behaved to my father as I would most wish, but this – how could such a thing happen? Why did no one stop him? My poor Isabella.'

'There is worse still, far worse—' Mr Knightley came and stood behind his wife, an upright dark figure reflected in her mirror, like a man prepared to face an executioner. 'My brother is in gaol.'

'Oh, Isabella, Isabella! In gaol, you say?' She turned and clutched him.

'It is the law. A lawyer cannot be above the law – although I think he hoped so. Let us sit down together and I will explain the rest.'

They sat either side of the fire, as Knightley told the whole sad story, not that there was much to tell. John Knightley had been convinced by another lawyer, a Mr Graham, an equally clever man who was already short of money and had seen this way of changing his fortunes; he had need of a partner to put up the greater part of the money. John Knightley, driven by whatever motive – perhaps merely the irritable jealousy of being the second son or perhaps, more honourably, out of anxiety to provide for his ever-growing family, had allowed himself to become convinced. He had invested everything, goods, house, wages – the money had gone out, for ever, irretrievable, but the canals had never been built. The colleague had disappeared – either himself duped and fled from his creditors to France, or himself the villain, it was not certain which. It did not matter – the money could never be recovered. John Knightley, himself a lawyer, had given up all hope. He was imprisoned and totally dependent on his brother.

'I cannot take it in!' Emma cried. 'What is the use of putting him in gaol?'

'No use. But it is the law. Until he can find the money he must stay imprisoned.'

'And his wife? His children?' Emma thought of her sister whose presence at Hartfield – much as it was looked forward to and enjoyed – was accompanied by a level of little anxieties which almost rivalled their father's. How could she deal with such a ghastly stroke of fortune?

'Isabella knows very little. John she thinks merely away on business – she is brave about that.' Knightley managed a smile. 'Far braver than I would have foretold – but her condition makes her health uncertain. I had hoped to bring her and the children here, but her time is too close, she cannot be moved. I have paid enough bills for them to stay in London for the present.'

Emma felt herself sinking under the waves of greater realisation but could find nothing, except exclamations – 'Oh, Knightley! Oh papa! Poor papa!' – to add. It was outside her experience; she felt like a country boy faced by a press gang – a dread of what was to come but no means of escape. 'Perhaps the two older boys could be sent here?' – in a murmur.

'Isabella will not be separated from any of her children. She is full of hidden fears – only half believes the reason for John's absence. She has transferred her fear for him – for John – for herself – on to their little shoulders. Oh, Emma, earlier you cried – so justly – 'Why did no one stop him?' That is the question I ask myself every moment, when I am not actively trying to further his cause. Why did I not know? I cannot but reproach myself, blame my own blindness—'

'But how could you know if he had not told you?'

'I knew his nature; he is my younger brother; I knew his weakness for money. Do you remember once he said to poor Jane Fairfax (as she was then) that he preferred a business letter over a letter of friendship. I can repeat his words: "Business may bring money but friendship hardly ever does". She accused him of a lack of seriousness but the words rang a knell in my heart. There was a time when we were both young – when he narrowly escaped grave embarrassment owing to an over-regard for money and a not great enough regard for honesty – Ah, nothing is served by looking at the past. Suffice it to say that I should have followed his affairs more closely – when so many lives depended on him. What is my excuse? I thought your sister's sweet gentleness, her deep affection for him, his fondness for her and their children, had taught him to curb his wayward instincts. I thought it because I wanted to think it! I should have known better.'

He was sobbing! Mr Knightley was sobbing, the manly shoulders heaving. Emma looked with horror; not only for the whole tragic situation but for herself. How could he give in to his emotions so completely! Vaguely, she felt herself displaced, her reactions taken over by him. Too young to appreciate the powerful effect that complete exhaustion of the body can have on the strongest of men – Knightley had only slept one night through in the past week when he lay at Hartfield – Emma stared, amazed, and her own tears, which were about to fall, receded, leaving her head aching all the worse for containing them.

Knightley rose. 'I am not myself' – a stifled voice. 'I shall sleep in my room.'

This was a cruel, ungentlemanly cut – to be left on her own and no prospect of sleep. 'Please – I—'

'I shall tell you more in the morning' – a little recovery, a voice not so blurred. 'The situation is not without hope – no, not at all, my dear—' He hesitated and then returned to where Emma sat in all hopelessness. 'What is one more night's sleep lost? Come, my dear, let me be your maid.'

Tender fingers undid the buttons at the back of Emma's

dress, made her step out of it and held her for a minute, then he sighed and left the room. Emma lay in bed waiting for his return.

The night was dark, cold; she clutched at the air, eyes wide open; it seemed that their whole life must be changed but she could not see how; he would tell her; he would ordain. She recalled his heaving shoulders, his sobs; and his tender fingers at her back . . . She came to no conclusion, except that it was not a Mr Knightley she knew. She could not think of John Knightley in gaol, of Isabella's future despair – of the wretchedness of the children. That must wait for Knightley's return. He was back soon enough, holding her comfortingly.

'Since Isabella cannot be removed from London – did I say she is confined to bed? – since the loving care of a sister is what she most needs, you, Emma, must come to her as soon as arrangements can be made for your father—'

'I – to London?' Emma's voice was faint.

'It is inevitable,' said Mr Knightley with the kind of firmness for which Emma had conjoined her life with his.

13

Emma had never wanted to go to London in her life; she had wanted to go to the sea and she had gone – her first days of marriage would be forever linked with the October light streaking a bottle-green sea, with many coloured pebbles running backwards and forwards under the thrusting waves, with the wild cry of the seagulls when she woke in the morning, with the fishing boats setting out at night. The sea had not disappointed.

But of London she had no expectations – except the worst. The reasons for this were hardly rational; until this latest tragedy, her sister had lived there very contentedly for many years; despite all the stresses of a growing family. The most likely reason was the influence of Mr Woodhouse who considered London as full of dangers as the high seas; Emma had grown up to believe that she would never be allowed to leave her father's side for that destination; believing this, she made the best of what she could not change – which required her to make the worst of what she could not have.

Yet now Mr Knightley advised, nay, commanded her to go – and as soon as she possibly could. And under what circumstances!

The day dawned with little light in the sky; but breakfast must be sat through; Mr Woodhouse given the merest hint of trouble – enough to prepare him but not to send him into a panic. 'Isabel a little under the weather' – that would do.

Mr Knightley had ridden out and on his return they met together in their upstairs parlour. 'I have visited Miss Bates,' he began at once, in this morning light his faculties as clear and sharp as ever.

'Miss Bates?' wavered Emma, too much on her mind to do more than wait.

'She is willing to come to Hartfield as soon as we desire her presence. She will stay as long as she is needed – as long as you are needed by your sister.'

They had talked of this the night before, but the swiftness of the actual happening startled Emma; she felt she had no part in it except to quieten her father – that had always been so much of her days—

'She asked but one favour – a favour I understand you had already undertook to arrange for her—'

A blush began on Emma's cheeks; despite everything, Miss Bates' favour brought memory of Frank. 'The pianoforte!' she exclaimed.

'Precisely. I do not understand exactly— She feels it something to do with her mother's death – you had offered to remove it? she was not clear.'

'You were away. She still wants it gone?'

'So I understand. She seems in dread of it.'

'I had meant to ask if it could go to Donwell?'

'Whatever you think best, Emma.'

'But if she is not in her rooms?'

'She was most particular – she wants it gone, until Mr Churchill returns to claim it. Donwell will serve, I have no doubt.'

At the name of Churchill, Emma's blush increased but she felt no temptation to reveal their meetings.

'I will have Robert Martin arrange to remove the pianoforte. I must be away back to London again.' He was hasty, his manner brusque, his face hardly turned towards her. 'Two days I will give you and then you must be ready.'

'My father?' queried Emma.

'Mr Woodhouse is not expecting a baby,' said Knightley in a brutal voice that astonished Emma. 'Miss Bates will keep him comfortable. She is not loquacious at the moment but I have no doubt that when her first grief has abated the words will take over from the tears and she can express her gratitude to your father in so many sentences of goodwill; that all his mind will be turned on when he can be allowed to express his fears of what passes in London. He will know nothing of the bankruptcy, of course. I am assured that those two will manage very comfortably together. Their words will mix like the waters of the Amazon and make a great double flow.'

So be it. If it were to be done, it were best done quickly; Mr Woodhouse must be told at the last minute when all the new arrangements for his comfort were in place. Miss Bates, who had never been housekeeper for more than a few rooms, must be taught to deal with Sterne in a way that made that headstrong cook take responsibility as she had always wished but never been allowed to do under Emma's governance. Mr and Mrs Weston must be informed and recruited as advisers to Miss Bates and comforters to Mr Woodhouse – it was as well Mrs Weston's health had returned. James must be given orders to prepare for the sixteen-mile journey to London and yet persuaded not to inform his master immediately.

These arrangements and more – she felt it necessary to check every store in the house, personally – kept Emma so busy that she had no leisure to think of herself. The dark image of London became dimmer. All her energies were devoted to departing from her father in a way which left him, if not happy, at least content; that seemed nearly too much to hope.

Miss Bates was soon in the house; her silent burden of sorrow battled with her wish to speak compliments of the great state in which she found herself, so that she would utter a few words, fall silent for a few seconds and then start again, rather as a pump, improperly handled, gives its water in fits and starts. She did, however, make much of an effort to smile which, in Emma's view, gave promise of more sanguine times ahead.

She chose to break the news of her departure on her last evening, after dinner when Mr and Mrs Weston had come for a visit. They would support her.

'Papa, I have something to tell you.'

'What can you mean, my dear? I hope James is not unwell. He has been acting very strange of late; if I did not know it to be impossible I would say he hid from me behind the door this morning.'

'Oh, papa. You must not be worried but I am to go to London!' It was a fearful cry, her own anxieties surfacing at a most awkward time.

'Isabella!' cried Mr Woodhouse.

'Mr Woodhouse, dear friend,' Mr Weston, smiling, Mrs Weston, smiling, Miss Bates, smiling, drew close. 'What cannot be changed must be endured. Mrs John Knightley is in excellent health, excellent – I have it from Perry – but she is a little tired.'

'Five children,' smiled Mrs Weston. 'Having only one, I know the amount of work that such joy must be earned by. It is natural that she should want her sister to be at her side.'

'Emma!' gasped Mr Woodhouse.

What cannot be altered must be endured. As Emma recovered herself enough to smile too, Mr Woodhouse found himself surrounded by a wall of cheerful faces and, if one of them were to leave, three were to stay behind. After an hour of investigating every vexatious circumstance he was even able to abandon the contemplation of his own discomfort for long enough to consider his daughter's. 'But, my dear, I recollect you dislike London excessively.'

'Mrs Knightley cannot dislike a place she has never visited' – Mr Weston firmly. 'She can only dislike the idea; and ideas have seldom much grounding in reality. In my view, ideas and imagination do more damage—'

'We must also consider,' interrupted Mrs Weston, 'that Mr Knightley's business has required his presence in London recently and that he is in residence there at the present time and it never does for a man to be separated from his wife.'

'Alas!' By the feeling in the word, it was clear Mr Woodhouse saw this as a reference to his separation from his wife twenty years ago. 'Alas, poor Mrs Woodhouse!'

There was a silence, broken only by a dreadfully large gulp from Miss Bates who had quite given up her smile. Mr Woodhouse turned to her and his kindly eyes met hers – wide and welling.

'Ah, poor Miss Bates. Poor, poor Bates!' Such a wealth and depth of sorrow was shared and exchanged between these two that the others could not presume to enter it. They exchanged glances, however, which expressed the consciousness that they had brought together two feeling souls who would find satisfaction in a similar understanding of life's woes. All had been done that could be done to prepare for Emma's departure.

All, that is, for her father. It was an exhausted young lady who found herself in her room at nine o'clock at night with her clothes laid out but none packed, none examined for imperfections, none chosen.

'Oh, Merry,' she cried when the maid appeared. 'I am going to London tomorrow and I have not brought a pair of new stockings nor trimmed a bonnet.'

'London's the place for trimming, ma'am,' said Merry

longingly. 'I've heard there're ribbons made of gold with sparklers dropping off them like icicles off a roof-edge. You won't be wanting Ford's trimmings once you're in London.'

Emma sat on the bed and looked at her stout, rosy-cheeked maid. How she would be looking forward to a trip to London! 'Now, I will sit here and command while you pack.'

It was as much of a surprise to Emma as it may be to the reader that this exercise, not thought of, except to be rather dreaded, raised Emma's spirits considerably. It was not that her wardrobe was inspiring; apart from a few new gowns made around the time of her marriage; she had little more fashionable than a second-hand study of Isabella's magazines and a country dressmaker could provide – but it led her to the thought that, even with the dismal reason for her visit to the capital city, she must, nevertheless, venture outside of the house, on occasions, if only to accompany the children. She must see sights that she had heard of only from books; she might do more – visit a theatre or, at least, an interesting church. There were shops, galleries, public buildings, parks.

By the time Emma lay down and closed her eyes, her head was spinning with visions of London which gradually became strangely similar to scenes from the novels of Smollett and Fielding, as if Mr Weston's proscription of ideas and imagination versus reality had taken root in contrary mode. Faces, darkened, smiling, grimacing, threatening, turned around as if in a kaleidoscope.

Just before dawn, the kaleidoscope stopped and Emma sat up abruptly. 'What if Frank Churchill should not have kept his word to me and is still at Donwell? And the pianoforte, his pianoforte, about to arrive?'

Up till now, she had not doubted Mr Churchill's intention to leave. Why should he want to stay, with no food, heating, light? But night fears made the worst seem possible.

Without waiting to wrap herself against the cold, Emma went through to her upstairs room and sat at her little desk.

Dear Mr Martin, I had intended to apprise Mr Knightley of my suspicion that some person had broken in at Donwell Abbey – through a pane shattered in a side door – but Mr Knightley has now left for London. Would you therefore do me the favour of ascertaining whether there are any grounds for my anxiety while conveying the pianoforte thence – I see no point in worrying Mr Knightley at the present time—

Many drafts produced this short note; it would have to do. It was not elegant, but the point was made; and Mr Martin was a conscientious man. She need not worry further – except to pass the letter to James with instructions to deliver it to Abbey-Mill Farm on his return from London.

Skipping her cold feet across the polished floorboards, Emma re-entered her bedroom where Merry wonderingly attended her mistress's return from such an unusually early visit to her desk. She held out a pair of not very warm curling tongs.

'Shall I heat them, ma'am?'

'No,' cried Emma, 'London must take me as it finds me!'

14

The day was colder than of late, but bright. Emma, sitting close to the window of the carriage so that she should miss nothing passing – neither grand house arising out of its shrubberies like a head from a ruff, nor grand equipage dashing along the road at great risk to her own humbler conveyance – felt the absence of rain a great blessing. Rain always made her sad and would have made her task of raising the spirits of the Knightley household far more taxing. A bright sky made a bright face.

Now that Emma had time on her own, she could feel the weight of the responsibility Mr Knightley had put on her. She must keep Isabella, so close to her confinement, cheerful in her husband's absence and ignorant of the true reason. She could not believe that a wife so devoted to her husband had not guessed that something was amiss. On the other hand, John Knightley had always struck Emma as a very close, secret sort of man so perhaps he did not confide his business affairs to his wife. Moreover, his legal work had sometimes caused him to stop away for more than a week or two. To which might be added Isabella's occupation with her children. 'Yet I hope Knightley would have told me anything half so important,' she said to herself.

Sixteen miles was all that had stood between Emma and the city for her whole lifetime. Now the miles disappeared under James's horses and the wheels of the carriage with startling rapidity. One minute they were in the country with a signpost saying they still had six miles yet, and the next they were crossing a fine stone bridge over a river that could only be the Thames – the bridge was called 'Westminster' – then they were among houses and even over a patch of cobbling which made the horses' hoofs ring.

Emma sat as close to the window as she could without sacrificing propriety, and was just beginning to feel herself in the centre of the noisy, bustling, jostling, dirty city that she had thought she most dreaded – so many people in one spot as she had believed impossible – her heartbeat fast, her cheek flushed – when their way had turned and it seemed they were almost come to the country again. There were cows, sheep, hedgerows, a fence with a style in it, even a brook. Perhaps James had mistaken the path. She tapped on the window. He guessed her meaning even before she spoke.

'Five minutes to Brunswick Square, ma'am.' He was confident, calm. There could be no mistake.

Emma had set herself to becoming calm – to finding an even temper that would sustain the distressing scenes she must witness – Isabella in bed, desolate, the children wild and sorrowful – when James called again, 'Bedford Square, ma'am!' 'Russell Square, ma'am!' 'Brunswick Square!'

They were passing through – or around: Bedford Square was gated at either end so they may not enter – a series of large and elegant spaces surrounded by tall houses. The size, the grandeur, the proximity to grass, trees and sky was quite unlike anything Emma had expected of London. Why had Isabella not told her? It was true that she had often refuted their father's anxieties about their health with descriptions of their part of London being very 'airy', very healthy. Emma was surprised, impressed, and hardly felt as if she were in London – at least the London of her imagination – at all. The carriage came to a standstill.

Casting out topographical questions, Emma composed her face into quiet sympathy; it was not difficult. Now that she was outside Mr John Knightley's own front door, she felt the magnitude of his falling even more keenly than she had before. This was a large front door, tall, broad and ornamented with a brass doorknob and knocker. It was at the top of a tall, wide, marble flight of steps and above it arose a wall of windows, of wrought-iron balconies. It was an imposing residence, made – as she thought to herself with some surprise since she had never seen the like before – more imposing by the identically magnificent houses to which it was affixed on either side and which continued round the square.

Their neighbourliness, their nearness, their upright jaunty look – although stately too – was not like the country. After all, she was in London. Here, she could already see, where people lived in rows, not by ones or twos, it would be terrible to lose your place, like a soldier who falls out of line – a shame and humiliation. Poor, poor John Knightley.

Such unhappy ideas occupied Emma's thoughts in the few moments she stood outside the house, quite long enough to lower her spirits to an appropriate level.

'I shall knock,' announced James, seeing his mistress apparently reluctant. But before he could do so, the door burst open and two figures flew out towards Emma.

'We have been waiting all morning!'

'We saw you arrive from the nursery but Nurse made us brush our hair.'

'We have set up a game of spillikins!'

Where was the sorrow, the gloom, the despondency? Wildness, perhaps, was present, but a gleeful wildness.

Emma was pulled inside by either arm, through a high-ceilinged hallway and into a pretty, finely furnished sitting-room.

'But your mama!' – an expostulation. 'I cannot sit down with you.'

'She's sleeping!'

'Sleeps tight as a mole! – We looked in.'

Emma confessed herself touched by the scene before her, the table set with three chairs, the spillikins expectantly arranged; it was clear the boys were resolved to enjoy their aunt's company from the first moment of her arrival.

'Papa is teaching me chess,' said Henry, the elder, 'but he has been too much away for me to progress very far.'

'I wanted cup and ball!' cried John, the younger. 'But Henry felt certain you would be too tired. But I said I had never seen you tired at Grandpapa's so I did not see why you should be tired in London, just because you've sat in a carriage for a few hours.'

Emma smiled, her relief at their childish high spirits allowing her to be persuaded to 'just one game of spillikins before I unpack' – and 'just one more before I visit your dear mama' – and 'this is the very last, Henry, and you must not press me further'.

But the light, sun under thin cloud, turned the corner of the square and came through the wide windows and she was still sitting with the slender pieces of carved ivory – quite as intent on winning as her nephews – when Mr Knightley entered the room.

'My dear! Emma!' None of them had heard him coming into the house and he was able to take in the contented scene of domestic harmony before Emma rose hastily, the colour of her cheeks deepened by a guilty blush.

'Oh, Knightley – the boys – it is too dreadful – and I have not seen poor Isabella yet – I have not even visited my room!'

But Mr Knightley looked at her with such loving approbation and the boys danced about crying that she was 'the spillikins queen' or some such nonsense so that she gave up her guilty look and kissed Mr Knightley instead and told him she thought London a bright, lively place – not at all the dark dreariness she had expected. 'It is quite as sunny as Hartfield,' she said, pointing at the streaks across the carpet.

'The sun shines on all alike, if it is allowed to—' he stopped himself.

'Ah!' Emma glanced at the boys as she recognised that Knightley was thinking of their father's sad incarceration.

'You must know, my dear,' Mr Knightley sat down and crossed his legs, 'that this area is quite new, built on land owned by the Foundling Hospital which you may walk around if you wish. We are hardly in the city – although it is but ten minutes' brisk walk from Lincoln's Inn Fields, whence I came today, where my brother carried on his work.'

The boys soon tired of such talk and left to see if their mama had woken. On their uncle's inquiry whether they had not a nursemaid to attend them, they fled even faster, with scornful cries of 'Nurses are for the babies, not for us!'

Knightley observed after their departure that it was high time they were sent to school, but Emma found herself laughing.

'I must admit I did not expect such a smiling reception.'

Knightley moved his place so he could sit close to her on the sofa. 'I am glad of it. There is much unhappiness to come. But if only I can ward it off until after your sister's confinement – if I can do that and release my poor brother from a different sort of confinement – if this can be done, the house held on to a few months longer, then it may not be so bad.'

Over his face came the grey, despairing look that aged him so and had so frightened Emma at Hartfield. She stood.

'I shall go to Isabella or it will be time for dinner.'

'Yes. Do not overtax yourself after dinner—' he hesitated, took her hand, 'I must tell you that there is no bedchamber big enough for us both here – I am in lodgings. It is a modest place but clean enough – in Henrietta Street.'

'Oh, Knightley!'

'It is not as I would wish it' – bitter – 'but then nothing is as I would wish it.'

Something more was hidden in this 'nothing' but Emma must go to her sister, must overcome her own disappointment that her husband would not be at her side during the nights and greet Isabella with all the affection that she very truly felt.

Her sister stood by her mirror, welcoming.

'Look! I am dressed in your honour! I had grown so slovenly in my dear husband's absence.'

'You did not have to dress for me, Isabella. What does your doctor advise?'

'Dear Mr Wingfield. You will meet him tomorrow, I have no doubt. He has been in attendance every day. I have absolute confidence in him and he in me. Rest, it is all he prescribes. So I rest; it's the boys who suffer – but you have been with them. Did you find them well?'

Isabella's pride in her children was as great as any young mother and as she went through the different virtues and (very few) vices of each of her five children in turn, Emma understood that it was not so odd that she suspected little of the disaster that had struck her husband. Her outlook was so narrow, so limited to her family circle, of whom John Knightley was an honoured but not intimate member, that she had no time or will to think of the world outside. The set-aside position of Brunswick Square could only encourage this tendency.

'If you can keep the boys from going wild, that will be

such a service. How dull that sounds! But you will not be dull. Although I shall rest, you shall have visitors – go out to the shops – Mr Knightley must arrange seats at the theatre!'

'You are kind, Isabella – but I have come not on my own account, but on yours—'

'Yes. Yes. But do not believe I am such a poor-spirited creature that I wilt entirely under my husband's absence. He is often gone on business; no man has ever worked so hard. I am glad you are come, however – very glad and only sorry that we cannot house Mr Knightley here also – but you who have never seen London must take advantage of your visit. When Harriet Wilson came—'

'Ah, Mrs Martin!'

'Yes, yes. The marriage was arranged in this very house, you know. She and Robert Martin and the children went to Astley's – I wonder if you should enjoy that, although you are already married!'

As Isabella laughed at her own witticism and said, if her sister would give her the benefit of her arm, they must go down to dinner directly or Cook would give in to her fierce temper, Emma reflected that she seemed anything but downhearted. Whether that would make the blow to come more cruel she had not the leisure to consider but, if Isabella could insist – which it seemed she would – on her, Emma, going about the town, like a regular visitor, then it would be hard to think of a reason why not. It was a strange position Emma felt herself in – a great sword hung over the family, had wounded already its most important member, yet inside the house all was merriment. She must take the advice of Mr Knightley.

The time for this came after dinner when all the children and Isabella had removed themselves upstairs.

'It seems odd, Mr Knightley, that I have caused such

an upheaval in my father's life to come and lead a life of pleasure—'

He looked startled.

'Isabella insists I go out – she talks of visits – theatre – shops—'

He attended closely.

'It is odd that I know what she doesn't know.'

'Poor Emma – to keep such a secret! I must warn you that my efforts towards secrecy may not serve and then your presence will be a necessity and there will be no pleasure. Meanwhile, do as you think fit; my brother's situation will not be made worse by the smiles of his family. I shall be busy too often, I fear, to take you around very much and my mind is too heavy; but take advantage of what comes your way. I would not be the one to stop you in any pleasures, even if Isabella did not insist—'

'—But the creditors?'

'Trust that to me.' He turned away – 'I must take my leave.'

'I shall take over the running of the house from Isabella.'

'Yes. Yes.' He was impatient to be gone, she observed, out into the cold darkness, not even telling her when he would return.

Emma stood beside the curtain long after his firm steps – they *were* firm – had disappeared; and then, sighing for a husband who was not confiding everything in her, sighing for Hartfield and for home, she made her way upstairs.

15

'There are two visitors for you, ma'am.'

Emma was upstairs superintending the boys' lesson – for their tutor seemed in want of a little assistance in the line of discipline – when the maid knocked at the door. In the two days since her arrival she had found plenty to occupy herself and not so much need to push away the 'pleasure' that her sister had spoken of.

The house was not so well ordered, after all. Isabella had indeed been resting and, as Emma was soon informed by Mr Wingfield, the attentive doctor, must continue to do so if she were not to incur dangerous risks. Emma knew herself needed; it was a message she was glad to hear and she was so ready to oblige that she had only stepped out of the house to accompany Henry and John on the smallest expedition – time enough to take notice of the palatial Foundling Hospital that Mr Knightley had spoken of, which quite dominated the scene – time enough to see another fine square so like their own as to be indistinguishable (she held to her view that the country style was far more individual) but no time for shops, churches, public buildings, of which, it was true, there was no sight.

Her main occupation was inside the house and, since the weather had become very cold for the early days of November and Mr Knightley attended only for dinner, she had not regretted any further chance for exploration. But now there were visitors.

Checking her clothes with the confidence of someone who knows that a pretty face and fine figure makes her appear well dressed in whatever she happens to be wearing, Emma nevertheless called in at her chamber to exchange her present shawl for a better.

'Who is it?' she inquired of the maid, since Isabella must not be disturbed.

'The Reverend Mr Dugobair Tidmarsh,' said the girl, not without an indication that she knew the name had a ring, 'and Mrs Tidmarsh. They are often here.'

Armed with this information, Emma entered the room bravely; a vicar held no fears for her – not even a vicar of the London variety.

'I do hope we are not disturbing you – so keen to make your acquaintance – Mr Wingfield told of us of your arrival, your sequestration with the poor invalid – both husbands occupied—' The woman came forward, talking; the man behind, silent.

Since these were the first example of Londoners that Emma had met she looked at them attentively. Mrs Tidmarsh was elegant, fiercely elegant, hair as black as a raven's wing, brows flying above dark eyes, tall and strikingly dressed in amber shades, trimmed with black velvet. All this Emma took in at a glance while her visitor talked in a voice deep rather than light.

'We have come to take you out,' she concluded, 'we have hired a carriage so you cannot refuse.'

Indeed, there outside the window stood a carriage – not a very smart one, it is true, and its driver was trying to set light to a most unpipe-like pipe, but a carriage even so.

'You are very kind.' Emma tried to glimpse Mr Tidmarsh but he seemed to be sheltering behind his wife. She could discern, however, that he was slight, dark and young – younger, by some years it would seem, than his wife.

'I am impulsive,' she said. 'You may feel I am too impulsive for a stranger. Come, Dugobair, add your pleas to mine.'

'We would be most honoured if you would accompany us on a small tour—' at last Mr Tidmarsh had a voice, a quiet, gentle voice like his face – 'We thought perhaps St Paul's Cathedral, the river, Covent Garden?—' He ended in hesitancy and question.

'My sister—' began Emma.

'Your sister comes to Mr Tidmarsh's church – she is very fond of him. But you must ask her. We will wait.'

What was it about this woman, so apparently domineering to the point of rudeness, that made Emma wish to take the proposed carriage ride? The obvious energy, the humorous delivery, the sharp, clever look in her face?

'I shall be a moment!' she cried. And a moment it was; Isabella, awake now and playing with little Emma, on the bed, told her sister she must go at once because she, herself, had set it all up with Mr Wingfield, and she had not forewarned her in case it came to naught. 'Philomena is most self-willed – she cannot be made to do anything she does not want. She is very good too,' Isabella hastened to add in case she seemed severe on a friend. 'Her work for the poor of the parish puts me to shame' – a smile of satisfaction – 'but then, dear lady, she has not been blessed with a fine family of children.'

Still a little discomposed by the speed with which her situation had changed, Emma found herself seated between Mr and Mrs Tidmarsh and making speed towards the centre of London.

'St Paul's Cathedral is a good enough place to begin,' Mrs Tidmarsh was all enthusiasm, as if she must bind

Emma's attention more certainly; and it was true that Emma thought one moment how she should have brought Henry and John – but it had not been offered – and the next – this a more severe distraction – that she wished Mr Knightley had been at her side; he should have been the one to give her a view of London. But such misgivings could not last long under Mrs Tidmarsh's determination.

'Two entire days and you have seen nothing. Dugobair, tell Mrs Knightley what the great doctor says about our city—' An aside to Emma, 'Mr Tidmarsh is the repository of all the words I need – my memory, as a consequence, is lamentable!'

> Here Malice, Rapine, Accident, conspire,
> And now a rabble rages, now a fire;
> Their Ambush here relentless Ruffians lay,
> And here the fell Attorney prowls for Prey;
> Here falling Houses thunder on your Head,
> And here a female Atheist talks you dead.

Mrs Tidmarsh tried to stop him with mock anger, 'No! No! He teases me. The other—'

'When a man is tired of London he is tired of life—'

'Yes. Yes. I love the sound of that, although I would that Dr Johnson had thought to add "woman". There are occupations for women,' she began and then broke off all of a sudden to ask Emma in serious interrogation, a frown appearing, beetling her dark brows, whether she liked to shop.

'In Highbury, there is Ford's – a general draper – I like to shop there well enough, although the choice is small.'

'I do not refer to one shop' – emphatically – 'I refer to a plurality of shops, to an avenue of windows as long as an avenue of trees leading to the greatest of shops – I refer to Oxford Street!'

'Oxford Street?' questioned Emma, feeling more ignorant and humble than she ever had in her life.

'Shall I tell her, dear Mr Tidmarsh?'

'You will not be able to resist, dear Philomena. When have you been ever able to resist?'

The sharp face swivelled close to Emma's. 'I recently made an investigation into the items for sale in Oxford Street and I discovered there are—' her voice began to race, as if she were an impatient child reciting her prayers – 'thirty-three linen drapers, ten straw hat manufacturers, two silk and satin dressers and dyers, twenty-four boot- and shoemakers, five woollen drapers, two drapers and tailors, three fancy trimmings and fringes manufacturers, one India-muslin warehouse, three plumassiers—'

'You must not be confused,' Mr Tidmarsh interjected with his kindly gaze on Emma, 'Mrs Tidmarsh speaks out of hate, not love. Mrs Tidmarsh hates shopping – this act of learning is an act of self-flagellation—'

'I am relieved!' exclaimed Emma.

'Good. You are of like mind. No shopping. We have cleared the way for churches, coffee-houses and bridges. To walk across a bridge is my chiefest delight—'

'The weather is hardly clement,' interrupted Mr Tidmarsh. 'Non omnia possumus omnes, as Virgil observed.'

'You may lecture us now, Tidmarsh. I shall take a rest.'

With Mrs Tidmarsh silent, fine eyes actually closed, Mr Tidmarsh explained to Emma some of the historical growth to this giant city, that the cathedral had been finished over a hundred years ago, that the dull smokiness in the air, of which Mrs Knightley must be only too aware, was due to the burning of fossil coal forms and that, if they could make their way through all the jostle and busyness, they would drive on down to Covent Garden and then through to the wider streets of Mayfair where they would stop at a chocolate house. His habit of slipping occasionally into Latin added to his authority in Emma's eyes, even if it proportionately diminished her understanding.

'Coffee,' intervened Mrs Tidmarsh, opening her eyes in a flash.

'Chocolate,' insisted Mr Tidmarsh. 'And we may have just time enough to catch a glimpse of the elegant St George's Hospital at Hyde Park and even see the walks and lake of the park itself, before we return you, exhausted, cold, desperate, to your comfortable Brunswick Square.'

'Will we not set foot to ground in an ambulatory motion?' asked Mrs Tidmarsh, tapping her foot – well shod, Emma noticed, with a good strong boot which hardly accorded with her fine pelisse.

'Unless we hold our feet in the air, they must touch ground at the chocolate house—' the word 'chocolate' was emphatic – 'but my ambition is to show Mrs Knightley few of the individualities of our city but rather an impression of the whole. It is a way to approach—'

'I am most grateful—' began Emma.

'You will be more grateful to be home—'

'I am sure—'

'And now we are at Sir Christopher Wren's masterpiece. Philomena, perhaps you would be good enough to remain in the carriage, for I put no trust in this pipe-torturing driver to control his horses and at least you may direct him back, while I take Mrs Knightley inside.'

'But I understood—' began Emma.

'Viewing a church is not walking – it is floating—'

'You are fanciful, Mrs Tidmarsh. May I help you out, Mrs Knightley? Now direct your eyes upwards – Veni, vidi . . . Ah! If I tired of such a sight, I would—'

'Dr Johnson said it better, my dear!' called Mrs Tidmarsh from the carriage.

Never had Emma endured such a day. They had squeezed their way through the streets in company of chaise after chaise, coach after coach, cart after cart; through the din and clamour of thousands of tongues and feet, of bells from the church steeples, postmen's bells, street organs, fiddles of itinerant musicians and cries of the vendors of hot and cold food at the street corners.

By the time they emerged into the purer light and air of Mayfair where there were stone pavements and fine tall buildings which Mr Tidmarsh advised her were the London clubs where gentlemen gamed away thousands of pounds a night, she would have drunk gin, if it had been offered her. Instead she was guided into a small chocolate shop by Mr Tidmarsh who apologised that he must abandon the ladies for a few minutes while he executed some parish business.

'This is tolerably elegant, do you not agree?' Mrs Tidmarsh looked around her at the oak-panelled room with its glass-fronted bow-window.

'Oh, yes. Your husband has been so very kind, so patient with my ignorance—' she hesitated at Mrs Tidmarsh's look of bewilderment.

Then 'My husband!' – a laugh so shrill as to attract notice from the next table – 'Dugobair, my husband! Oh, I am so sorry! But it is such a very droll notion. Mr Tidmarsh – I see how it occurred, Mr and Mrs Tidmarsh – perfectly natural you should think – but I am Mr Tidmarsh's mother!'

'Mother!' exclaimed Emma, for there could not be as much as ten years between them.

'I shall tell you my life story – if your ears have any room left after this morning's lectures. I was married to Mr Tidmarsh's father – he was upward of twenty years older than me – his first wife who was French died in those terrible years that poor country suffered which I do not wish to think about. Dugobair – my late husband believed it is some sort of French name, although I hold that the first Mrs Tidmarsh invented it in the belief it was very

English – Dugobair (you see the Frenchiness at the end) – was born in France where they were living – my husband, Mr Tidmarsh, had taken orders but his life was devoted to music – from where they returned to London and I made their acquaintance. The late Mr Tidmarsh, although so much older, was the noblest, truest, most brilliant, most informed—' she sighed and fell silent.

'Mr Knightley is nearly seventeen years older than I am,' Emma, out of ordinary politeness, thought to lift the sadness but, as she spoke the words, she found herself shocked that she should communicate something so personal, so private, to a stranger, to someone who had been a stranger only a few hours ago. Not even with Mrs Weston had she discussed the difference in age between herself and Mr Knightley. It had been too tender a point – although she did not quite know the reason – to be aired abroad. But now she had pronounced the words – in public!

'Would that his health is good,' said Mrs Tidmarsh heavily.

'Oh yes! Yes! He lives such a hearty, outdoor life. You would think him ten years younger.'

'I had been surprised to see you so young,' said Mrs Tidmarsh with increased interest, 'knowing Mr John Knightley was the younger brother and Isabella the older sister by many years.'

'It is strange,' Emma blushed; the perfection of Mr Knightley stood in front of her. For some reason she wished to convey this further to Mrs Tidmarsh but could not find the words. 'He is – so – honourable – good—'

'Handsome, too, I trust.'

'Very handsome.'

'Mr Tidmarsh was not handsome; his health was too ruined by his experiences in that country I will not think of. But when he held a bow' – again that sigh.

'He fiddled?'

'The cello. But he was principally a composer and a historian of music.'

'He has published— ?'

'Indeed. Handel relied on his opinion. We met through music – I play the harp tolerably – it shows off the bare arm so well—' she laughed; but Emma could not help but be aware that ever since the name of her husband had been introduced, her high spirits had been overlaid by a depression; she admired her for it; it showed the depth of her feeling for Mr Tidmarsh. How lucky she was to have Mr Knightley, even if she could hardly own to much of him at the present time – and in such good health!

'Now – my dear son approaches – we must stiffen our sinews – Come, Mrs Knightley, we have exchanged our husbands and we are friends; soon you will call me Philomena and I will call you— ?'

'Emma' – blushing a little.

A day such as Emma passed could hardly be taken in at the time – a new city, a new friend, two new friends; and, although in some ways her inferior – she could not be insensible of the hired coach and a growing awareness that Mrs Tidmarsh's clothes, if stylish, had a very rough, homemade look about them which, together with other remarks made in the course of the drive, led her to conclude that they were sadly lacking in money – she could not help but be greatly drawn to them. Isabella would tell her more; meanwhile she waited with expectation for Mr Knightley's tread so that she could share some of her day with him.

'Emma! My dear Emma – you are pale. Are you well?' He held her so close – how warm! How comfortable to be together!

'Oh, yes. Extremely well' – a pause – 'I have been viewing London!'

Mr Knightley sat down. 'I see. London, you say. The whole of London – no wonder you are pale!'

'Very nearly the whole—' Emma laughed; she sat beside him. 'We began at St Paul's Cathedral where a smoky pall is due to—'

'We?' inquired Mr Knightley.

'Isabella's friends. The Reverend Mr Tidmarsh and his stepmother.'

'Ah, a vicar. I wondered my unsociable brother allowed Isabella any friends. But a vicar and a doctor may pass. And a stepmother, you say?'

'She was married to Mr Tidmarsh's late father – you may guess that—' Emma smiled at herself.

'He was a fiddler – admired by the great Handel—'

'A veritable Methuselah then!'

'Indeed, he was older . And she plays the harp and – and will not go into the shops, although she can recite them all. Mr Tidmarsh is very learned, full of Latin, full of quotations – a reading man – he gave me so many lectures on the town, on each of the bridges – there is a new one, you know, just constructed – and oh, Mr Knightley, if we had only been here a winter or two past, when the whole River Thames became frosted over and turned itself into a great street – with a name, even – but I have forgot the name. There is so very much to remember.'

'And where else did my dearest Emma go?' – indulgently.

'Through Covent Garden – a mad rush of a place.'

'Covent Garden!' – a frown.

'What is it?' – anxious.

'I am foolish. It is nothing – my lodgings, as I said, are in Henrietta Street – near Covent Garden. I had thought to give myself the pleasure of showing you—'

'Oh, Mr Knightley!' – the day was spoilt! That she could be the cause of any sadness when he bore so much, so bravely. 'I would never have gone – I should never have gone – If you knew how I talked of you—'

A proud look – 'Talked of me, Emma?'

'Thought of you,' she corrected herself, 'Lacked your presence. Oh, my dearest, how can we go on like this, apart!' The day had turned to dust and ashes. Mr Knightley was displeased with her; her conscience was not clear; she had talked of him. 'I did not even know the place of your lodgings – we might have driven straight by it—'

'Sshhh, Emma, my dear. I am glad you have been happy. I had wanted to walk with you on my arm, my dear, pretty wife; it is mere whimsicality! I have you here, now. I thought the weather too cold for walking—'

'But we did not walk! We drove everywhere – to gain an impression of the whole.'

'You did not walk?'

'We floated around the churches—' a smile, irrepressible, appeared. 'But you shall be the first person to walk with me on the streets of London.'

'My pride is quite restored,' said Knightley ironically; Emma could see he had been hurt but had now decided to be content.

'Could you not stay here?' she asked. 'My room is not so very small and I am sure I am thinner than when I arrived. And you certainly are.'

'Oh, Emma, Emma. If you could only know how I long to be with you—' he embraced her then, showing a depth of passion which surprised Emma – particularly in the drawing-room. She drew apart, patted her hair, 'The children—'

'The children. Yes.' He composed himself. 'You must stay a little longer. Even if there were room here, I could not see Isabella every minute – when I am to visit poor John or have come from him. It would be beyond my powers of deception. Tell me, does Isabella talk much of John?'

'A little, yes. She is anxious at his prolonged absence, I make no doubt. Sometimes I feel she knows more than we guess. But she says nothing or merely sighs and repeats as if to convince herself, "George is not worried, so I am not worried, I have perfect trust in George", and once she added, "It is not good for the baby if a mother is down-spirited so I shall not allow myself such a luxury."'

'Poor Isabella – and you, too, my dear. The strain is great but I feel it for the best. I will not be jealous of any outing that comes your way. I am not a city man. I would rather trace a path across my meadows than the most elegant street in London; I warn you, however, that I have tickets for the theatre. It is the celebrated Miss Eliza O'Neill, at least I am assured she is celebrated. I am advised ladies must bring at least two handkerchiefs and gentlemen present a tolerably clean shoulder.'

This discussion between Mr and Mrs Knightley proved that a loving couple, after spending a day in which their experiences have conducted them into utterly different directions of thought, may nevertheless come close together if a high degree of love is combined with a reasonable degree of goodwill.

Nevertheless there was a wistfulness in Mr Knightley's eye as he presided over dinner. Isabella had not felt well enough to descend from her room, so Emma faced him at the other end, with the children, on their very best behaviour, ranged on either side. He looked down and could not but wish that this was his table – even his children – transported of course to Donwell Abbey. What a joy that would be! But he was too practical a man to live with what might have been or even what yet might be in the future.

'A further slice of ham, my dear?'

'No thank you, Knightley,' Emma had just recollected Mrs Tidmarsh's comment that God gave gentlemen louder voices so that they could command and ladies softer voices so that they could gossip – and she spoke abstracted and with a smile. Following her train of thought she did not at first hear little Bella's lisped question, 'Why do you call Uncle, Knightley?'

'I know,' answered John. 'It is because he was an old man when she was a silly maid like you.'

They all laughed, Mr Knightley too, but it was not a comfortable sound.

16

Mrs Philomena Tidmarsh and Emma became close; it was inevitable. There had been a thirst for friendship on Emma's side ever since Miss Taylor had married, Harriet Wilson had proved herself a fool and Augusta Elton a bigger one. A husband was not the same as a friend, Emma owned it to herself – particularly when he was so seldom in the same place as his wife. A gentleman not only spoke differently from a woman but thought differently also; it was delightful but it left a space for someone else; Philomena Tidmarsh became that person.

'I am glad that you and Philomena have become so close,' Isabella sat up in her bed, surrounded by three of her five children. 'To drive all the way to Bushy Park without even a leaf to see on the famous chestnuts – such friendship, such exertion! I declare that I take more pleasure in your explorations than if I were to undertake them myself. You have seen more in two weeks than I have seen in the eight years I have been here! What are you to do today?'

'Today she is to play me her harp. We go to St Peter's – their house—'

'I am glad not to follow you there. A gloomy place and the harp runs up and down without ever a variation. I fear I fell asleep when she played to me – not that she is so keen to play—'

'You are in good spirits today,' Emma looked approvingly at her sister.

'I am always in good spirits when the time comes near. It is the waiting – but I must not put you off—'

'No. No. Perhaps I should stay—'

'Not at all; it is a good day for you to visit when poor George visits Hartfield.' Isabella sighed, her face cloudy for a moment, 'What weight of business our dear husbands do support; John has never been from home so long—'

'In Scotland, you must remember—' this as agreed with Mr Knightley – 'at the mercy of weather, roads—'

'You frighten me – If he would but send me a letter—' but the fear and the hope were equally short-lived for little Emma, the baby for a few weeks longer, must snatch Bella's doll and the two children, struggling energetically, be removed by a nursemaid. It was time for Isabella's rest, Emma persuaded her sister, and mentally told herself to see if it were at all possible that John could write his wife a reassuring note.

Indeed motherhood transports a woman into such a private world that she is scarcely part of the human race, thought Emma, as she walked, in the company of a servant, across Brunswick Square – for the church and the house at its side, where Mr Tidmarsh lived, was not far off.

'I have decided my fingers are too cold for the harp!' announced Philomena on Emma's arrival. 'We will sit by the fire and talk, drink coffee, toast muffins, perhaps read poetry. Do you admire Byron?'

'Oh, no!' exclaimed Emma with feeling. His was a shocking name, she knew, although not having read a word.

'Then Crabbe. But maybe we shall have no time for anything but talk!'

Emma, who had been used to taking everyone in hand but Mr Knightley – who used to take her in hand – was still surprised by how much she enjoyed being led by Mrs

Tidmarsh. She no longer felt overwhelmed, however, for she saw she was quite her new friend's equal in intelligence; but very much below her in experience. Besides, there was a frankness which she could not but admire.

'I cannot quite perceive how you became so close to Isabella,' she said, once they were installed either side of the fire – necessarily very near because the rest of the room was as dark and cold as a mausoleum. 'Your natures are so very different; she so bound up with her children, you so ready for new ideas—'

'It is strange, I acknowledge. We met through my son, of course, and I suppose I see in her something I have never been, will never be now—'

'A mother!'

'Yes. A happy mother, with healthy children, a good, loving husband—' she paused, a long pause.

Emma looked into her cup, blushing that the truth was so different and could not be told now but must be known some time soon; the elegant house sold, servants dismissed – The blush subsided, pallor replaced it.

'You are sad?'

'No. No.' This secrecy, this falsity was the only jarring note in her friendship with Philomena. Yet in this she was bound by Mr Knightley's direction. He had not yet succeeded in obtaining his brother's release from gaol but he said it was a matter of a week or two. Money would be forthcoming – he had not told her how. Isabella would have her baby – Christmas must be passed – the baby put to a wet nurse – and a new life must be started on a humbler scale for Mr and Mrs John Knightley and their family.

'You frown. You are silent. You are vexed.'

'Vexed?' – if only such a small word could encompass what was a perfect tragedy. 'I am a little tired – a little expectant, too – Today Mr Knightley has gone to Hartfield

– and tomorrow I will know how my father does, have letters, hear from all my friends.'

Mrs Tidmarsh put her elegant head on one side while she considered this. She already knew Emma's circumstances and showed a curiosity, remarkable to Emma in one who had travelled so widely, in all the details of life at Highbury. 'You are anxious of bad news?'

'No. Not exactly. But my father has poor health. It has always been my responsibility to keep him happy. I cannot easily believe another can do it so well, although all the reports are good. Perhaps it is pride in me—'

'That another can supplant you so readily.'

Emma assented with a smile. 'And such a one as Miss Bates whose voice is like the patter of rain on a roof.'

'But she is kind?'

'Oh, yes, she is kind enough. She cared for her mother until her decease; she gave up her own life to it.'

'I can never understand such sacrifice.'

Emma looked surprised. 'But surely it is only natural—'

'—that a younger should make sacrifice to an elder. I do not feel it. When my dear Mr Tidmarsh passed away, I was melancholy, very melancholy, but I could not regret that I had been spared long years of chasing after a querulous, complaining old man.'

Emma could think of nothing to say; she was shocked.

'You may say he would not be querulous; but all old men are; they cannot help it. It is their nature. Many younger men are too but they can help it. I shall never marry again, for that reason. I do not like men, in general. I worshipped Mr Tidmarsh; but he was a genius. His playing was the least of his talent; by the time he passed away he had written half a dozen books; you may have heard of his *Rules for Playing in a True Taste on the Violin, German Flute, Violoncello and Harpsichord*? No? Well, it does not signify – Have I told you I am writing a novel?'

It was such talk – a combination of the shocking and the exciting – that made Emma take such pleasure in Mrs Tidmarsh's company and that sometimes also gave her a sense of disquiet. 'I would always look after Mr Woodhouse,' she said, formally. 'Perhaps that is my nature.'

'Yes. You are better than me – I have no doubt of it—'

'I did not mean – it is what I wish to do – not a sacrifice—'

'But now Miss Bates does it,' Mrs Tidmarsh laughed, 'and you are worried lest she should not be as good as she should and you are worried lest she should be too good.'

In conversations such as this, in the agility and sharpness of Mrs Tidmarsh's mind, Emma had food enough for thought in the long hours she spent on her own at Brunswick Square. Until this meeting, she had been entirely unconscious of herself as she might appear to anyone other than Mr Knightley. He had been her sole adjudicator; but now she had another – and someone whose viewpoint was altogether more daring.

'Did you sustain your wits through the harp?' asked Isabella on her return.

'She did not play. We talked.'

'How dear Philomena talks! I do not listen to it any more than I listen to the harp, she runs up and down just the same. But I believe it is very clever.'

'Oh, yes,' agreed Emma, sighing. 'Now I have promised to read to Henry and John, although I fear, by their faces, they sometimes think my voice sounds very like Mrs Tidmarsh's harp.'

Mr Knightley's return from Highbury the following day was awaited with a high degree of expectation by all at Brunswick Square. He would come at a good time for Emma since Mrs Tidmarsh had informed her that for the next few days she would be entirely occupied in teaching those who could find none better at the Foundling Hospital, that spreading building which Emma passed every day without ever exploring.

'It is James!'

'It is James bringing Uncle!'

The boys' cries brought Emma to the window, heart beating. Knightley was already out – Henry and John jumping up at him like dogs.

'Oh Knightley! Knightley!' She flew down the stairs and into his arms.

'I see what I must do for a warm welcome; I shall plan a visit to Hartfield every day!' Even Isabella was out of bed and the questions came so fast that Knightley protested he must give a general report first or no one would hear anything he had to tell. This was agreed and they all managed to sit down more or less quietly, although little Emma had to be restrained in her aunt's arms and Mr Knightley kept a hold of John's leg.

'First,' the tone was solemn, 'Mr Woodhouse is most fearful of having caught a cold, a sore throat, which may lead to a putrid fever because the front door was opened on my arrival and, although this unfortunate door was closed as soon as my second leg and arm were in the hallway, the ensuing draught—'

'Oh, dear papa!' cried Isabella, 'putrid fever—'

'He is making fun, Isabella dearest,' Emma smiled reproach at Mr Knightley. 'What Knightley means us to understand is that our papa is as he always is – thoroughly taken up with fearing for his health—'

'And not just his own – he could hardly believe I had taken a public conveyance in such weather and insisted poor James be turned out to bring me—'

'Dear papa – so thoughtful,' agreed Isabella.

'He has a new gravitas to his thoughtfulness – a new

responsibility which he takes with commendable seriousness—'

Neither of the ladies could make out this reference so
Knightley continued, 'It is neither old nor young, neither
male nor very female; neither big nor small—'

'A riddle!' cried Henry.

'—neither fast nor slow, except in its tongue which races
as if James had his whip on it—'

'Miss Bates!' cried both boys as one.

'How are they dealing together?' asked Emma once the
laughter had died.

'They are capital friends. Mr Woodhouse has found a
companion who will drink gruel, shut windows before
they are open, play quadrille – with Mrs Goddard and the
Coles—'

'The Coles!' exclaimed Emma.

'—live off thin food, little wine, take never more than
three turns round the shrubbery – in short, he is a despot,
who has found a subject, a most willing subject. Miss Bates
has aged ten years and Mr Woodhouse has lost ten. They are
in perfect accord. Indeed they scarcely had time for me—'

'Oh, George!' cried Isabella. 'That cannot be true!'

'Of course it is not true, Isabella.' Emma was delighted
to see Mr Knightley in such a playful mood. Something
good had happened, she felt sure. She had not seen him
so cheerful since the terrible news of his brother and she
could not wait to have him to herself so that she might
know if her observation were correct. But first there was
the whole of Highbury to be inquired after – the Westons
must take a good half-hour on their own, even though Mr
Knightley had brought letters for both sisters from Mrs
Weston.

'They are in exceedingly good health. Anna has made up
for the loss of two of Mr Weston's teeth by gaining two new
ones of her own—'

'Oh, Mr Knightley,' protested Emma. 'Mr Weston's teeth are nearly as famously good as his wine.'

'Nevertheless he has lost two of them – while visiting the farm at Abbey-Mill with me – pearls before the swine, you might say!'

Emma had never seen him so exuberant and wondered that the others did not notice the change from the grey, hollow man that had been there before. He had brought cream, eggs, butter too, and a whole side of pork – 'a special present from Miss Bates, I understand.'

There was still much left undiscussed – the Eltons, for example. Had Augusta Elton yet secured a visit from her intolerable (in prospect, at least, since no one had met her) sister, Serena Suckling? But dinner could wait no longer or Cook's temper would be taken out on the lamb – she could burn the sweetest meat from the other side of the kitchen. They must eat; Isabella must rest; happy recollections of Highbury would sustain them for a week or more. Henry banged the gong and they all went to table.

Emma's impatience must be curbed for at least another hour.

17

'My dear, I have some further news – an arrangement I have made that I hope will not cause you displeasure.' Emma and Mr Knightley sat together on the sofa – at last alone. Emma, who had longed for this moment, looked at her husband with surprise.

'What should cause me displeasure that you have arranged? It is impossible.'

'You are generous. I am perhaps being too wise – but I recall; it is not so important, after all. I have brought Mr Robert Martin to London with me; he stays at my lodgings.'

'There is room enough for another!' exclaimed Emma before she could help herself.

'I have taken a further room. We have business together. He—'

'Yes?'

'He will call tomorrow.'

Emma bowed in assent. Of course he would call tomorrow; she might not think him quite a gentleman but she was not so prejudiced as to want him banned from her sister's house. In person she thought him a fine, sensible man.

'He carries particularly fond memories of Brunswick Square. It was when Mrs Martin was staying here – still Harriet Wilson – that they came to an understanding.'

'I know it,' assented Emma, yet in wonder that their conversation dwelt so long on Mr Martin when she wished to uncover the reason for the tranquil glow of contentment in which Mr Knightley still bathed.

'You recall also that I mentioned I had tickets for the theatre?'

'Oh, yes!' This was more positive. 'I have been looking forward to it, to walking with you like an ordinary married couple, quite on our own—'

'I have invited Mr Martin to join us—'

'Oh!' – a gasp, big eyes.

'I have a box – there is room; he is in London for three or four days and I have a particular reason—'

'Oh, Knightley!' It was too cruel – for their *tête-à-tête* to be broken for such a man. The disappointment was so great that, coming on top of the last weeks, Emma found childish petulance overtaking proper resolution – 'To go to my first theatre in the company of one who is hardly more than a servant!'

'Emma! He is a gentleman.'

'A gentleman-farmer, as you once informed me, it is hardly the same as a gentleman.'

'You are unjust. You may recall that on Mrs Martin's visit here, she and Robert Martin took Henry and John to Astley's; they did not think him not good enough!'

'Astley's is for children – dancing horses and suchlike – re-enactments of battles – the sort of stupid things little boys like and uneducated men!'

'Emma! I had not believed you could say such things—'

It was dreadful – they were quarrelling. Tears came into Emma's eyes – their first quarrel – and over someone as unimportant as Mr Robert Martin.

'You are overtired,' Mr Knightley became more gentle as he saw the tears. 'I cannot disinvite Mr Martin – it is not possible – nor would I – but I had hoped to please you with another guest. Your friend Mrs Tidmarsh – and her stepson, if that would be right. Emma, what do you say to that?' He lifted her chin, humouring her like a child.

She was conscious that she needed such treatment; she had borne the responsibility of the Knightley household and of keeping John Knightley's terrible secret from it. 'I say it is a happy thought—' she managed a watery smile – 'Philomena will not know the difference between a gentleman-farmer and a gentleman.'

'Philomena, is it?' was Mr Knightley's only comment but his face wore a look of relief that the quarrel was over, the affair settled. The tranquil glow – still unexplained – returned, even if a little dimmed.

Mr Martin duly called the next morning for what he immediately announced as a brief visit; and Emma was struck afresh by his handsome unpretentiousness.

'Mrs Martin is well, I trust?'

'She is happiness itself, I thank you.'

'And your mother and sisters?'

'All in good spirits.' He paused. 'Miss Elizabeth Martin is enjoying the pleasure of the presence of a superior instrument, the new pianoforte, at Abbey-Mill.'

Emma saw this was an opening, if she wished to take it, to follow up her note to him with a further inquiry; it was sensitive of him. 'That other pianoforte I wrote you about travelled from Highbury to Donwell without injury, I surmise?'

'Indeed. It is in the driest corner of the house; I am confident that everything is as it should be at Donwell.' As he spoke, he looked at her closely, an odd, questioning look.

'It is very good of you. I was probably over-anxious.'

'I would do nothing less – my respect for Mr Knightley.'

Was this a reference to her request in the note not to inform Mr Knightley? Much to her annoyance, Emma found herself blushing.

'Please give my regards to Mrs John Knightley. And Mrs Martin's—' he hesitated and Emma guessed that he was undecided whether to remark that the confinements of both ladies would come nearly together. She smiled coolly – and he decided to remain silent.

'I am meeting Mr Knightley.' He rose, bowed.

It was done. Emma returned to her seat to try and discover what it was in the meeting that had made her feel uncomfortable. Surely she could not be uneasy because he had behaved so well, so irreproachably well! Then was it the note, the secret note? The ghost of Frank Churchill hovering. She was glad to be called away to mix Isabella's chocolate, 'in the way only you, dearest Emma, know how'. She was good for making hot drinks, at least.

Mrs Tidmarsh expressed herself delighted at the invitation to see the celebrated Miss Eliza O'Neill, in a piece, quite coincidentally, called *Isabella*. 'I will be intrigued to see her torture the English language on the excuse of drawing tears from our dried-up London ladies' – as she put it, somewhat to Emma's surprise. 'My preferred female performer when my dear Mr Tidmarsh was still with me – and his ear for a voice was prodigious – I must confess was Mrs Billington – such purity of tone! – such technique! – such independence of spirit! But she belonged to the whole of Europe and could seldom be spared to delight her home country! I shall be glad of Miss Eliza O'Neill – at least she is a female!'

The Reverend Dugobair Tidmarsh, however, declined Mr Knightley's invitation, although professing himself very much honoured, et cetera. He proclaimed pressing parish business as the reason for his unavoidable absence; but his stepmother informed Emma with a laugh, 'He can bear nothing in the dramatic form but Greek tragedy – and that in the written mode. I sometimes tell him he is quite allergic to the spoken word.'

The party, therefore, would consist of Mr Knightley, Mr

Martin, Mrs Tidmarsh and Emma. A light meal would be had at Brunswick Square so that Isabella could enjoy at least a part of the evening's festivities; Mr Knightley ordered quails, Emma oysters. Mrs Tidmarsh looked out a dress with a train and Emma, torn between happiness in Mr Knightley's spirits – for his glowing air still prevailed (still unexplained) – and her own misgivings as to the peculiar mix of Philomena Tidmarsh and Robert Martin – she could not think of them in the same breath – altered between all expectation of a cheerful outing – 'My dearest,' said Mr Knightley, 'you know, this evening is for you' – and a foretelling of doom. 'The Drury Lane Theatre was at its zenith when Mr Garrick presided but that was nigh on a hundred years past' – Mrs Tidmarsh could be very cutting.

Nevertheless days must pass, dresses must be freshly trimmed, shoes and gloves bought new. 'London is very hard on shoes,' sighed Isabella who was glad that her dear sister should have an outing. 'You must look your best so that Highbury would be proud.' Isabella's spirits, in decline over the last week or so, had risen noticeably after a letter from her husband had arrived by special messenger. She did not divulge the contents to Emma who wondered what good cheer John could possibly have found to impart, but she kept it by her bedside as if its physical presence gave her courage. 'He promises to be back before the baby finds his thumb,' was Isabella's only hint at his message.

'Highbury', the word murmured on in Emma's head even as she dressed for this great event – even as she was admired for the jewelled feather in her hair and the piece of new lace across her bosom. Henry and John and Bella admired and thought their aunt like a queen or, at very least, a princess.

'Then I am satisfied,' Emma smiled, although 'Highbury' still sighed in her head. Only Mr Knightley could banish it, arriving with Mr Martin, both so scrubbed and red-faced and as nobly elegant as any country gentlemen come to town. For, Emma, had to admit it, Mr Martin looked more the gentleman than she would have credited.

'I am late!' cried Mrs Tidmarsh, arriving shortly behind them. Her elegance was of the dramatic sort – in emerald green with her favourite black velvet and necklace and earrings of fine jet. 'I must report that my maid mislaid my gloves, despite my informing her that a lady without gloves is like a soldier without a sword!'

The gentlemen bowed; introductions were made; they moved to a table from which at the last minute Isabella had absented herself.

'To think I am the only true Londoner!' cried Mrs Tidmarsh.

'Were you born in London?' inquired Emma, with real interest because she could scarcely believe anyone could not be born in the country – despite five, nearly six nephews and nieces to prove the contrary, besides a foundling hospital on her doorstep.

'Ah. Ah,' responded Mrs Tidmarsh, if it could count as a response, and said no more.

'I am very taken by London – such as I have seen of it,' Mr Martin was deliberate.

'On behalf of the city, I accept the compliment,' smiled Mrs Tidmarsh.

'I should like Mrs Martin to visit it again.'

'Indeed,' agreed Mrs Tidmarsh, smile fading.

The high spirits of the whole company was remarkable, Emma could not help but think, and she could not help but think also of poor John Knightley when his house was used for such merry-making. But Mr Knightley must be allowed a little relaxation.

With talk of London, music – 'I am at my most severe where music is concerned,' said Mrs Tidmarsh, tapping her fan at Mr Martin – to fill any gap in the conversation, the meal passed with such rapidity that the arrival of the carriage took them all by surprise. Not a serious word had been spoken and near two hours passed.

'Your friend is quite a flirt,' whispered Mr Knightley in Emma's ear as he laid her cloak about her shoulders.

Emma had no time to utter more than a surprised disclaimer when they must bustle into the conveyance and set off with a rush.

'I hope I am not too close,' said Mrs Tidmarsh to Mr Martin. 'You are broad and I am narrow, which should fit the space in equable manner – except that ladies are inclined to spread.'

'Thank you. I have ample room,' replied Mr Martin and Emma felt Knightley squeeze her fingers. It was so unlike him, so lacking in his usual dignity, that she thought she had imagined it until he whispered close in her ear, 'You perceive my earlier meaning.'

Their progress was at first perfectly quick and, as they reached the vicinity of the theatre, perfectly slow.

'Look, dead souls!' Mrs Tidmarsh bent her head to the window. It had begun to snow; white flakes floated through the dusky evening air.

'Why d'you call them that?' asked Mr Martin, his curiosity caught.

'Why? Because I always have. Do they not look like dead souls to you!'

'You could hardly have an alive soul,' commented Mr Knightley *sotto voce* to Emma.

But Mr Martin, so sensible, so practical, such an unfanciful countryman, seemed quite taken with the idea and the discussion between him and Mrs Tidmarsh on the subject of souls and death and snow and winter continued until they reached the theatre.

The press of people there was so intense that Emma was glad to hang on to Mr Knightley's strong arm and took very little notice of her companions until all four of them were safely seated in their box. The consciousness of grandeur, of red velvet and gold tassels – a sort of grandeur she had previously associated with such as Serena Suckling and would have despised but which now seemed part of the theatrical experience – gave her heart an extra beat.

'It is altogether another world!'

'False,' said Philomena, smiling at Mr Martin.

'If the theatre were not false it would not be theatre, it would be life,' said Mr Knightley.

'Great art is more true than life,' again Philomena bent her gaze on Mr Martin who looked, however, somewhat out of his depth. Besides he, like Emma, was keen to crane about and see everything that went on. The theatre was completely full, surrounded with the noise of hundreds of voices all shouting at once – some from one side of the theatre to another.

'The last time I was here,' said Philomena, although no one listened, 'I saw Kean doing Shylock. London is full of Jews, you know. Mr Tidmarsh numbered them among his dearest friends.'

'The lights are dimming, my dear,' Emma addressed her husband. 'Will you not take your place?'

'Two boxes along, where the front curves,' Knightley was leaning forward, 'sit Mr and Mrs Campbell. Look, Emma; I met them, you know, on my failed search for Frank Churchill. They returned from Ireland just as I gave up all hope of him being in England. Emma!'

But Emma, it seemed, could not take her eyes from the stage for a moment – curtains parted and drama about to commence. The deepened colour of her cheeks must be attributed to excitement rather than to any discomfiture caused by the name pronounced by her husband.

Such was the press during the interval that despite Mr Knightley's intentions, they did not meet the Campbells till both parties were leaving and they found, by chance, they stood together on a cold pavement waiting for their carriages.

While Mr Martin listened to Mrs Tidmarsh confess – although it sounded more like a boast – that both the handkerchiefs she had brought were dry, Mr Knightley bowed at Mr Campbell and brought Emma forward. Introductions were made; Mr Martin and Mrs Tidmarsh summoned to make their bows.

'You must call, Mrs Knightley,' Mrs Campbell was civil. 'We are still melancholy at the loss of poor Mrs Churchill; it will do us good to meet such an old friend of hers as you are.'

Emma received the invitation with a sorrowful face which hid many different emotions. 'I will be glad to.' Their carriages arrived; they parted; and Emma was left on her own very soon after, for it was not thought sensible for the gentlemen to come all the way back to Brunswick Square when their lodgings were a short walk away. Mrs Tidmarsh would be with her almost all the way.

It was a disappointing and disturbing end to the evening. Emma sat in her little room – the house dark around her – and tried to write out some of her anxieties by answering her old friend Mrs Weston's letter to her:

It is late but I cannot sleep; you will say it is too much pleasure – it is that – and pain. Tonight we attended the theatre – such crowds, such stuffiness and Miss O'Neill with a voice as loud as a dragoon – although very beautiful. But afterwards we saw Mr and Mrs Campbell and their kind, sad faces made me think so vividly of Jane Fairfax – how little I helped her – how little I liked her! And why? Because I thought her cold – that is what I believed to be my reason but was it not because I knew her to be inferior—

As Emma wrote these words, she was stabbed by the knowledge that she had addressed them to someone who must never read them – for Mrs Weston, too, had been inferior, a governess, as Jane Fairfax was to have been, until her marriage. In both cases, marriage had saved them, raised them – but poor Jane had not lived to enjoy it.

Emma scrumpled up her letter and mounted into her little bed. On the morrow she would write to Mrs Weston of Isabella and the children, air, of Westminster Bridge and Hyde Park. Such thoughts as she had started to pen must be left behind with the dark night and guttering candle.

18

Emma's epistolary resolution reckoned without visitors.
She had scarcely dismissed Isabella's maid who had become
quite as good as Merry at setting her curls round her face,
when the first carriage was at the door.

'I am far too early, I own it, I apologise for it, but we have
decided to travel up to Yorkshire to visit poor Jane's child.'
Mrs Campbell sat, but would not leave her coat. 'But I did
not wish to leave London without seeing you. It was you
that brought it all back to us again. We so much wish to
see her child, we cannot even wait for better weather.'

'I understand,' said Emma, 'She was like a second daughter to you.'

'It is true—' a pause; 'you knew Mr Churchill too, I
recollect,' a question; yes, it was certainly a question.

'Mr Churchill was at Highbury on and off during that
summer that he was engaged to Miss Fairfax—' a pause,
'Mr Weston, with whom he stayed, is an old and dear friend
of ours.'

'So you saw a good deal of Mr Churchill?'

Emma nodded.

'You grew to understand him.'

Emma did not nod. 'He was carrying a secret – his secret
engagement to Miss Fairfax. It is not easy to understand
someone who carries a secret. You may think so at the

time but when you are proved by subsequent events to be under a misapprehension, then you lose faith in even the generalities of understanding.'

'Quite so. Quite so.'

'I could not say I understood Mr Churchill but now I am very sorry for him.'

'Ah, yes.'

There was a silence, during which it was borne upon Emma that this sensible lady had come to tell her something – not merely for the sake of politeness – and that now she debated whether to proceed. She leant forward, studied Emma, and then stated abruptly, 'The past is history, do you not think?'

'I have little in my past,' smiled Emma, 'that could count as history.'

'Yes. Yes' – and Emma had an even stronger sense of a confidence edging tentatively towards her.

Mrs Campbell stood and, as if the motion released her anxieties a little, said, quite loudly, 'Mr Churchill was never what he should have been, I am much afraid. Neither before his marriage, during, nor after.'

'Oh!' Emma found herself picturing the haggard man she had seen at Donwell – a man in danger from his own despondency. She stood too. 'He has a capacity for strong emotions, I believe. Mrs Churchill was the centre of his life.'

'You say so – yes, perhaps. But he did not make her happy.'

'No!' This was too sad; Emma did not want to hear more. She saw Mrs Campbell understand this and pull on her gloves. She produced a sociable smile.

'He is not here to defend himself. I am partisan. I am sorry, Mrs Knightley, if I have said too much. My sorrow – you understand—' She went to the door, Emma in attendance. 'Yet I must own that I am glad that he has gone to Europe.

I cannot but believe that little Frank Churchill will grow up better without such an influence as his father must exert.'

The words were cruel, the face intelligent and good; Emma was left distressed but had no time to dwell on an explanation before the second visitor was announced. It was Mrs Tidmarsh.

'I must say thank you; thank you, dear Emma, thank you!'

'Why so many thanks?' Emma laughed at her friend's sincerity. It was a relief, after her previous visitor, to feel such open warmth.

'Last night has restored my faith in *la nature humaine*.'

'Ah,' said Emma, 'so you enjoyed Miss O'Neill.'

'I do not talk about Miss O'Neill; Miss Eliza O'Neill's nature cannot improve—'

'But the nature of man can?'

'Ah – you mock me. You who know above all the justice of my new faith. Such gentlemen as Mr Knightley and Mr Martin! You may be used to such company – they say custom stales the greatest—' she broke off, 'but you frown?'

'No! No!' Emma did frown to hear Mr Knightley coupled with Mr Martin. She would not have expected Mrs Tidmarsh to lack such discernment. 'Mr Martin is an upright man – a farmer.'

'Yes, I understand he has a veritable paradise of a farm. He describes such sunsets, rivers hung about with willows, meadowland—'

'He is a tenant of Mr Knightley's' – stiffly. Emma did not exactly doubt the verisimilitude of her visitor's description of Mr Martin's conversation; perhaps he had talked of the land – it was his work, his means of employment – but she suspected that Mrs Tidmarsh's romantic imagination had supplied the sunset and the draping willows. 'Mr Martin is a happy man; he has a young wife who thinks him the centre of the firmament, a mother-in-law who dotes on him, sisters who listen for his step as if he were a king—'

'Ah! Happiness!' Mrs Tidmarsh sighed. 'Tell me again about Highbury – how I love your stories of that little place. Last night as I lay abed, I found myself turning against London. I said to Mr Tidmarsh over breakfast, perhaps London has lost its most vociferous supporter – perhaps I have been in the smoke and grime too long—'

'It is not at all smoky and grimy where you are—' interjected Emma.

'I speak in metaphor. All night I saw those green meadows, clear skies, pure water—'

'And wind and frost and rutted roads—' laughed Emma.

Mrs Tidmarsh laughed too but persisted all the same. 'I am resolved; I must come to the country; if you will ask me, I shall leave my beloved London and see what happiness trees and rocks and hills may bring me.'

'There are no rocks in Surrey.'

'A detail' – long elegant hand waved. 'I have showed you the beauties of the town and now you may show me the beauties of nature! But do not worry; I will not force myself. It will be when it suits; when you are back, comfortable, once more established?'

'Of course you shall stay, dear Philomena, although I fear you may be disappointed—' Emma broke off – the future was still unknown and, until Mr John Knightley was rescued, full of dread. She was glad when her friend rose with her usual swiftness and grace.

'I must leave you – I have a pupil—' She stopped, hand to mouth, coughed, brought a lace-edged handkerchief to her mouth, but the word was out. Emma had suspected it for some time since seeing a young lady disappearing with a maid from the Tidmarsh establishment on one of her visits. Philomena not only kept house for her stepson, but also taught the harp. Emma blushed for her; blushed for herself; could think of no words to cover the awkwardness. For an heiress of thirty thousand pounds, married to a Knightley of Donwell, to make such a connection was indeed awkward. Constraint was on both sides and followed them to the door.

'I am sorry to have missed dear Isabella.'

'We are all in great expectation,' Emma was glad of the subject.

'She is well?'

'Mr Wingfield is very satisfied.'

'I am glad to hear it.' They parted on this quiet note and Emma, dissatisfied with herself, although not willing to own the reason, went upstairs to make sure that Isabella was as comfortable as she described. But once more the front door was swung open to the wintry cold and this time Mr Knightley entered.

'My dear!' They clung together.

'Dearest!'

'Isabella?'

'Not yet. I am expecting the doctor any minute.'

'Then we can sit together.'

'Oh, yes.' They found that sofa which would always be the heart of Brunswick Square for Emma and sat close. 'Your hands are cold,' said Emma, for Knightley was silent.

'And yours are hot. Did I see Mrs Tidmarsh as I came away?'

'You did!' Emma heard the note of defence in her voice and wondered at it.

'She is your friend so I shall say little but I did not quite like her manner with Mr Martin.'

'He did not object to it!'

'He is a man.'

'Ah,' Emma took away her hand, which was indeed very hot. 'Ah, a man may encourage but a lady must discourage.'

'He did not encourage – but I do not wish to argue.' His wish, however, was too late.

'He talked of sunsets, glistening rivers, graceful willows—'

'Mr Martin? Impossible!'

Since this echoed her own view, Emma was too honest to push it further but returned to the earlier theme. 'You hold that a lady must behave better than a gentleman. And yet it is gentlemen who govern us, make the laws—'

'Manners are more important than laws.'

'I imagined that you might pronounce the word "morals".'

'According to their quality, ladies aid morals, they supply them – or they totally destroy them.'

'You refer to their place in the family?' Emma questioned and continued as Knightley bowed in assent. 'It is all, therefore, in the hands of the female sex?'

'All that is most important.' A pause. 'Dear Emma, you are grave. So much philosophy because you have a friend who I reproach a little. She is clever, of course, witty, and admires you greatly. I should have started with that. Now give me back your hand.'

Emma did so gladly; but she could not shake off the subject of Mrs Tidmarsh so easily.

'I believe Mrs Tidmarsh—' she began hesitantly. 'Her rooms are cold and she does not have a maid.'

'The gloves? – "like a sword to a soldier" – the maid who forgot them?'

'I believe she teaches the harp – she is afraid to show me her proficiency because she is ashamed.'

Mr Knightley inclined his head. 'You understand her.'

'She is brave. She admired Mr Martin extremely as an example of a countryman. She is very keen to visit the country; to visit Highbury. She is worn down by London.'

'I see.'

A pause. Silence. They both considered.

'Sometimes she puts me in mind of poor Jane Fairfax. Not her exterior,' she added, at Mr Knightley's surprised look. 'She is all emotion, Jane was all coolness – at least to my eye. But their situation, their situation as Jane's might have been if she had not found a husband. That is why I say she is brave.'

'And that is why you wish her to visit.'

'I cannot say that I wish it; I feel she is so much a part of the bustle of London that I fear the quietness of Highbury would hold little appeal for her. She wishes it.'

'Yes?' prompted Knightley.

'I was never kind enough to Jane Fairfax.' The sentence hung there and Knightley may or may not have been forming a comment when there was an urgent knock at the door and Isabella's maid put a scared white face through the crack.

One look was enough for both Mr and Mrs Knightley to spring to their feet. 'And now there is no time to say what I came for,' muttered Knightley but Emma was already out of the room.

The successful advent of a new soul to a household – a female soul, as it turned out – is always a matter of great rejoicing, even when there are five little ones in place already and when the master of the household is unaccountably absent. For two weeks and more, nothing else was thought of but nurses, cots, shawls, warming pans, hot drinks, cold drinks, nightlights, sleep, or lack of it.

Emma's role in all this was neither too easy; nor too arduous. She must keep the children occupied so that Isabella might have enough rest to regain her health. Despite the continued cold weather and Philomena's 'dead souls' wafting across from one end of the square to another, she took the older children on a daily walk. As they bowled their hoops across the frosty ground or raced each other down to the tradesmen's mews and back again, she found herself contemplating the Foundling Hospital with more curiosity than heretofore.

One afternoon when the children were engaged with a special religious instruction under Mr Dugobair Tidmarsh, she resolved to walk inside the great doors. She knew already that visitors were welcomed. She was not prepared, however, that the first face presented to her curious gaze, should be that of her friend, Philomena Tidmarsh. The lady herself looked equally taken aback, although she recovered quickly enough.

'You catch me at good works! You have enough at home. But I must go out and find them!'

An elderly woman joined them – perhaps once a nurse, Emma deduced, respectable but hardly a lady. Introductions were made. She was a Mrs Fennell. She began at once.

'Mrs Tidmarsh is such an inspiration to us – her talent – her responsibility to the Foundling Hospital when many in her position might want to forget—'

As the good woman talked, Mrs Tidmarsh became noticeably uneasy but then a look of patient resignation came over her features. It was unlike any expression Emma had seen before on a face that was usually notable for its vivacity. Gradually, it was borne on Emma that everything that Mrs Fennell said – as to 'gratitude', 'old friends', 'improved situation' and, finally, 'Mr Tidmarsh, our excellent musical patron, our genius of the cello' – led to one conclusion: Mrs Tidmarsh had herself been a foundling, only plucked from it for marriage to Mr Tidmarsh!

The news was almost incredible! That a friend of hers – chosen by her – should be a foundling – poor babies left, on occasion, as Mrs Fennell described it, in a hole in the exterior of the wall! The contrast between the scenes even now taking place at Brunswick Square and such tragic abandonment, pressed closely on her.

'And would you like to see some of our educational facilities?' inquired Mrs Fennell kindly. 'We like our children to read and write wherever possible.'

Pleading duties to her sister, Emma escaped. Neither Mrs Fennell nor Mrs Tidmarsh attempted to detain her and, as Emma cast a look over her shoulder, she saw them still standing together, the older woman talking in her good-natured open way and Mrs Tidmarsh silent, unmoving, dejected.

19

The weeks passed. Mrs Knightley still saw Mrs Tidmarsh, although less – both ladies finding themselves too occupied for more than an occasional expedition to a gallery or, on one bright afternoon, a breezy walk accompanied by Mr Knightley across Westminster Bridge. 'It is so long since I first crossed into London—' Emma had sighed. A concert, too, was shared, where Mrs Tidmarsh and her stepson both showed themselves admirably at ease with 'rallentandos' and 'glissandos' and 'appoggiaturas'. But for intimate teas across glowing coals, for muffins and confidences, there seemed little time.

'You are not such friends with Mrs Tidmarsh,' commented Mr Knightley.

'I am ready for Hartfield,' said Emma.

'I had hoped you might say that. I would not like you to have lost your heart to London. Particularly now that the time has come to prepare Isabella for the change in her circumstances. I am counting on you to paint the most glowing picture of life at Highbury because that is where they must reside. You must write to Mr Woodhouse also. Illness will be the excuse – it will appeal to your father and he will look no further.'

'Oh, Knightley!'

'It is hard for you. I know it.'

'I did not refer to my part in it. I am not so selfish. But I must presume that this means Mr John Knightley is safe!'

'He is.' Knightley bowed.

'When?'

'A few weeks past. But only now—'

'I knew it. When you were so glowing. At the time of Mr Martin's visit—'

'You are correct. Mr Martin is much concerned in the affair. But tomorrow, you will come to Henrietta Street.'

'He is there!'

'He is there. See him. Prepare Isabella and we will have him back here for Christmas and spend New Year together in Hartfield.'

'Oh, Knightley! It is too good. All these many, many weeks – But how? – How?'

'Come to Henrietta Street tomorrow.'

Such was Emma's happiness that she need no longer picture her brother-in-law among the rats and the squalor of a prison cell – although Knightley had constantly assured her that his care made sure John was never in a place so dreadful – that she did not pursue the 'how' too far. Her duty was to pen a letter to her father that would prepare him enough, but not too much, and give Mr and Mrs Weston a report by the same post containing rather more information, so that they could comfort the fears at Hartfield with firm good sense. The word bankruptcy had lost its terror for Emma over the weeks and they must learn to face at least a hint of it too. John Knightley had failed himself and his family but the best must be made of it. He, no doubt, had suffered for it and would continue to do so.

The truth of this judgement was brought home to Emma when, the following morning, she arrived at Mr Knightley's lodgings in Henrietta Street and at last found herself face to face with John. He was old, bent, thin, grey and, more unlike his old self than all of these, humble. He took Emma's hands and looked pleadingly into her eyes.

'You have seen Isabella, the children, the baby! Oh, how I long for that! How I have longed for it! I do not deserve it! You are good – my brother, how can I ever repay it!'

'Do not talk this way, John.' Mr Knightley stood, arms folded. 'No brother would have done less. It was my duty. No virtue attaches to it.'

'But Abbey-Mill!' he exclaimed in a pitifully thin voice as he sank into the chair. 'That my wild thoughtlessness should be paid for in such a way—'

'Enough! Now we are provided with roast beef, we must eat. Emma.' He glanced at her and she obliged but her looks were all questions. Why had John Knightley made reference to Abbey-Mill? What had Mr Knightley kept from her? What was the link with Mr Martin? She could not understand and must know. But John Knightley must eat first, be calm. She would have to wait.

Two hours passed in which she tried to satisfy her brother-in-law's thirst for news of his family; the thirst was unquenchable, but she did her best, supplying every detail of the most cheerful nature – Never had Henry and John seemed such paragons of every virtue, nor Isabella so strong and healthy.

At last, when darkness had already fallen, Mr Knightley put Emma into her bonnet and cloak and said he would take her to Brunswick Square.

'I am exhausted!' cried Emma as eventually they managed to secure a hacking cab off the crowded streets. Mr Knightley handed her up.

'Yes. He is like a drowning man clutching at those who have rescued him.'

'You have rescued him.' She paused. 'He talked of Abbey-Mill Farm. You talked of Mr Martin. I believe there is something you are holding from me.'

'You are ever right, Emma.'

'You did not used to say that.'

'For a long time you have been right. Mostly right.'

Emma laughed. 'I would not have believed you if you had not added that.'

'I am so glad you can laugh. Your laugh is better than any music.'

'But I am serious. Tell me.'

'You remember that I once told you that you would not like my arrangement – I prevaricate – I have sold Abbey-Mill Farm to Mr Robert Martin!'

'Sold! Abbey-Mill!' Emma could hardly take it in.

'The money has paid off all John's debtors; he is a free man and with a small sum to help him as he sets up as a lawyer once more.'

'It is impossible! Abbey-Mill is part of Donwell. It is impossible you should sell it—'

'The entailment was at first a difficulty but I took legal advice—'

'And to the Martins! The Martins! It is too horrible! Altogether wrong! Against nature!'

'Emma, you do not know what you are saying' – gently – 'John is my brother. I am the elder, it is true, Donwell is mine, Abbey-Mill was mine. But should I have hesitated for a moment when so much was at stake? I thought not. If there had been any other way – there was no other way – I loved Abbey-Mill Farm – I love—'

'Oh, Knightley!'

'But I could not put that kind of love first – I cannot put that first.'

They had reached Brunswick Square and the driver looked for directions to the house but there was so much still unsaid and no opportunity to say it once they were inside. 'Drive at walking pace around the square till I tell you to stop,' commanded Mr Knightley.

'There is something more you will not like,' he turned again to Emma. 'You have not asked where Mr Martin found so much money that would pay off poor John's debts.'

'I cannot think practically,' Emma held her head. She pictured the little farmhouse, old Mrs Martin, Harriet Martin marrying beneath her and now the wife of a man with an estate of his own – a small estate, certainly, but very different from being a tenant.

'The money has not come from Mr Martin. It has come from Mrs Martin, Mrs Harriet Martin.'

Clip-clop went the tired horse round the dark square; clip-clop went Emma's head.

'Harriet Martin's father died,' continued Mr Knightley, 'quite recently, as I believe you know. I remember you told me they had bought a new pianoforte. He was a tradesman of course but not an ordinary one. Now you have been in London and seen those miles of shops in Oxford Street you may understand better than before how a great fortune can be made out of trade – greater perhaps than out of land – in money terms, at least. Harriet found herself inheriting a large sum.'

'Harriet Wilson an heiress!' Distractedly, Emma recalled the time when she had imagined just such a development and then, as she thought, discovered it untrue.

'Round again?' called the driver and receiving no answer, he muttered to himself, 'I'll turn the other way about or the poor old nag will be so giddy he'll fall off his legs.'

Neither occupant of the cab noticed the reversal of direction. 'Harriet Martin is a fine heiress,' continued Mr Knightley, 'who once owned nothing. It is our good fortune that Mr Martin wanted no more grandeur for his family than Abbey-Mill. He talks of adding on a room or two but to him it is the most beautiful spot in the world.'

'He talked to Mrs Tidmarsh of the sunset—'

'Perhaps he did. So there you are. Everything as it is. You will come to think about it as I have. As a joyful piece of good fortune rather than a source of sadness.'

'But your land, your property! Generations of Knightleys – bought by the money from a common tradesman!'

Knightley said nothing for a moment but held her hand tight. He understood how hard it was for the mistress of Hartfield to accept such a change.

'If you want a merry-go-round!' called the driver, patience gone, 'be off to the circus!'

'We'll stop at the next house along!' returned Knightley.

Emma had one more thing to say; one painful reproach but she found, as they drew up in front of the house in Brunswick Square and the gaslight lit up Knightley's concerned face, that she did not have the heart to say it. Nevertheless, as they entered the bright hallway, children overflowing down the stairs towards them, the words repeated in her head, 'Why did you not take me into your confidence when all the Martins – even Harriet Martin – knew of it?' It could not be the main theme of her thoughts with so much to consider, but it gave her a melancholy sense of separation from Mr Knightley's vital concerns. Such a cutting-out of what was important to him had happened too often.

John Knightley returned to his home two days before Christmas. Isabella had already been informed by his brother of the bankruptcy and also warned that his health had suffered as a consequence and she bore the change in her husband with surprising fortitude. It was impressed upon her that her husband should not bear the principal responsibility for the disaster; his colleague, Mr Graham, was allowed to be the guilty party, John Knightley his dupe – more blameworthy for foolishness than anything worse. Soon Isabella was able to confuse the time of his illness and think it the cause of his bad judgement rather than the result.

'You have hoped to make poor John your patient for these many years,' Emma laughed as she saw Isabella, remarkably recovered from her confinement, brewing yet another potion for her husband, 'and now he is at your mercy.'

'You must not laugh, Emma dearest. If I do not watch John, he will be off to work again in some even less God-fearing place than Scotland and then he may not return at all! You must read the parable of the Prodigal Son and you will see a little of how I feel.'

Isabella's innocence and muddle astonished Emma. Certainly, her sister had not been informed of John Knightley's incarceration but her expectation that the broken man who moved so humbly about the house was ready to slip the wifely leash and return to gainful occupation – travelling, moreover, to a remote place – seemed ridiculously optimistic.

She said as much to Mr Knightley. They had escaped Brunswick Square and taken a barouche to Hyde Park where, muffled to the eyes against a cold wind, they took a walk beside the lake called Serpentine. Mr Knightley did not agree with his wife's view to the extent she had predicted. 'My brother is a ghost of himself at the present, but he has powers of recovery. I have seen him as a child; when his health is recovered, he may surprise you. Isabella's confidence in him can only help – as long as she does not kill him with her doses; I saw a pot of some noxious substance that you would not give a horse.'

'It is papa's gruel!' smiled Emma. 'He has sent the recipe by special post today and Isabella is delighted both by his paternal solicitude and our brother's obedient reception to it.'

'Times have changed!' Mr Knightley's tone was a little ironic, for the unbankrupted John Knightley had been

known for his impatience with his father-in-law's preoccupation with his own and others' health.

'It is not only that he is a willing patient – or at least an
unrebellious one – but that he has become of positive use
in the house. I own that has surprised me.'

'Ah!' Mr Knightley's pace quickened with his interest.
'That terrible lassitude of humiliation leaving him? That is
a good sign.'

'Only this morning he inquired of me how the coal came;
and yesterday he asked to see the tradesmen's bills—'

'I had not hoped for so much so quickly! Oh, Emma,' he
turned, 'if this could be settled without more anguish.'

'The loss of Abbey-Mill Farm will always be a source of
anguish,' replied Emma bitterly.

'You still dwell on that.'

'You do not?' Emma stood still and watched the wind
ripple across the lake waters. A duck quacked and appeared
from behind an overhanging shrub. It quacked again and
another appeared; and another and another – until a whole
train of ducks came quacking up to where they stood.

'They think we have bread,' said Knightley absently. 'Tell
me, Emma, would you have been made quite so unhappy
by the loss of Abbey-Mill if it had not been Harriet Martin's
money that had bought it?' It was gently said; but the
sentiment cut Emma deeply.

'I am not such a fool as you think me!' She flung out the
words, scattering the ducks with her vehemence so that
they retreated with hysterical quackings.

'I did not mean to insult you—'

Emma's mood changed again. 'Oh, Knightley, if only we
could be safely at Highbury. We never quarrelled before we
came to London! I feel that you are hardly my husband at
all – I cannot bear it—' a sob broke from her. 'I am not brave
like Philomena, you know! I want things to be easy and
comfortable again! I want our quiet evenings at Hartfield

back again – just the two of us and dear papa with his little complaints – I would even drink gruel for that!'

Mr Knightley took her arm; it was too public a place to do more. 'You are brave, my dear – as brave as you need to be; no one can be braver than that. Perhaps Mrs Tidmarsh has a greater call for bravery. As to Hartfield, our quiet evenings, I sometimes thought you dissatisfied and restless. I am not so sure that you will be so happy to be back – not after the first pleasures of our return. London has provided you with new standards.'

'London perhaps!' cried Emma savagely. 'But not Londoners; they are all like ducks, quacking and crowding together in rows; even the houses do it!'

Knightley began to laugh. 'I have never seen a quacking house, for sure.'

'But they are in rows – it was the first observation I made.' But she smiled too; it was so long since she had managed to entertain Knightley enough to hear his laughter.

'You will go back to Highbury soon,' said Knightley as, tucking her closer to him, they began to walk again. 'If half of what you have told me of John's resurrection is true, then soon he will take over everything you have performed so nobly and you will be left free as air. I must go to Donwell once more before Christmas; perhaps we shall be going together after that. It has been an unnatural life we have been leading.'

20

The unnatural life must be continued through Christmas; Emma knew it but her impatience to be gone grew stronger each day. Isabella saw and felt sorry for it. She sat in her chair with a basket full of children's stockings all in need of a mother's loving darn. Emma, with far less to do now both adults were taking the burden from her, sat at the piano but her fingers remained obstinately stiff and unmusical. It was two days before Christmas and Mr Knightley had not yet returned from Donwell.

'Dearest Emma, you have done more for me than any sister should expect.'

'Yes. Yes.' Emma went to the window.

'Mr Knightley will not be back till tomorrow.'

'I am not looking for Mr Knightley. I was looking at the Foundling Hospital.'

'Ah – poor children! To be without parents! I can hardly bear to think of it!'

Emma returned and came to sit with her sister; she looked into her sweet, kind face.

'What is it, my dear?' Isabella pulled a thread through a little stocking and broke the end off with her teeth.

'You approach life with admirable simplicity!'

'I am no intellectual being, it is true. I leave such things to others.' A pause. 'Did I tell, my dear, that I have invited

Mr Dugobair Tidmarsh and Mrs Tidmarsh to our Christmas dinner? They are so dark and lonely in that great gloomy house of theirs and I thought it would please you.'

Emma nodded and turned away; for her cheeks would blush at the thoughts she must hide.

'One of the joyous gifts conferred by children,' continued Isabella comfortably, 'is that one may never be melancholy in their presence. When I consider that this will be the last Christmas I may spend in this house where all my children have been born and lived, a sadness overtakes me; but then Henry or John or Bella enters with a plea for the cup and ball I hid when they broke the kitchen window and one look at the rosy face, the contrite frown ready to break into a laugh or purse into a kiss – they know they will always get their way with me – and my sadness is disappeared as if it has never been.'

'Your happiness resides in your children, sister; you are fortunate; you are good.'

'And with my husband, Emma dear. A husband must come first.'

'Yes. Yes.' Once more Emma wandered to the piano but this time she did not even attempt a note.

Isabella's words proved very true. A Christmas that should have been a melancholy event was turned into a happy festivity by all the joyful noise and tumble of children who saw their father restored to them after a long absence, their mother back in their midst after her confinement, and their much-loved uncle and aunt in case they should need further attention. They were cheerful, unspoilt children and seemed quite unaware that their presents were diminished greatly in quality and number from the previous year.

The food was simpler too and the wine less abundantly served but, as they sat down, ten at the table, Emma thought it would do very well as a last supper. She turned to her left where Mr Tidmarsh waited hungrily for the mutton to be carved.

'Mr Knightley and I will leave earlier than the Mr John Knightleys.' Mr Tidmarsh knew the situation and had been a great comfort to Isabella throughout the days of her husband's return.

Mr Tidmarsh bowed. 'I shall endeavour to be of service.'

'You are kind.'

'Mrs Tidmarsh will also do everything in her power to help your sister.'

Now it was Emma's turn to bow. She had never managed to know Mr Tidmarsh very well, his learning proving a barrier to friendship, either in reality or in Emma's imagination. Whenever she was with him, she learnt, and, although she enjoyed the learning, she could not be altogether comfortable with the sensation of inferiority it inevitably brought with it.

The meat arrived and Mr Tidmarsh, instead of falling eagerly upon it as was his usual habit – Emma suspected the meals provided in his home by Mrs Tidmarsh were inadequate for the needs of a young energetic man – took to poking about the slices in an absent-minded way.

'Gravy, Mr Tidmarsh?' inquired Emma, as a reminder.

'Mrs Tidmarsh is not as strong as she appears,' he said suddenly. 'Her spirit sustains her body—'

'Oh!' Emma could think of nothing better.

'I had thought that country air—'

How Emma blushed! And was angry, guilty, vexed and embarrassed. 'I – we—'

'Not now – not yet – the cold—' He, too, blushed, poked his meat furiously.

'Please – I beg you—' So Emma muttered and blushed as Mr Tidmarsh muttered and blushed but she did not give an invitation for Mrs Tidmarsh to Hartfield – she could not.

'Well, then—' finished Mr Tidmarsh and, at last, began to eat.

It struck Emma as she watched his satisfaction that he might not have noticed the absence of the invitation he had sought.

The dinner continued – everybody in the best of spirits – and even John Knightley's haggard looks were disguised by a brighter colour.

Afterwards, while Mr Knightley sat beside Emma on their sofa, Isabella and Mrs Tidmarsh left the room and soon there was a sound of heavy scuffling and a bang on the door before it could be opened.

'Mama has prepared a surprise,' said Henry, coming in importantly like a little footman. 'You must pull your seats round.'

The servants appeared next, dragging a load with Isabella darting smilingly around and Mrs Tidmarsh, self-conscious, wearing a grand air and an uncharacteristic bloom on her cheeks, followed. It was a harp. All was explained: Philomena Tidmarsh had been prevailed upon to play; this was a rare treat; they must applaud her even as she sat on a little gilt chair and raised her arms to ripple up the strings just as her cape sleeves rippled down her naked arms. At very least, it was a splendid sight.

'I thought she would not admit to professional talent,' whispered Mr Knightley to Emma.

'She has given up the deception.'

'So now she gives us pleasure.'

Emma looked to see irony in her husband's face; but there was none, could be none. As soon as Mrs Tidmarsh embarked on 'Strike the Harp in Praise of Bragela', it was clear beyond doubt – even to Emma who was an imperfect judge of the instrument – that here was a very superior player. Even the children sat still while the room filled with noble sounds.

'I think of Highbury,' whispered Emma to Mr Knightley; she bethought herself further, 'and of Donwell'.

Mr Knightley smiled and inclined his head closer to hers. The weeks of anguish were replaced, for one evening at least, by the joys of a happy family life – raised to a higher pitch by Mrs Tidmarsh's art and the consciousness of what had gone before. This house might have reached the end of its era as the John Knightleys' home – they must leave it in ignominy in the world's terms – but this evening, this *tableau vivant* told another story. They were happy and this happiness of an hour or two would always be more real than cleverly-set bricks, a fine staircase and a broad front door.

'I thank you. I thank you!' John Knightley did not try to hide the tears in his eyes. His thanks enlarged to include everyone in the room.

Mrs Tidmarsh breathed deep and lifted up her arms again; the music seemed to come out of her white brow and elegant nose, her red curled lips.

Emma sighed and shut her eyes. The river between Donwell and Abbey-Mill sparkled, fast and quiet, in front of her; willow trees trailed their long fingers above, weeds stretched hand upon hand below. Emma sighed again.

'You are tired,' whispered Mr Knightley.

'A little.' Ah, the secrets, the secrets! Emma saw Frank Churchill's hangdog but jaunty back disappear along the bank, Harriet's plumply pleased figure at the gate of Abbey-Mill. Frowning, Emma brought herself back to the present, to the white sinuosities of Philomena's fingers, to her back straight as a pillar – but then even that turned itself into the dignity of a woman left behind in the hall of the Foundling Hospital, the dignity of someone who stood beside a woman who was not quite a lady. Once more Emma closed her eyes and this time it was Jane Fairfax she saw; and heard her slender fingers make music from the ivory keys.

21

A home-coming must always be a delight – particularly when an elderly and much-loved parent, unseen for very many weeks, awaits in welcome.

'Ah, my poor dear child! You are just as sickly as I feared. If you knew how I have suffered on your behalf – Miss Bates and I – we have talked of nothing else!'

Mr Woodhouse stood in his hallway, on a December day when the wind blew, a signal of his true affection for his daughter and his urgent need to see her at the first opportunity. Behind him, Miss Bates peered humbly around, like a squirrel behind a tree, although now and again she abandoned this natural role to stretch to her toes and twitch Mr Woodhouse's shawl closer about his shoulders.

'I am in remarkable health, dear papa. Tell him, Knightley, how well I am and Isabella and all the children and let us have the cold meats which I can see on my kind round table for I am as hungry as anyone who has been up since before dawn, forgotten to eat breakfast and arrived many hours later at their own dear home with their own dear papa! Oh, papa, I am so glad to see you and—' she caught a glimpse of the flickering squirrel – 'dear Miss Bates who, I can already perceive, has looked after you so well.'

'Yes, indeed. She is a good lady, very good. Come, Miss Bates, do not hide—'

'No, no, I'm sure – the family together – a joy—' Miss Bates was too overcome to continue and Mr Knightley, ever kind-hearted, gave her his arm to follow Emma and Mr Woodhouse into the parlour.

The reunion with Mr Woodhouse must be followed by a reunion, nearly as emotional, with all the inanimate but much missed old friends of sofa, chair, tables, hangings, bookcases, staircases, windows and vistas from the windows. Mr Knightley had ridden immediately to see Mr Martin so Emma had plenty of time to feel herself truly at home again, to find nothing important had changed – merely a few rearrangements downstairs of chairs and cushions which she soon restored to the original (dear Miss Bates had never much of an eye for such things). In a few hours, after interviews with Sterne who was no more disobliging than usual and Merry who confessed to being very under-occupied, she was able to feel that Hartfield and she were on terms and that she might read the notes left for her in her upstairs parlour.

Mrs Weston must come first. At her late age to produce a second child, another healthy daughter, and to be yourself in good health and good spirits, was more than enough to thank God for! Mr Weston could hardly believe such fortune; the only cloud – an anxiety that must be cleared sooner rather than later – was that Frank's child, Mr Weston's grandson, was said to be ailing. Old Mr Churchill had written with such a report but Mrs Weston's calm nature allowed that Mr Churchill's distress at the continued absence of Frank – he knew not where – and his own solitariness following the death of both Mrs Churchills might have led him to exaggerate the baby's illness. Mrs Weston felt sure it was nothing more than the slightest of ailments. Nevertheless, it had inspired Mr Weston to feel a greater responsibility for his grandson that might result eventually in the baby being brought, even before the good weather, to Highbury where he could keep a better eye on its welfare.

The second half of this letter Emma read with fluctuating emotions and she turned to a letter from Harriet Wilson rather quickly. Here, too, there was news of a safe delivery – as if every one of her acquaintanceship was intent on enlarging the human race, she thought a little sourly. The baby was a boy, 'the image of his father', and Harriet was all simple pride and satisfaction; no mention was made of the new ownership of Abbey-Mill Farm. For that, at least, Emma must be grateful.

There were other letters and invitations – from the Coles, from Mrs Goddard and from Mr Elton who clearly knew more about John Knightley's altered circumstances than any of the others and spoke of 'the mysterious ways of God who raised up only to cast down'. Emma felt moved to cast down this letter to the floor and only picked it up again when she saw a long postscript on the back of the paper penned in Mrs Elton's hand:

My dear Mrs Knightley, I understand in the sadness of your family's times of tribulation you may not be in a mood for merriment but I hope you may make an exception for a dinner I shall be giving in the New Year when Mr and Mrs Suckling arrive on a visit. They have suffered the misfortune of a part of Maple Grove falling to the ground. It seems that the heavy autumn rain followed by severe frost shortly before Christmas caused cracking in stone so particularly venerable. A further misfortune caused the cracking to reveal itself in the wall to the dining-room where a great dinner had just been laid – utilising, as a tribute to the season, their best set of Sèvres china. Suffice it to say that only one

gravy-boat survived and that only because Mr Suckling
held it aloft in his hand as they fled the room. It was
a miracle that only that which can be replaced was
lost, while the irreplaceable – I refer to my dearest
sister and her family – emerged unscathed. They are
now in excellent lodgings in Bath but I have prevailed
upon them that a family environment (however inferior)
may lift their spirits after such a horrible experience. So
I ask you to dinner – first, as always. As I observed to
Mr Elton, Mr John Knightley's follies cannot be laid at
your door.

Down went the letter again and up jumped Emma to stamp
her feet and cry, 'I wish the Eltons' house would fall down
as well as the Sucklings'!'

On the whole it seemed to Emma that her inanimates
gave her better welcome than the animates – saving those
in her own household, of course. Merry did her hair so
neatly and the rooms, although very quiet after a house so
filled with children, gave all the pleasures of country light
and space. When Knightley returned, she was able to pass
him the Eltons' letter quite calmly and ask how Isabella and
John's situation was to be explained in the village. There
was sure to be talk.

She had tried to say this without sadness or reproach on
her account but could not subdue a blush that gave away
the depth of her feelings.

'Oh, Emma, you should not have to bear this,' he took
her hands.

'You have had to bear far more – Abbey-Mill—'

'Yes. But I do not have your pride—'

'You criticise me?'

'No. No. I am older, that is all I meant by it. I have
had my dignity knocked once or twice. You are new to
the sensation. I sorrow for it but I console myself that at

least, now, here, we can face whatever unpleasantness may follow together.'

'Oh, yes!' cried Emma. 'I did not mean to complain on my own behalf – on behalf of my pride, as you term it – but merely to inquire how far we will explain the circumstances of my sister's visit here – of John Knightley's changed appearance (for it will be remarked on) and their continued stay, when before they could never spare more than a week or two.'

Mr Knightley let drop Emma's hands and stood. 'They may not be here so long as you imagine. You have already seen my brother's powers of resurrection—' He stopped abruptly.

Emma waited for more; but no further explanation came. He looked down on his wife kindly but with the eyes of someone who saw a child. He did have more to say but he did not mean to confide in her. Yet again he did not mean to confide in her.

'I have no doubt you found time to visit Abbey-Mill Farm,' she said in a spiteful tone.

'I did.' No emotion.

'You had much to discuss, I may be certain.'

'Indeed.' He bowed and gave her his hand; his meaning was clear – this private conversation was closed and it was time for dinner.

But Emma evaded his hand and, smiling falsely, went, fast and furious, alone to the door. 'I also may be certain,' she cried over her shoulder as she reached the head of the stairway before him, 'that you saw Mrs Robert Martin!'

He made no answer, perhaps did not take it in; then they were in the hallway – in the drawing-room – and following happy Mr Woodhouse and happy fussing Miss Bates to the dining-room; there they sat together, the picture of contented reunion, one each side of the table. Emma must talk; Emma must smile; yet her words cried over her shoulder, echoed in her heart – she scarcely knew why or what she had intended by them, and yet how they echoed!

'I am out of sorts tonight,' she told Knightley.

They stood outside the bedchamber, the long evening, the evening of home-coming, over, sadly undergone when it should have been so gay.

'Emma—' He put out his hand. She turned away; her heart was cold, stunned by that echo, unfeeling. Sleep was all that she cared for. He watched her face, her clear young profile; he bowed. 'You are fatigued.'

She gave the smallest of curtsies and went into the room; the door closed sharply between them.

Torrents of cold rain fell on Hartfield, Highbury, and the surrounding countryside. Mr Knightley, on horseback early, had not perceived the force of descending water and found himself soaked through, with insistent trickles even managing to insert themselves down the insides of his riding boots. Not being foolish and being unwilling to risk catching a cold, he put in as soon as possible at a warm fireside where, moreover, he was also likely to be offered the breakfast that he had, in his haste to get away, left Hartfield without.

'Oh, Mr Knightley!' cried Mrs Martin – old Mrs Martin, her skirt bundled up and her hair not quite neat, but she did not think of that – 'Come in! Come in! To be sure, you are more like a waterfall than a man. Take off your wet things where you stand.'

Leaving behind in an outer room his streaming hat, coat and boots, Mr Knightley made his way with many protestations of gratitude and apologies at the earliness of the hour, to the warm and cheerful breakfast room. Robert Martin and his sister stood by the table where they had been sitting until a moment ago, in front of steaming platters of bacon and coddled eggs, while Harriet still sat in a corner chair, by the fire, her fat, dimpled baby asleep on her knee. She still wore a bonnet and a loose wrapper and the mixture of embarrassment at the unfinished nature of her toilette and the consciousness at making a perfect picture of motherhood made her glow like a beacon. She had never looked so pretty.

Mr Knightley bowed, glanced in her direction just long enough to admire, and then took his place at the table where Mrs Martin had already laid a full platter.

'We are simple here,' said Mr Martin, his words suggesting only satisfaction at such a state, 'no ceremony, no attempt at ceremony.'

'Not for very much longer if Harriet has her way—' Any criticism implied by Mrs Martin was contradicted by the fond look she directed towards her daughter-in-law.

'Oh, mama!' Harriet blushed redder than the fire. 'You will let Mr Knightley believe I am not satisfied with how we are—' turning her appealing blue eyes on their visitor. 'It is only that the parlour is small with so many of us now—' here she hid her blushes with a kiss on her baby's smooth brow – 'and there is a place so rightly waiting for a drawing-room – so flat – facing south – with a view of the river – it barely needs more than a few tiles to roof it in—'

She broke off at the smiles and even a hearty laugh from Mr Martin. 'How can I refuse her anything, when she asks so sweetly and there is so very very little to be done?' he asked Mr Knightley.

'Oh, Robert, you mock me!' cried Harriet.

'Indeed I do not. You have quite convinced me of the rightness of your argument. You shall have your drawing-room and your new pianoforte shall go in there and, when you pace up and down and discover that five couples could stand up in it, without any squeeze, I shall not be surprised at all but suggest that, if we were to push the bow out a little or even, perhaps, dance across the hallway, we might run to ten couples – for, after all, there is Elizabeth to find a husband—'

'Robert!' cried Elizabeth.

'Look, Mr Knightley, how dreadfully he mocks his ladies!' cried Harriet.

'He is a very lucky man,' said Knightley, his smiles becoming a little serious. 'If I were him, I'd build a drawing-room east, west, north of the house if it would please—'

'Oh, Mr Knightley! Now you are mocking me—'

'Never. Now, I must see how my clothes dry?' He looked to Mrs Martin but she shook her head and told him it would be longer than half an hour before they even stopped dripping, so he had no choice but to sit in the midst of this cheerful family and fill himself up with food, tea, and friendly talk enough to last him for the day.

Emma watched the torrents of rain from her bedroom window while Merry took an age with her hair and told her the Highbury gossip she had been saving up for weeks.

'The rain runs more heavily in the country,' Emma sighed. She had woken with a dull head and a feeling of guilt at her emotional behaviour of the night before. She had intended to be simple and lively, to recapture the happiness of her arrival, to put things on a proper comfortable footing between herself and Mr Knightley. But these good resolutions were undermined by his absence – even before breakfast and on such a day, as if he had fled the house. Now she must eat with her father, submit to more questions about Isabella which were hard to answer since it was agreed that Mr Woodhouse must not know the full extent of John Knightley's difficulties, and do all this under the ever-watchful and sincere eye of Miss Bates. This good creature did not talk as much as she used, it was true, for her time seemed entirely taken up with seeing to Mr

Woodhouse's comforts – like a friend, servant, worshipper! thought Emma, aware that, despite all her good intentions, she was already giving way to disagreeable instincts.

'And I expect, dear Mrs Knightley,' said Miss Bates, 'you will be happy to see your own pianoforte again.'

'I had little time for music,' began Emma shortly, before recovering herself. 'Thank you. Indeed I am sadly out of practice but I shall take my accustomed place as soon as I have finished the housekeeping with Sterne. Perhaps you would like to attend on this first occasion since my return?'

'Oh, no – yes – whatever you think best – your superiority in such matters – my own humble attempts – Perhaps I may be of use—'

This was penance for Emma but she welcomed it and did not even allow herself to wonder when Miss Bates might resume her place in her own lodgings. She took her penance further by duly taking her position in front of the piano keys where she was repaid by fingers as stiff as spoons and a memory of no music beyond that which she had known since childhood.

It was thus Mrs Weston, come by carriage to welcome Mrs Knightley back, found her erstwhile charge, thundering out 'The Grand Old Duke of York'.

'Mrs Weston! How pleased I am to see you!' Emma jumped off her stool and ran towards her.

'My dear. My dear.' The two ladies kissed, held hands. Miss Bates, chancing to come to the door, made sound enough to attract Emma's attention which was followed by such a frown (an unconscious frown, one must hope, for the sake of Mrs Knightley's good intentions) that she retreated instantly.

'In such weather, this is nothing short of heroism!'

'Mr Weston had to engage a carriage for a meeting at Richmond, so I took advantage of it to come to you. My dear Emma – all these weeks in London – so much sadness, difficulty, joy – dear Isabella – another little Knightley daughter—'

'And you? How is your new little one? I see you have escaped your motherly duties.'

'Indeed I have. But you know I have in my time replaced the duties of a mother towards you, dearest Emma. Let us say that I am the most fortunate of women – let us pass from that, to you. How is it with you?'

As Emma felt herself under inspection from that calm, loving eye that for sixteen years had been all she knew of a womanly affection – indeed of a motherly sort, if it could never replace that of a true mother – she felt a great urge to cry and howl like a baby.

'You are a little pale, I think. Perhaps London—?' Mrs Weston hinted delicately into the silence.

'No. No. My human frame is just the same as always – strong and healthy – my body does not let me down—'

'But? There is a but, I feel it coming.'

'Mr Knightley—'

'Oh!' Mrs Weston looked down at her hands; her expression was not encouraging; at least Emma did not find it encouraging. Nevertheless she persevered; if she did not talk she must howl.

'Mr Knightley and I – a quarrel – no, a coldness – he does not confide – there is a want of openness in him,' her voice strengthened, 'and yet it is he who has always convinced me of the greatest value of openness—' A fleeting image of Frank Churchill's passionate face made her hesitate, but that secret was long over. 'He has now on several occasions taken action, kept secret – oh, it is hurtful!—' she gulped, stopped.

Mrs Weston looked up. 'Mr Knightley is a man of sound judgement,' she said. 'He approaches forty years of age, of which only one of those years has been spent with a wife.

He is used to relying on himself and himself alone. His takes the most manly road in which he bears full responsibility. If he does not apply to you for your opinion, it is because he is sure of his own. You are still very young, however brilliant your intellect—'

'Oh, don't tell me such stuff!'

'Emma!'

'I am sorry. I am sorry for such rudeness. But you have always led me to believe that I am clever, whereas in London I learnt just how limited my knowledge and understanding and education is – and now Mr Knightley makes it clearer still. He sees me as a spoilt child – he used to tell me so! – he likes me well enough, my looks well enough – but only as he might like a doll!'

'You a doll?' despite Mrs Weston's distress at Emma's unhappiness, she could not help smiling at this unlikely image that her intemperance had called forth.

'And now you smile too! As if I were a child in a tantrum—'

'No. No. You mistake me. I am your friend. But I cannot agree with you about Mr Knightley. If he does not tell you everything he knows, then he must be right not to do so. You must rely on his judgement in all things. He is your husband. You must endeavour to submit yourself to his will –'

'Oh! Oh!'

'You do not like such talk. Perhaps I seem old-fashioned in comparison with your London friends—'

'I had no time for London friends.' But as Emma spoke, she thought of Philomena Tidmarsh, of Mr Tidmarsh. They would not have lectured her so – as if Mr Knightley was a god, not a mortal man. Besides, how could Mrs Weston pretend that a wife must submit to a husband in everything when they both knew perfectly well that Mr Weston's easygoing nature looked to his wife for guidance – only seldom the other way around! Why should she play the role of unquestioning slave just because she was married to a man of strong, intelligent character? It was not right; she knew it was not right – but she also knew that calmly determined expression on her old governess's face; there was no more to be gained by continuing the conversation.

'Mrs Weston, my dear Mrs Weston,' said Emma, trying to still the trembling in her voice, 'I apologise, the strain, poor Isabella, John – the journey from London. I have of course the uttermost respect for Mr Knightley's views.'

'We will not talk of it again,' Mrs Weston sat up, managed a smile. 'Now, show me what you have purchased in London, for I am sure, from the descriptions in your letters, that you have ribbons and trimmings and lace that will set all Highbury green with envy.'

'It is the cut of the sleeves where I learnt most,' contributed Emma, very nearly calm again. 'Tell me, is it true that the Sucklings' house has fallen about their ears? I would laugh heartily, if I did not understand from Mrs Elton their misfortune might at last bring them to our doorstep –'

'Oh, it is a terrible prospect, but I believe we must not hold our breaths for I saw Mrs Elton only yesterday and her face was long with stories of the Sucklings' being too much in demand at Bath for them to wish to desert it for the humble pleasures of Vicarage Lane.'

'I am relieved.' Emma took a breath. 'And what of young Frank? The baby?'

'On that subject there is much to say—' And with this introduction Mrs Weston settled down to the absorbing story – to her at least – of slatternly wet-nurses, unregulated behaviour, childish weakness and strength – She had had it all from Mrs Campbell who had been up to Yorkshire to see for herself.

The rain continued to come down outside the window as she spoke – on and on, as it seemed to her companion.

The evergreens took on a darker shade, the branches of the trees and shrubs that had lost their leaves, striped grey and black. It was a dismal sight, Emma thought, and found herself contrasting it to the colonnades and porticos, the bow-windows and trim brick, the bridges and gardens and lakes of London. How could it be that after only a day back in her beloved home she found herself harbouring such disloyal comparisons!

'In short,' concluded Mrs Weston, who did not seem to have noticed Emma's wandering gaze, 'we will have the poor creature here as soon as ever Mr Weston can arrange the journey. That is what he has gone to Richmond about, for old Mr Churchill stays there now and is talking of shutting up Yorkshire and removing to Richmond permanently. Poor Frank must be in great anguish of mind to stay away so long, when he must know the pain his continued absence will cause those he most loves—'

'The one he most loved has left him,' Emma spoke with a blush.

'That may be so; but there are many left behind who bear him lasting affection—'

'Ah – indeed – a passionate man may feel that affection is no exchange for love—'

Mrs Weston looked at Emma, surprised. 'There may be both together – I do not separate the terms—'

'What does it matter?' Emma turned her eyes on the melancholy vegetation again. 'We are agreed – we forgive him – you because you have a forgiving nature and I because – because I admire one who can love so deeply as to ruin his life—'

'And ruin others with him?' Mrs Weston's tone now seemed a little sharper than her nature, as described by Emma, should make it be.

'Ruin? Do not let us talk of ruins.'

A silence fell as both ladies tried very hard not to think of John Knightley as a Gothic castle.

'I believe the rain has slowed to nothing more than drips.' Mrs Weston stood and went to stare out of the window.

'If you mean to go,' said Emma, joining her, 'then I must call papa; he will never forgive me if you leave without sitting a little with him—'

'Your dear papa! How glad he must be to have you back!'

'He says so – but I would never have believed how comfortably he and Miss Bates have dealt together – sometimes they seem to speak in the same voice. I must admit it has been a surprise to me – I had not thought Miss Bates quite so excellent a companion—'

'And Sterne? The other servants? Do they have complaints of her management?'

'Not one bit – and she does not flutter half so much. She will sit without speaking a word for up to half an hour – I noted it last night.'

'She is a good, dear creature – she was needed and she came – and now?'

Emma sighed; it seemed that no subject was without its problems. 'There is such an appeal in her eye – yet she cannot stay for ever.'

'Perhaps when Isabella comes—' Mrs Weston hinted delicately.

'There will not be room; my thought entirely – every bedchamber occupied—'

'Quite. And now there is even a spark of sunshine. Look, how it makes the laurels shine.'

'I shall fetch you to papa.'

Emma found as she left Mrs Weston and Mr Woodhouse at a table of backgammon that her head was less heavy than before. She felt quite able to manage various necessary arrangements and regretted all the more her outburst over Mr Knightley's lack of openness. It had been mere foolishness. No one was married to a better man!

It was with real warmth of spirit that she saw Mr Knightley, handsome and glowing, ride up the gravel drive, give up his horse to be taken into the stable, and take his usual firm stride into the house.

'How early you left!' She smiled, helped him off with his coat. 'And in such a downpour.' She held the coat next to her cheek, 'And yet you are hardly wet at all!'

'I sheltered for the worst of it at Abbey-Mill – dried myself through – and had such a breakfast! My dear, you must find time to visit the Martins today; they are asking after you.'

Emma's head gave a throb. Knightley glanced at her as she made no answer.

'You must not allow prejudice to overwhelm good manners.'

'No. No. Indeed. I shall visit them this afternoon.'

'Thank you, dearest Emma. I expected nothing less.'

To be married and in harmony is happiness complete; to be married and to be in disharmony turns the whole world black. Emma and Mr Knightley ate dinner together, spent the evening in the same room, lay together and breakfasted the next morning together. But they never looked into each other's faces and their voices – as they spoke politely of plans for Isabella and John Knightley's arrival; of the Westons' determination to succour little Frank Churchill or of that traditionally diverting subject, the Sucklings – did not penetrate to their thoughts. Their thoughts remained private, sad and undefined. Soon Mr Knightley, with his usual purposeful calm, announced that it was his day to be a magistrate and left Hartfield. Emma did not watch him go.

What had come between them? If questioned, neither would have showed themselves certain. Knightley, the man of action, hardly wanted to believe there was a separation – or only such a separation as might come between two people, however loving, who had over-taxed their strength. Emma, more used to considering her motives, felt a lack of sympathy from Mr Knightley, a wish that she should be someone rather different than she was or than that person she should wish to be – although what constituted this person she was perfectly unclear. It was not exactly disapproval that she sensed but a kind of insistent weightiness. This weightiness, felt whenever Knightley was near (and to some extent even in his absence), carried with it, scarcely out of sight, an image of Harriet Martin at her garden gate – Mrs Robert Martin who was now a mother and owner of Abbey-Mill Farm – and whom she must visit that morning. It was unfortunate that the first words Emma heard at breakfast after Mr Knightley's departure should come from Miss Bates, blithely sure of having found an excellent topic of conversation: 'Mrs Elton assures me that Mrs Martin is determined to throw out a room at the back of the house twice as big as all their present rooms together; she talks of dancing!'

'I wonder, dear Miss Bates, whether you have misinter-preted—' said kindly Mr Woodhouse, scraping off what little butter he had first allowed on his bread till there was no more moisture visible than a veil-like film. 'Mrs Martin's father was a tradesman. Mrs Elton is prone to exaggeration; she had told me the Sucklings' house, Maple Grove, had fifteen bedrooms and it was only when I questioned her she revealed that half of these were in use by the servants; on the other hand she calls the Vicarage a "house for dolls", whereas it is perfectly spacious enough for two – even if Mrs Elton does have a few thousand to her name. You will tell me Mrs Elton is building a ballroom next.'

Miss Bates, smiling agreeably, nevertheless stuck to her principle. 'I am sure I am not as mistaken as all that; she was tolerably clear.'

'You know, dearest papa,' interposed Emma in a voice that sounded strangely sharp to her ears, 'tradesmen have the money of the future. If you had seen the shops in London—'

'I expect you are right, my dear. In London – you know all about London – I am quite prepared to let you speak for London money, but in Highbury, it is a quite different matter. In Highbury – or Donwell indeed,' he gave Emma a smile that was arch as well as complacent, 'it is land that counts. You will convince me of nothing else, however many visits you pay to London!'

Emma who, in her exasperation with her father's refusal to face facts (facts that she herself had been just as unwilling to face a few weeks earlier), had been about to mention the Coles – and, even, closer to home, Mr Weston's trading successes – became abruptly silent. The abruptness pleased Mr Woodhouse, convincing him of his rightful victory over London; but, in truth, Emma's silence and the blush on her cheeks denoted her sensibility that such talk approached the thin ice of John Knightley's situation. She must not be drawn into any conversation that might approach the reality: it was tradesman's money that was looking after Mr Woodhouse's daughter and six grandchildren. A lawyer had been hard enough for Mr Woodhouse to accept as a son; a bankrupt lawyer, although still very likely above a tradesman in his view of the world, would cause him the sort of pain and confusion that it was the duty of even the most hard-hearted daughter to make every effort to avoid.

'I am glad poor Isabella and John are giving up London for the country,' Mr Woodhouse was following a satisfactory train of thought. 'I know you have assured me it is only for a short time but I beg to differ; no one at Hartfield ever wishes to leave!'

Catching sight of Miss Bates whose smiling and winking face at this sally indicated that she wished to heartily agree but did not quite dare, Emma stood up and prepared to leave the room.

'She has let her egg become quite hard, that is the problem.' Mr Woodhouse's words followed her: 'Poor Emma; she would never have done that before she left for London.'

Emma could not catch Miss Bates' humbly murmured rejoinder but her father's words rose above the closing of the door. 'Another week or two and she'll settle down comfortably; change is always for the worse, I do believe.'

This conviction, so patently true in a way Mr Woodhouse could not possibly imagine, perhaps for this very reason, vexed Emma to such an extent that she had to exert extreme forbearance to avoid clapping the door shut with a violence that might have made a part of Hartfield follow the example of the despised Maple Grove, and collapse to the ground. Hartfield was not used to change or noise – even Isabella's children managed a quieter level. Emma had grown up with this knowledge and never before felt the need to question it. Indeed she did not now but merely rushed through her duties with a more forceful energy than was her usual practice and, before she left the house, looked in on her father with an unthinking flurry and no attempt to rearrange his rug which she saw had been quite wrongly folded by Miss Bates.

'Goodbye, papa. I am to go visiting. The weather is bright, as you see. James has the carriage out so you may be easy.'

She had gone, so quick that Mr Woodhouse had no time to voice a fear but not, however, quite quick enough to avoid Miss Bates who stood behind – almost inside – the grandfather clock in the hall, and clasped her hands beseechingly.

'I should have spoke at breakfast – you gone so swift and dear Mr Woodhouse – perhaps as far as Highbury – I may walk – my boots are stout, but—'

'Dear Miss Bates,' Emma moderated her voice, 'I will be glad of your company as far as Highbury. I see you have your coat on in readiness.'

'A presumption – I should not presume—'

'Of course you should. You have been far too generous

with your time to Hartfield. It is your rooms, perhaps, you wish to visit.'

'The damp – in this weather.'

'It is done. I shall be glad of your company.' As Emma spoke these insincere words and they set out together in search of James, it struck her that Miss Bates – her good nature, her loquacity, her general popularity – might be a useful emollient on her visit to the Martins. This proposal was received with much lively gratitude and, with some sense of shame, Emma was forced to realise that the past weeks had seen a severe curtailment in social life for Miss Bates, who, when living in the centre of Highbury, had been used to being surrounded by humankind – even if this merely led to a nod on the pavement or a word about the weather in Ford's or the post office. It would not have occurred to Mr Woodhouse that Miss Bates would wish to leave his side, so that any contact she would have with the world outside must come to Hartfield.

'I suppose the Coles and Mrs Goddard and Mr Weston and the Eltons called on you in our absence?' Emma questioned.

'Oh, yes! They are all so very kind – so very fond of your dear father – so attentive – as attentive as such busy people can be – We were quiet – but we wished to be quiet.'

By further questioning Emma discovered that the attentiveness of Highbury had been very limited indeed – and that Hartfield had almost slept like an enchanted castle. 'I am surprised rose thorns did not grow round the walls!' She laughed, but was a little vexed.

'No. No, Mrs Knightley. We were so content – three turns round the shrubbery, unless the wind blew too strong – backgammon, chess – I can give Mr Woodhouse a game now – the days flew by – and your letters – oh, if you knew how often we read them – my eyes being a little better than your father's, I read them aloud – It put me

in mind sometimes of the days – oh, I should not say—'
She stopped, a tear in her eye, and Emma could not but
be aware that she was thinking of those days when she
and old Mrs Bates had read aloud their letters from Jane
Fairfax.

The memory caused a slight rise in Emma's colour since
at that time her own principal interest had been to avoid
hearing these letters – letters from a paragon of every virtue
and talent – and she more than once had cut short the
doting grandmother and aunt. Yet it would be cruel not
to mention her now. 'Dear Miss Bates – she of whom we
are both thinking is at rest now – she is peaceful—'

'Yes. Yes. You are too kind.' The good lady dabbed at her
eyes and made every effort to sit straight and not give way
to grief.

'You must be in a fever to see little Frank Churchill—'
The idea came to Emma with something of a shock; she
did not look forward to it.

'Yes. Oh, yes. That is why I wished to look into my
lodgings. There is talk of the nurse taking him there –
the Westons' house is not large, you know; but perhaps
you have an idea—'

'No. It is entirely what you and Mr Weston decide – I
am no relative.' Emma had never quite managed to couple
Mr Weston and Miss Bates with total conviction – the one
so sturdy and self-supporting and the other so needful of
patronage, so this little piece of deference cost her an effort.
But the truth was there and she must not deny it. She was
surprised, however, that Miss Bates made no mention of her
own return to her rooms as companion to her nephew and
his nurse. Perhaps she was taking such a step for granted.

'I will only be a very few minutes,' Miss Bates assured Mrs
Knightley, her agitation at causing a delay in her hostess's
plans very plain.

'I shall come in with you. Ford's has no excitements

for me after London and another's presence may lighten your task.'

The rooms were very cold, small and dark. Emma had forgotten how small and dark; her eyes, inevitably, were drawn to the corner where the pianoforte had stood.

Miss Bates, whose humility did not hinder the efficient working of an observant eye, looked up from her search for mice. 'You remember what stood there – but we must not talk of that!'

'It is safe at Donwell – rest assured. Mr Martin has it in his care.'

'I am glad. Yet I cannot—' she hesitated.

'We will inquire after it.'

'Thank you – all the trouble – Yet I cannot like that piano!' the words came in even more of a tumble than before and continued in fits and starts as Miss Bates eased her troubled mind by a confession to someone whom she trusted and looked up to as the representative of all generosity. 'The piano sometimes seems to be – an indication of the bad – the bad in Mr Churchill – The secrecy of its arrival – money spent – Jane playing on it too long – wearing herself out – Mr Churchill leaning close to her face, my poor Jane – so worn, so pale—'

'Miss Bates, do not distress yourself! Sit down, please.' Emma was quite alarmed by the trembling figure and gasping face. 'They found happiness in marriage, we must remember that.'

'Marriage – happiness – ah, yes. They were happy – Jane's letters – happy, for a while. But his nature. Jane had no one to turn to. Oh, Mrs Knightley, how could he have left her so much alone! Was not that cruelty. She wrote to us of the long evenings in Yorkshire, alone with Mr Churchill who was not a man of decision – of any activity of mind. Sometimes – I should not even think such a thing – but I cannot but wonder that if she had not been so much alone she would have been stronger – Oh, poor Jane!'

'Jane was never strong, you must not make things worse—'

'You are right – of course – I have burnt her letters – I promised myself never to speak of her unhappiness – loneliness—'

'But if she were so unhappy, why did you not go to her?'

'Oh, Mrs Knightley!' A wail. 'How could I?! Do you not think it was my one desire to be with her? – oh, how I longed for it – but there was my dear Mrs Bates, and—'

'And?' prompted Emma.

'Mr Frank Churchill could not quite – we are humble people – in the grandeur of Enscombe – we would not quite fit in – It was for our own sakes, he said – we would not have been comfortable – but, if I had been able to move Mrs Bates to Yorkshire – probably not, most probably not – but if I had, we would not have needed to be introduced in company – but just to be near—'

'You must not blame yourself.'

'But I do! I cannot help it! I apologise – Mrs Knightley – so, so kind . . .' She could not speak more. Her silence gave Emma a moment to cogitate and to find consolation for the sorrowful creature in front of her. Eventually she ventured, in words more heartfelt because she truly believed them, 'You may be right in some points but I am sure you are overlooking the great love that Mr Churchill bore for your niece. After all, he risked his inheritance to become engaged to her. A young, handsome, well-educated gentleman who could have formed a connection with any lady in the land, chose Jane Fairfax, whose undoubted elegance, virtue and talent,' Emma forbore to mention her humble origins, 'shut out any other young lady. He loved her with single-minded passion. That alone is enough to make any young wife happy. That he could not change his nature, I can believe, but that he ever stopped loving her, I cannot!'

'Oh, Mrs Knightley.' Miss Bates sniffed and composed herself. 'You are so good – you cannot conceive – however, I will say no more. He did continue to love her in his way, I believe you are right in that.'

With such consoling agreement, the two ladies left the little rooms – scenes of such happiness and such misery – and set off to find James and the carriage at the Crown.

However, before they could dash away to Abbey-Mill, Emma had to put up with one more conversation she would rather have avoided.

'Mrs Knightley! Such London style and elegance!' Mrs Elton, shopping basket over her arm, came like an eager bloodhound along the pavement. 'I would have seen the difference in the dark.'

'I am dressed entirely from Highbury,' protested Emma. 'I did not go to London for shopping.'

'Ah, yes.' Mrs Elton's voice lowered to a knowing whisper, particularly annoying to Emma. 'Mr Elton has been most concerned. He has offered prayers in church, more than once, mentioning no names, of course. When do the Mr John Knightleys arrive?'

Heartily did Emma wish that Mr Knightley had taken her advice and not even hinted at any financial falling away in his brother's situation. A hint, for the Eltons, was as much as a clarion call to anyone else. 'They will be here as soon as Brunswick Square is closed. Mrs Knightley and the children first. We are all very satisfied that they come to us before Mr Knightley takes them away to his new post.'

'New post!'

'Oh, yes. In Putney, I believe. Or Chiswick. The details are not quite fixed. 'But somewhere further out of London – for the children's sake, you understand.'

'I see – I misunderstood.'

'Indeed.' Emma bowed, 'London is not the best place to bring up six lively children.'

'Six. Yes, I must congratulate—' Mrs Elton's voice became depressed; unconsciously she smoothed her hips, as gaunt as ever.

'The air – so unhealthy.'

Mrs Elton rallied, 'But I have always heard from Mr Woodhouse that the air is so particularly fresh in Brunswick Square – quite unlike the rest of London.'

'The air is very fresh – for London; but nothing like so fresh as in Richmond or Chiswick or even Putney. The air in those places is very nearly as fresh as in Highbury. Now, I am afraid we must take our leave—'

'Of course, Mrs Knightley. I merely wished to welcome you back, after so long – and dear Miss Bates, such a worthy companion for Mr Woodhouse.'

Seeing escape at hand, Emma could not resist one final barb. 'We were all most sympathetic to the trials of Mrs Serena Suckling. Falling houses is one of the risks of London but I have never heard it occur to a properly built house in the country. Please give my condolences to your sister.'

'Mrs Suckling is taking the opportunity to build two more chimneypieces,' began Mrs Elton but Mrs Knightley had made her curtsy and left, followed by Miss Bates, like the longboat bobbing in the wake of the cutter.

23

It was after midday by the time James drew up the carriage in front of Abbey-Mill Farm. It was a flat, grey day and the whole area, river, garden, apple trees, was no longer bathed in the golden glow that Emma had admired on her last visit. She could not help thinking that its low-lying position must make the house and its surroundings very damp in the winter. She said as much to Miss Bates as they descended and made their way to the garden path but Miss Bates could not agree, having always found Abbey-Mill one of the driest, cosiest places she had ever been in. Mr Martin called it paradise in his friendly way and she had never been one to disagree.

At this point, she saw Emma's frown and, misreading its cause, started on a eulogy of Hartfield which she was surprised to find only deepened Emma's frown. Luckily for her peace of mind, the path was not long and the door was already open before they reached the end of it. There stood the same cheerful maid who Emma remembered from her last visit, with the message that her mistresses awaited them in the parlour. Emma saw the change from the mistresses welcoming them in person on the doorstep, and allowed her cloak to be removed with an irritable shrug, before she schooled herself into better humour.

Indeed they had not reached the parlour before a great many Martin ladies had come to greet her, only Harriet lingering behind a little.

Congratulations on the baby – the reason for her visit – were dispensed with real goodwill. The baby himself was then produced – no wet-nurse for him – and, although his face was mostly hid by a vast white cap and he was disinclined to wake beyond a wide-mouthed, lolling yawn, Emma was able to pronounce him a fine, large child who did both his parents justice. If Miss Bates could not restrain a few sad looks, everybody understood the reason, forgave her easily and, out of consideration for her feelings – she who had never yet seen her only living relation – took away young Robert to another room.

'Now I know Mrs Knightley likes chocolate,' said old Mrs Martin kindly, 'but I must admit that we usually take something a little more substantial at this time of day. Harriet tells me it is not the proper thing to do but Robert has been used to a plate of cold meat or suchlike – it is hungry work looking after a farm.'

Emma bowed her head graciously, Miss Bates nodded and smiled again and Harriet, well, Harriet was so pleased with her life, so pretty and cheerful and felt her good fortune so obviously, that nothing could displease her and, it must be said, it would be an uncharitable person who could be displeased by her.

Emma sighed; she could not be that person. Harriet in the flesh was not the threat she had become in the veiled regions of her imagination. She was Harriet as ever, simple, good and affectionate; even her pretensions were so transparent as not to offend.

'We had thought, perhaps, of extending just a very little,' she began timidly, under Emma's questioning. 'I would so value your advice in the matter. Mr Martin—' she stopped for a blush.

'My son will do everything for her,' finished Mrs Martin. 'Now here he comes!'

With a mother's ears, she had heard her son's arrival before anyone and had them all nicely seated round the table before he came in, breezy from his walking, proud to see the visitors.

'Mrs Knightley. Miss Bates.' He bowed, gentlemanly, and took his place at table.

As Emma, who declined to eat anything more than a biscuit, looked around at the happy faces, all deferring to the man in their midst who in his turn listened to whatever they might say when he was not too taken with consuming what seemed to her prodigious quantities of food, she could not help but contrast this scene to that which Mr Knightley found at Hartfield: a querulous foolish old man, an ignorant old maid, and a wife who gave him no heir and scarcely concealed an unquiet heart. Moreover, this circle was soon to be added to by the sum of a brother who had brought discredit to the name of Knightley, a sister-in-law who was nearly as foolish as the father and six children who, much as Mr Knightley might love them, were not his own. No wonder he had the habit of stopping in at Abbey-Mill!

Such admirable clear-sightedness lowered Emma's spirits considerably. It did not hinder her from uttering all the polite civilities that are normal on such occasions or from advising Mrs Martin that her plan for a room facing south would perhaps lead to a shade too much warmth in the summer but would amply compensate for this effect by its beneficial aspect at all other times of year. 'Hartfield's aspect is all southern, I do believe!' interposed Miss Bates. But during the entire visit, Emma carried on a dialogue within herself which, in summary, went like this: 'Mr Knightley loves me; Mr Knightley is a good man; Mr Knightley has much to put up with; Mr Knightley is deserving of much sympathy, in particular from his wife.' So far it was all statements; but then came the questions: 'So why cannot I who have felt such an easy rush of feeling for him from the first moment he declared himself, why cannot I provide him with the loving that he merits? Why, instead, do I feel a coldness towards him? Why do I feel constrained in his presence?' No answer came to these painful questions and, at last, Emma forced herself to smile and put them away.

She must take Miss Bates and go and find poor James and the horses standing in the cold. But no, Mr Martin had found room for them in the stable and even now James held a steaming mug in the kitchen. At this further evidence of good order, Emma's spirits sank even lower, and she insisted she must not stay another minute or Mr Woodhouse would be made fearful of their safety.

This was understood by all to be sufficient reason to hasten their departure and – with such warm farewells to make Emma feel thoroughly appreciated – they made their way to the front door. It was here, as they stood waiting for the carriage to reappear, that Emma caught a look in Mr Martin's regard which surprised her and made her uncomfortable enough to take Miss Bates' arm as if for protection. What was it? Disapproval? No, that was too strong. But a puzzlement – a knowledge of something about her that concerned him. It was indeed a repetition of that look he had given her on his first arriving at Brunswick Square.

'Thank you, Mrs Martin, Harriet—' She turned her face away and, chiding herself for too much sensitivity, took her leave. She had visited Abbey-Mill as Mr Knightley had asked her and now she must return to her own home and prepare for the onslaught of the John Knightley family.

It was a measure of how much Emma felt her situation altered for the worse that an arrival that had in previous

years always been looked forward to with joyous anticipation now was contemplated by her with something
approaching dread.

24 ∫

New Year passed, marked by no more festivity at Hartfield than a dinner attended by the Westons and Mrs Goddard. Mr Woodhouse was able to make up a quiet table of cards, for both Emma and Mr Knightley were unwilling players and seemingly unable to play as a pair. Mr Woodhouse's expectation of the imminent arrival of his older daughter, which had reached fever pitch a day or two before New Year – 'They will wish to be here, comfortably, with their family, I make certain of it—' subsided. He turned once more to Miss Bates for company and revealed to Emma that 'Miss Bates showed a remarkable aptitude for jumping her knight and a firm hand with the queen' – high praise, indeed.

A week or so of dull blustery weather passed, in which Emma sat at the pianoforte more often than she had in a year; she was determined to bring at least one piece up to a standard that should please her ear, but this ambition seemed curiously evasive: if she conquered one awkward run of notes, a chord previously quite within her grasp dissolved under her hands. Eventually she overheard Miss Bates whispering loudly to her father, 'Dear Mrs Knightley – how she does work! I feel I know that charming little piece quite by heart.' The complaint behind the compliment was only too clear. She shut the piano and picked up her square of cambric – at least that was silent.

'It is nearly arranged,' Mr Knightley announced at last. 'I shall go to Brunswick Square tomorrow with James and he shall bring back Isabella and the older children the day following, and another carriage will bring the younger children, the nurse and the remaining maids. I shall stay for a day or two to finish closing down the house and make a few further arrangements.'

Hurt that this announcement should come as soon to Mr Woodhouse and to Miss Bates as to herself, Emma stabbed out yet another false cross in her embroidery and put it away. She said nothing, however, neither that evening nor that night and bid Mr Knightley goodbye the next morning with a fond admonition to keep his collar up against the wind. For a moment she saw a bright warmth in his eye and then he merely bowed and called to James. Lips pursed, Emma watched him go, watched the slick wheels spinning up the gravel and the leafless chestnut trees dashing their branches about in the wind. Shivering, she turned and went briskly back to the house; there was still much to be done in preparation for Isabella's arrival.

There is a special quality in a family home – lived in from childhood – which has the ability to make for the greatest comfort or the greatest pain. Emma who had in the last weeks, almost unknown to herself, begun to look on Hartfield as the cause of much of her dissatisfaction, watched Isabella's unaffected happiness at being once again in her dear old surroundings, with a surprise bordering on jealousy. It seemed months, years, a whole age, since she herself had arrived from London with just such exclamations of recognition and delight – 'Dear old round table!' – 'Sweet little buttoned chair!' – 'No curtain has ever been prettier than this!'

Emma watched her sister through the veil of her own anxious humour and found it only truly swept away – for a little time at least – by the affectionate antics of her nephews who, under threat of being sent away to school (when the money could be found, Emma presumed) were in particularly high spirits, whirling her into energetic games of cup and ball – at which activity she could be certain to excel – or forcing her out into the cold garden to play catch. Little Bella, too, had grown very fond of her aunt during her stay in London and, recently separated from a favourite nurse who had been turned away, attached all her affections – and her stubby little body whenever possible – to Emma.

It was nice to be wanted, Emma acknowledged; to feel the firm press of young flesh gave her joy and lessened the hurt she carried within her.

Isabella not only brought new life and energy – her staunchness in the face of their change of circumstances commanded her sister's continuing surprise and admiration – but also two letters for Emma, one from the Reverend Dugobair Tidmarsh, the other from Mrs Tidmarsh.

'They miss you extremely!' cried Isabella. 'Philomena has been unwell, but read the letters for yourself. They have been so kind in all the packing up – they and good Mr Wingfield – I cannot imagine how I shall manage without him – but he is a busy man, all doctors are – and I could not be near so neat and orderly without Mrs Tidmarsh and Mr Tidmarsh – I am quite in their debt.'

Emma took the letters to her room with a sense of unease. She opened Mr Tidmarsh's first.

Dear Mrs Knightley, London has been a sadder place without your lively interest; Mrs Tidmarsh and I cannot go to an exhibition, view a bridge or take in a concert without missing the companionship of Mrs Knightley from Highbury, Surrey. I, of course, have my work; although on occasions I find myself in agreement with Pliny, '—otiosum esse quam nihil agere' – but this is not central to my argument. I write of my stepmother; she has charitable work – she has musical responsibilities – but her mind is not diverted. Since my father's death, she has found no companion her equal – apart from myself, if I can commit such an immodest thought to paper, and I am engaged often at St Peter's. Philomena is a rare woman, her mind as tuned as a man's, but with no set subject, no object on which to concentrate its intelligence – I ramble. My message is this – Mrs Tidmarsh misses you; she is unwell; I am anxious. Perhaps, when the weather is more clement, I may, on her behalf, take up your generous invitation for her to visit the surroundings of Highbury, about which you have told us so much that we perceive it as a regular Arcady—

The letter closed with little more ado but the most sensible and grateful anticipations of Mrs Tidmarsh's future happiness in leaving the smoke of London for the sweet openness of the country.

Emma, even with Isabella's words of gratitude and the debt owing to both Mr and Mrs Tidmarsh, could not respond as she would have liked due to an irritable consciousness of presumption by one who was still hardly more than an acquaintance. Instead, she picked up, with a face somewhat set, the smaller note from Mrs Tidmarsh.

My dear, I could not let the opportunity of Isabella's removal to you pass without this little missive. With what pleasure I look back on our association – be it ever so short – in your life, so full as it must be, perhaps already forgotten. Yet a friendship outside one's own circle is always a little special and I flatter myself I provided that interest for you. Assuredly, you gave me much of something I had felt lacking in my life – a freshness, openness, a keen intelligence, without the cynicism which is the curse of our age and shows itself most particularly in a city like London when ambition is equated with labour and success with virtue. You gave me new hope and I thank you. I shall not trouble you further, but, if you ever find yourself at your desk – I picture it made of rosewood and by a window overlooking a park all green and brown and blue sky – and not altogether busy, then think of your London friend and pen me a note – and I shall treasure a breath from a freer, brighter world! Adieu my dear Mrs Knightley – Please convey my respects to Mr Knightley, Mr Robert Martin and to your dear father, Mr Woodhouse who – between you and Isabella – I feel I know enough to send the best of good wishes!

Emma put down the letter with a mixture of relief and guilt. She sighed – no mention here of illness or of a visit. Yet the voice spoke directly to her in that way she had found so attractive, so unlike any lady she met in Highbury. There was an appeal in it – but only for a moment, about 'a freer, brighter world'. Sighing again, Emma folded both notes and put them into her desk. Perhaps she would show them to Mr Knightley when he returned and see what opinion he took of them.

Another week passed – almost flew by with the house so full – before the two Mr Knightleys came riding into the Hartfield driveway. The sisters, standing at an upper window with their arms full of linen, watched them arrive.

'Look at the colour in John's face!' Isabella cried with delight. 'I do believe he is quite restored.'

Emma could not keep herself from reflecting that it would be a poor sort of man who could be so quickly restored after causing such damage to those God had entrusted to him to love and care for, yet could not help but be glad at Isabella's cheerful optimism.

'I should not be surprised if they have not good news!' she continued. 'You know John will never settle down here with papa – it would never do. Even in bankruptcy, he must be independent. Mark my words, he has found us a new home!'

Emma looked at her sister with surprise. Such an easy acceptance of the difficulties between Mr Woodhouse and John Knightley – between two such very important people in Isabella's life – showed a strength and willingness to face reality with which she would never have credited her sister. She, Emma, although priding herself on a greater understanding in such matters than Isabella, would not have been able to pronounce such words without pain, would probably not have been able to pronounce them at all.

'Come, Emma, let us welcome them!'

But Emma was looking at Mr Knightley, her Mr Knightley – how easily he swung off his horse, how handsome his face was turned full to the house – and her heart beat hard and quick. She wanted to run with Isabella – even after six children and reprehensible behaviour, her sister still ran to her husband – but she could not. She must walk, she must meet Knightley, already in the hallway, crowded with children and say, with the politest of smiles, 'We expected you yesterday! I fear your beef will have lost all its pink and look more like leather.'

'My dear, my dear Emma.' He took her hand and kissed it. 'I am pleased to be back. I would not care if the beef had turned to wood.'

No, but my heart is wood, thought Emma, mechanically, before joining the whole party to go into the parlour and greet Mr Woodhouse. 'Our lives are mostly lived in public,' she reflected further, 'and in public we are a loving couple.'

That night Mr Knightley held Emma in his arms and, as if to contradict her mood, he was affectionate. 'I have good news,' he said, 'the best there could be.'

'Ah,' thought Emma, 'he will tell me of the true depths of his feelings for me and cast away this strange shadow that has crept so subtly between us.'

'My brother has found employment and a house in Richmond. A contact through old Mr Churchill at Mr Weston's suggestion; it is not grand – the fall is still great from what he was before – but it is honourable. John may restore himself to a place of dignity and his family, although much reduced in circumstances, may follow him, if that is what Isabella wishes. She is being told of the circumstances this very moment, I have no doubt, and I suspect that, such is her attachment to her husband, as evinced by her entire lack of reproach through this whole sorry business, that she will wish to be with him, however cramped their quarters. Long holidays at Hartfield may be desirable for the children – they can hardly afford such luxuries as the seaside now – but Isabella will want a home of her own, beside John, I make sure of it. But, tell me, Emma, what is your view? You know her best.' He turned to her, face glowing with pleasure at all his efforts being crowned with this much success.

In the dim light of the single candle, Emma could make out his open, eager expression; although asking advice on her sister (about which he had already given a firm opinion), she was reminded more of a schoolboy seeking commendation for work well done. He deserved an alpha assuredly. Yet during his speaking, her heart had grown sad and cold; it was not what she had expected and hoped for. His happiness had nothing to do with her, with them. Perhaps he had not even noticed these days which had been so painful to her as she felt them estranged. Indeed it now seemed likely that any estrangement on his side was entirely because of his total concentration on effecting a new beginning to his brother's story. Now that it was achieved, he had time for Emma again, warm looks, loving hands that caressed her face and hair. 'You do not answer, my love. You are tired. So many in a household – so many fewer maids than usual – your father, Miss Bates—'

He was understanding. He had given up looking for praise; it did not matter, after all, so much to him for he knew he had done right. When did he not act out of the noblest principles with the most practical application? Strangely, this thought of Emma's which should have made her more loving towards her husband, gave a bitter twist to her mouth. She could not help thinking that this goodness and care for the whole world made him not so especially hers.

Frank Churchill's words – spoken in wild anguish – came to her: 'He is not passionate' – was that it? And then he had continued on to say that Emma and he, himself, were alike in their nature – passionate natures – his fingers clutching at her body as they stood swaying on the slippery bank. She had felt his passion turned towards herself, before tearing out of his grasp.

'You must sleep, then,' said Knightley, as Emma closed her eyes. 'I will just kiss you quietly.' He did so and the candle was blown out without her making a stir.

25

Another month or more passed until the occasional black frost alternated with milder days. The snowdrops and crocuses – about the latter in their purple and golden majesty Emma had written a note to Mrs Tidmarsh – were long gone, primroses in full flower and the green shoots of daffodils producing enough show to make believe that spring was round the corner.

'I do declare I have never seen such heads on them so early in the year!' exclaimed Miss Bates as she, Mr Woodhouse, Emma and Isabella took a turn or two about the garden.

'Every year since I can remember words, I have heard just that same announcement, with the same inflection of wonder!' laughed Emma. 'I cannot help thinking that daffodils do always intend to come up in March and it is we humans who expect them later, in order to give us a pleasurable surprise when they come earlier!'

'Oh, Mrs Knightley—' began Miss Bates, but thinking of no proper compliment, subsided.

'March is the most trying month,' sighed Isabella, 'They say it comes in like a lion and goes out like a lamb but I think it is as if the two were stabled together, one minute giving a great roar of wind and sleet and the next, like today, so mild I cannot get even the youngest child to keep his hat on.'

'I never uncover my head till June or July and then only when the sun is neither too hot nor the breeze too chilling,' contributed Mr Woodhouse.

'Poor Mrs Bates quoted me every year when the sun shone bright early on, "Ne'er cast a clout till May is out" but we never could decide whether the May referred to in that wise old saying was the blossom on the hedgerow or the month of the year. We argued more about that, I do believe, than anything else in all our long time together.'

'My dear Miss Bates,' said Mr Woodhouse with a most enthusiastic look, 'I believe I may come to your aid – the May in question is undoubtedly—'

Emma and Isabella exchanged a glance at this point and fell behind, comfortable in the certainty that a discussion about this foolish old saying would keep Mr Woodhouse and Miss Bates entertained for as long as they wished to circulate the shrubberies and probably longer. It was the most felicitous combination of their favourite subjects – health and the weather.

'Another week or two and we will be off to Richmond,' said Isabella, contemplating the blue sky and new grass. 'I cannot allow John to be alone much longer; his spirits become depressed and it is not good for his health.'

Emma knew her sister ached to start her new life and indeed thought it very likely that John Knightley should need a companion, lest he fall into some further misguided temptation. 'I will miss you.'

'You will miss me and I will miss you and the children will miss you most dreadfully. Mr Woodhouse, however, will take it without much sense of loss, I surmise. Miss Bates is the most enterprising companion. Dear papa is never dull for a moment, scarcely complains, and is in altogether better spirits than I have seen him for years.'

'"Enterprising", you call her.' Emma appeared to ruminate on the word.

Isabella laughed. 'It is odd, is it not, that poor old Miss Bates for whom we have had nothing but pity ever since we were children, should have such a commanding effect on someone so much her superior – but that is the way of the world, I do believe, or human nature, at least. I hope you will not think of turning her off from Hartfield.'

Emma did think of this – often – but was too clearsighted and honest not to recognise that the good creature's presence would be far too much missed by her father to justify such a step. Besides, she could not now wish to go back to those days when it was her primary duty to see to the happiness of her father. 'No. Miss Bates must stay,' she smiled at Isabella. 'Although she must take care not to improve her chess game any further or she is in danger of defeating our dear papa.'

'I think we can count on Miss Bates to avoid such cruelty.' Isabella also smiled but then paused for a moment in their walk and turned her full attention to Emma. It was so seldom that the two sisters were together without the presence of children with their constant demands or some essential household activity in train, that Emma found herself surprised by the keen intelligence in her sister's gaze. They were more intimate than they had been for years – partly owing to John's downfall and partly owing to the family's extended stay at Hartfield – but Isabella's complete preoccupation with her motherly responsibilities had stood between any deep confidences. Yet now she spoke with a determined air, as if the thought had been turned over and prepared, 'I wonder, dear sister, with papa so comfortable, you and George do not consider opening up Donwell Abbey. It is a sad thing, when the world is so short of houses, that that beautiful old building stands empty. Does Knightley not speak of it? I know he talked of it to John – although only to suggest we might remove there. But that would not do. John must be where he can work and my place is at his side. I do not mean to interfere—' continued Isabella, faltering a little as she saw her sister's flushed and frowning face, 'but I have always seen how Mr Knightley loved Donwell. Now his responsibilities take him there daily—'

'You have said enough! Do you think I do not think of it! My own husband leaving his house for me – but what can I do? You call Miss Bates "enterprising" – yes, she does well enough when I am here – we are here – but to leave papa for ever in the hands of a woman who has lived off other people's charity all her life – who has no thought in her head but to say the next thing that will please whoever has just spoken before – Would you condemn Mr Woodhouse to such a – such a narrow fate!'

'You are passionate – yes, she is not a clever woman – but then neither am I and our father is happy—'

'Oh, Isabella, how you have changed.'

'Yes, perhaps – my situation—'

'Dear Isabella – I did not mean—'

'No. No. You meant only for the best; and so did I – but it will be forgotten – it is not my place. Dear papa, how he does like us all to be happy! Now let us rejoin them.'

So the division between the two sisters ended in affection but left behind, for Emma, an uneasiness. What should be done? Was it possible that her sister should see such matters more clearly than herself?

'The day is so fine, I believe I shall take a walk to Randalls,' said Emma, an hour or two later. 'And if I am long away, I shall have gone further, to the cottages. I have sadly neglected them this winter. But now I can make a note of their needs.'

Such combining of pleasure with virtue caused little stir among the acute activity of Hartfield. Only Miss Bates paused a moment from her reading aloud to Mr Woodhouse – they had both taken a fancy to reports of great personages in *The Times* newspaper which had come into the house since Mr Knightley's advent. 'You would not credit what energetic lives people lead!' became a ritual exclamation.

'You are so good, Mrs Knightley,' said Miss Bates, glasses on her nose and finger on a column inch.

Armed with such unwanted commendation, Emma left the house and began a brisk walk along the path to Randalls. She had not yet learnt the lesson which rules: virtue first, pleasure after, so she went directly to Randalls, noticing, with some surprise, that the distance which she had always assumed a barrier to daily intimacy with her old friend, Mrs Weston, seemed to have shrunk over the last weeks so that its friendly four-square walls were in view after scarcely more than ten minutes passed. 'I would be there in five,' the thought flew unbidden into her head, 'if I were mounted on a horse!' She smiled at her folly and yet ladies did ride over the countryside. She could have been in Highbury in a flash and at Donwell as soon as Mr Knightley. The only drawback to this plan, she admitted it as she came across Randalls lawn, was that she had never learnt to ride. How could she have done such a thing to Mr Woodhouse? His heart would have given out at the very idea!

Approaching from the side of the house, Emma only saw the carriage in the driveway as she was close upon it. Mr Weston stood beside it, Mrs Weston behind it with her children's nurse, all attention fixed, however, on a woman just emerging from the vehicle which had four horses, was much splashed with mud and gave every impression of coming from a long distance.

Unnoticed, Emma drew closer and was able to see that the woman, who wore shawl and bonnet of an unfashionable cut, carried a large bundle. The moment her feet were set on the gravel, both Westons, with irrepressible exclamations of excitement, crowded forward and bent over the bundle – from which a loud cry issued. Emma could no longer disguise from herself that by some strange law of coincidence she was witnessing the arrival of little Frank Churchill at his grandfather's. The greatest curiosity debating with the fear that she might be interfering in a private moment, she hung back, undecided, still however watching closely the scene in front of her.

'Oh, fair curls – fat cheeks – he does not look sickly as I expected!' Mrs Weston exclaimed, her usual calm tones raised more than ever Emma had heard them. Oh how she doted on babies!

'Come, my dear. The day is fine enough, but he is best inside.'

They would have turned and gone inside without ever seeing Emma, had not one of their maids, less occupied, dropped a curtsy, all of a sudden, saying 'Mrs Knightley, ma'am.'

'My dearest Mrs Knightley – see what the warm wind has blown our way! What a happy chance you should visit just now! Do you see, it is Frank's baby! Such a boy!' Mr Weston's unaffected pleasure in her joining the welcoming party, made it inevitable that Emma should admire the rosy-cheeked baby – just like his father, as everyone agreed at once (and certainly there seemed nothing of the fine lines of his mother there) – and be drawn in to the merry party. In the confusion and happiness, Emma was swept up to the nursery where the Westons' little Anna jumped up and down shouting, 'Baby! Baby!' and where little Frank was unwrapped like a parcel and sat solidly on the floor with his thumb in his mouth. Then downstairs again to the parlour where Mr Weston, beaming with goodwill, felt it right to offer his visitor some refreshment – 'although the house is all at sixes and sevens with this addition,' he remarked, with a poor show of regret, 'and we are as likely to get sieved prunes as a glass of tea!'

Laughing heartily at his joke, he sat closer to Emma than he would usually and asked, as if there were a choice of answer, 'So what do you think of the boy, eh?'

Emma, who was determined to disguise her emotions at viewing Frank's child, smiled. 'Oh, I do not think much of him – a poor creature.'

'What?' began Mr Weston, amazed.

'No golden curls, rosy cheeks, blue eyes, handsome features, no legs, arms, fingers, toes . . .'

'Mrs Knightley!' Mr Weston returned to his laughter.

'I am so very glad for you,' Emma found herself able to be more serious. 'It will ease your worry on his behalf to have him in your own nursery.'

'It will. It will. Mrs Weston is most convinced it is the right course of action – once we had old Mr Churchill's permission – although the space is not great, we will manage, we will certainly manage—' he hesitated.

'Space must always be of secondary importance where happiness is concerned,' encouraged Emma and she thought of her sister's determination to join her husband.

'Just so, just so,' agreed Mr Weston, but the air of concern remained. 'There is one development which I must look on as a further blessing, although it is also a source of disquiet. The manner – the secrecy—'

'Yes?' prompted Emma.

'Frank Churchill was in Yorkshire. Old Mr Churchill had already left for Richmond; Frank came to Enscombe – but only found the housekeeper—'

'He did not see his baby?' asked Emma, and then

suddenly remembering Frank's wild designation of the baby as 'a murderer' she blushed hotly.

Mr Weston was far too concerned with his own preoccupation to notice his companion's change of countenance.

'He did not see little Frank, although that was the object of his visit. The housekeeper told him – indeed, he is the father and has a right to his son – where the wet-nurse lived, where he could find little Frank – but apparently he did not go there. His manner was not calm – I have a letter here from the housekeeper – I have hardly had time to take it in – Forgive me if I have burdened you—'

'No. No. If I can be of any help—'

'I think it is poor Frank that needs help,' Mr Weston sighed. 'Would that a grown man was as easy to help as a five-month-old baby!'

It struck Emma that this was the best-judged remark that she had ever heard Mr Weston pronounce and she could think of nothing to add to it. An awkward silence fell. The preoccupations that had drawn Emma to Randalls had been overwhelmed by circumstances; it was perfectly clear that this was not the moment to invite Mrs Weston's views on a removal to Donwell – even if it had been possible to separate her from the nursery, which seemed unlikely.

'I must not keep you further.' Emma stood. 'Besides, I have promised myself a visit to the cottages—'

'They will benefit from your attention, I have no doubt.' Mr Weston bowed a little abstractedly.

Emma thought, equally abstractedly, that she might benefit from the visit even more but, as it turned out, neither side had the opportunity – for, just as she reached the end of the driveway, a heavy shower of rain, come out of a cloud racing from nowhere, forced her under the trees, which, being leafless, afforded her but little protection. In a second she was wet, in another wetter. Despite the return of the blue sky, Emma decided there was nothing for it but to return to Hartfield.

The house when she entered, disposing of her outer garments with alacrity, was unusually silent. In the parlour she found Mr Woodhouse asleep but Miss Bates, *The Times* folded at her side, bright-eyed and expectant, looking at her over her stump-work.

'You did not reach the cottages, I collect?'

Was Miss Bates suggesting she had failed in her duty? A guilty conscience made Emma frown.

'It came on to rain, a sharp burst, now over – but it caught me just as I could find no cover.'

'Mr Knightley is returned too. He has gone to help the boys with their Latin. Poor Mrs John Knightley declared it quite beyond her wits and has retired for a rest. Mr Knightley was most energetic and assured me that it would do his head good to study a well-constructed Latin sentence.'

'Mr Knightley is good at everything,' said Emma, repressing her surprise for she had never connected Mr Knightley with the classical writers. She sat down, however, declaring she would not disturb him in such a mission. It had struck her that here was a private opportunity – so rare in this house – for telling Miss Bates of the arrival of her little great-nephew. It would give her time to get over her flutters and settle herself.

'I found news for you at Randalls – more than news, in fact – an arrival—'

'Oh, Mrs Knightley – oh—' her hand was at her heart, her sewing dropped.

'A happy arrival. Little Frank Churchill has come with his nurse.'

Emma was not disappointed in Miss Bates' reaction. The depth of her feeling was touching – although Emma found herself not altogether touched – and her reiteration of her poor dead niece's name eventually produced tears that could not be contained, try as the good creature might. The tears fell, however, with many side glances at the sleeping Mr Woodhouse and admonishments to herself not to wake him.

'It is happy news, I believe,' Emma reminded her more than once and eventually this fact overwhelmed Miss Bates' old memories of sadness and, after fifteen minutes, she was composed once more.

'I shall put on my little glasses,' she said, 'and then if your good father does wake he will not notice anything amiss. But perhaps you will have a cup of tea.'

Emma declined this offer and instead went slowly, stair by stair, to the schoolroom. The interview with Miss Bates had calmed her emotions on the subject of Frank's baby. Entering quietly, she had time to see Knightley, in his shirtsleeves, sitting between Henry and John at the scrubbed table where Emma had once studied (though not Latin) with Mrs Weston, then the independent Miss Taylor. Knightley leant from one boy to the other, correcting their work with an eager, good-humoured look, while they questioned him in the same jolly way. It was a scene bound to please the eye, yet Emma frowned.

'I did not know you had Latin to add to your accomplishments.'

'Emma! Oh, I am a fraud. The boys have found me out already. Now their father could carry on a conversation in Latin. But he was always ahead of me in matters intellectual.'

'And much good it has done him,' thought Emma but a look at her quick-witted nephews taught her to stay silent. She watched still as Knightley set a few more tasks for Henry and John and then together they went down to their own parlour – still preserved for their private use. Emma led her husband there for the sight of him in the schoolroom had reminded her of the nature of the man she had married and, with sudden resolution, she had seen that the news she had to impart – of little Frank's arrival in their midst and his father's being sighted in Yorkshire – provided just the opportunity for her to unburden her heart of the secret of his presence last year in Donwell. Knightley was a good, kind man who loved her; she must not shirk this duty another day.

With such admirable resolution, she handed him his coat – for the fire hardly burned – and sat at her little desk, although swung round to face him, where he stretched on the wider chair.

'I can see you have news. You were at Randalls, I know. Let me guess. Can it be? No! So soon after the last! That Mrs Weston has acquired a third child!'

'You know already! Oh, Knightley' – a reproach. Why could she give him nothing?

'The whole of Highbury knows and most of Surrey. The carriage stopped at the Crown to ask the way – the baby cried – Mrs Goddard was passing by with a train of girls – Mrs Elton met Mrs Goddard further down the street – You see, nothing can be secret in Highbury!'

Emma blushed a little at her consciousness of the untruth of it. Knightley, misreading its meaning, continued, 'But I left you the pleasure of telling Miss Bates.'

'I did. It brought back poor Mrs Churchill to her but I left her tolerably ready to revel in blue eyes and golden hair.'

'You may describe him to me, Emma. I have not seen him, you know.'

But now the weight of what she must confess began to bear in on Emma, and she did not expand more than 'A stout, healthy child' – she paused – 'the picture of his father.' Now she must continue.

'His father?'

'Frank Churchill has been seen – in Yorkshire. He was looking for the baby.'

'Well, let us hope he does not find him!' the tone was vehement, the brow dark and heavy. 'You did not tell Miss Bates, poor lady, of this?'

'No – I—'

'You were right. I have come to believe that I was correct in my first estimation of his character. Everything he touches turns to pitch. Poor Jane Fairfax. Poor child. When he was needed, he ran; now that times are more settled, he will come to make problems. If I were Mr Weston, I would ban him from the house—'

'But – I—' Emma felt resolution faltering, slipping away; this was passion indeed in Mr Knightley! She tried once more – 'Surely a man has a natural right—' But broke off at the thought of little Frank at the mercy of his father's violent nature.

'Natural! He has a natural right if he is a natural man but a man like Mr Frank Churchill is as unnatural as—' A simile failing him, he stopped, looked at Emma's pale, anguished face and shut his mouth as if clamped. A look which Emma had not seen before, containing, among other emotions, something resembling shame, took hold of his face for a moment, then disappeared again. He stood up, came over to Emma and took her hand. 'I cannot retract my view of Mr Churchill but it does not do to shout. You are not his keeper – you should not be shouted at – it was not gentlemanly of me. Forgive me, Emma.'

'Oh, yes. Yes. But I—'

'Not another word. You will change for dinner and I will return to Henry and John. How fond I have become of those two boys and how sadly I will miss them when they leave us!'

'I cannot but agree,' said Emma in a low voice for her

heart still pounded, even though she was already facing the certainty that her secret must remain untold. She looked at Knightley and thought, 'You would like a son, above all things,' but she did not say that either.

26

As the weather became fair and stayed fair for several days, instead of hours, at a time, Highbury – that is, the part of Highbury that could boast a dining-room and a driveway – always closed down to some extent in winter – showed signs of an intention to become a livelier place.

'This is the third invitation since Tuesday!' Emma held up the cards to her sister at breakfast.

'You are quite right, my dear. It is an imposition, a danger to our comfortable circle that must be resisted.' Mr Woodhouse picked up the butter-knife as if ready to ward off outside forces with any weapon to hand.

'My dear papa,' Emma smiled, 'I was saying it as a source of pleasure rather than pain. I am afraid you will be out-argued now that John is not here to support you.'

'I am sure Miss Bates will not want to be out at all hours. I expect these are dinner engagements we are invited to.'

Miss Bates, recognising that she might be faced with the choice between disagreeing with father or daughter, became so busy with the teapot that it was clear she could neither see nor hear anything beyond its elegant spout.

'Besides,' continued Emma, more for the sake of argument than because she wished to dine out daily, 'it is the Westons, the Goddards, the Coles – with dancing proposed, the Martins, and now, today, although I believe

we should not hold our breaths for this one, the Eltons
announce—'

'The Sucklings!' Isabella finished for her. 'I am glad you
will have some gaiety when I am gone, Emma. Papa, you
must not allow your own disposition for tranquillity to
overwhelm Emma and Mr Knightley's right to company
– particularly when Mr Knightley is not here to speak for
himself.'

'My dear, but of course Mr Knightley and Emma shall go
where they please – it is only myself I speak of. I shall stay
quite happily – it will be quite like old times – Miss Bates
and I – Miss Bates never wishes to leave Hartfield, I know
– nor need she—'

This kind thought was interrupted by a loud noise
as Miss Bates dropped the lid of the teapot. Her look
of regret and distress must be attributed to that rather
than any dissension with Mr Woodhouse over her wish
to stay every night at Hartfield. Once the tea stain had been
sprinkled with salt, Emma took up Isabella on her plans of
departure.

'You will at least have dinner at the Westons',' she said,
'since their dining-room is already built. However, you may
be able to avoid the Martins since their room is only four
bricks high so that a brisk wind would sweep the food from
the table.'

'You are not planning to eat in the open!' exclaimed Mr
Woodhouse with a look of horror.

'Only from our waists up – or for Miss Bates hardly below
her shoulders—'

'Emma, you are too high-spirited—' Mr Knightley had
come in at the door. He had been out already – for this was
a busy time of year at Donwell – and come back hungry for
eggs and bacon.

'Emma always keeps us merry,' said Mr Woodhouse and
would have said more if Emma had not suddenly risen and

moved so swiftly to pull the bell to the kitchen that her sleeve caught her teacup.

'Oh dear, oh dear – what did I set in motion— !' began Miss Bates, eager as ever to take the blame.

So breakfast was completed in a very snowstorm of salt, and far too many rearrangements of the table to make Knightley comfortable, and to allow for any more discussion of social engagements or any words at all other than those of politeness, apology and goodwill.

A few hours later Emma sat at her desk in her parlour engaged in an activity she could not have imagined only a few weeks ago. She wrote a long letter to Philomena Tidmarsh. In front of her lay Mrs Tidmarsh's last letter; it was not long but told of being sadly disappointed in a visit to Drury Lane where 'upward of three thousand people laughed at veritable rubbish, but perhaps the odious fumes of the theatre was too much of a strain in my present state of being'. She had admitted under Emma's close questioning that she had suffered from an indisposition – an old weakness of the lungs which struck her particularly at this time of year – but she had thrown it off enough for everyday life and it now usually left her alone unless a pupil at the harp made 'the sort of a caterwauling that would make an archangel weep'. Her teaching was now a matter of openness between them and was often the source of human material for Mrs Tidmarsh's favourite disquisition on 'the natural superiority of the female sex until distorted by the male's shameful need to prove them inferior in brain-power, application and organisation'. According to Mrs Tidmarsh, the younger the pupils came to her the higher their confidence and the greater their power of learning. It was her view that by the time they reached twenty, they were 'sliding backwards down a slope which led them to become willing slaves in a world dominated by their fathers, brothers and husbands – called the stronger sex, but in truth, the weaker since they must subdue women for fear that they might equal or surpass them . . .'

Such ideas were very new to Emma and whereas, face to face, she might have found them distasteful and unladylike, in a letter – written in Mrs Tidmarsh's graceful hand, with much wit and many felicitous expressions – she read of them rather as she might a novel, with eager interest and only partial belief. In the letter which Emma had presently in front of her, Mrs Tidmarsh confided her belief that Mr Tidmarsh – her late husband – had chosen her in particular for her youth and that an older lady would not have provided him with the independence of thought he so valued. She concluded the letter by asking, 'I wonder whether the same conviction persuaded Mr Knightley in his choice of you, dear Emma' (in correspondence they had returned to first names) 'when he was looking for his life's partner? The great disparity must find a cause somewhere; can it not lie here – in your youthful, *untamed* quality?'

Emma smiled and finding Mr Knightley entering the room, asked him gaily, 'Mrs Tidmarsh holds the belief that you married me for my "untamed" quality? It makes me sound quite like one of your farmyard beasts!'

'I have always held Mrs Tidmarsh to be a clever woman; I would not dare refute any opinion of hers on my reason for doing anything – least of all on my attitude to you, my dear. I am sure she knows you far better than I ever can.'

Emma could not quite make out this speech, whether Knightley joked or was vexed; deciding it suited her best to believe the former – for she never wished to be on contrary terms with Mr Knightley, however often it turned out that way – she smiled more and asked him if he stayed in the house long.

For answer, Mr Knightley sat down and inquired with a meditative look, 'What else does your friend – because I believe she is your friend once more – write to you?'

'She believes that women are the equal of men if they are allowed to be.'

'I should be afraid lest the sex should lose in softness what they gain in force. Yet Mrs Tidmarsh is correct; in their own sphere, women may surpass men.'

'I am not sure she would agree with that "in their own sphere" – it has an ominous ring.'

'And do you?'

'My own sphere is a very comfortable one. I would be ungrateful indeed to ask for more.'

'So she writes you turbulent philosophy and you – what do you write to her?'

'You are not jealous, by any chance? I have never known you so interested in my correspondence. But my letters would disappoint you. Mrs Tidmarsh cannot get enough of the hedgerows, the hawthorn, the ducklings, the lambs and, now and again, as if for a change, the people of Highbury.'

'You paint the picture of a perfect Arcadia.'

'She thinks so.'

'Oh, Emma!' he started, sighed, stopped and stood. 'I was at Donwell today, the buds are already fat on the lime trees and the primroses seem to go on and on but the garden is becoming neglected – how sadly I miss good old William Larkins! Perhaps when Isabella has gone and you are less constantly occupied— ?'

'You forget our invitations,' said Emma gaily, although why she so put off his suggestion, couched quite like an appeal, she could not fathom. It was some perversity born of these weeks of estrangement which she felt so deeply and he did not seem to recognise – it was that and his comment, 'I should be afraid lest the sex should lose in softness what they gain in force.' She did not want to be soft.

'And besides, I may perhaps expect a guest.'

'A guest? I take it you refer to an invitation extended to Mrs Tidmarsh.'

'I have not given any such invitation.' Indeed, until this moment she had no intention of doing so.

'But you may do so?'

'With your permission.'

'My dear, you do not need my permission. I am not your master,' he tried to smile. 'And I do sincerely believe that I appreciate the qualities of Mrs Tidmarsh a vast deal more than you allow. She is an intelligent friend for you to have and if I do not agree with all her opinions, then that is a reason for discussion, and discussion can never be bad.'

'You are so fair, so balanced.'

'I make my apologies for it,' he bowed gravely.

'I did not mean—' Emma broke off; she could not lie directly, and she had meant to criticise, for it was in his balanced judgement that she saw a want of emotion, a lack of passion—

Mr Knightley walked to the door but, as he reached it, turned back to Emma. 'As for Mrs Tidmarsh, I would suggest to you that her opinions on the position of the fairer sex are not held with the kind of steadfastness that could not bend to circumstances.'

With such gnomic utterance as her companion, Emma must continue the rest of the day; it was all of a piece, she thought, with any intimate conversation held between them recently: it ended in disagreement either lightly clad in humour or more heavily in politeness. Neither disguised a want of real warmth between them, which only seemed to show itself in the tenderness that still sometimes led him to hold her close in the night hours.

It was with relief that she turned to her paper and began, in sprightly style, a letter to Mrs Tidmarsh:

You would not believe how busy I am about to become

– Isabella leaves in a week, but Highbury puts on its fine feathers. Dinner with the dear Westons – an invitation extended entirely so that we may admire the clutch of babies including now Frank Churchill's, a most blooming representation of his father, showing all the evidence of the latter's unconfin'd spirits—

Emma found she needed a pause here before continuing the letter which ended, despite many protestations of affection, without an invitation to Hartfield.

The dinner at Randalls took place two nights before Isabella's departure and the Westons' parlour was, as Emma had foretold, as thickly decorated with babies as the ceiling of an Italian chapel may be decorated with cherubs. Putting forward this idea to Mr Elton as they waited for dinner to be served, Emma could not refrain from adding, 'The difference being that, whereas the painted article are blessedly silent and immobile, the human variety have the vocal chords of a pack of hounds in full throat and much of their activity also.'

'There is one other difference,' Mr Elton put his fingertips together as if to make a theological pronouncement – which indeed Emma quite expected since he was more full of pomposity every time they met – 'the human babies are clothed, whereas the heavenly are naked as God intended.'

'Oh, Mr Elton!' cried Emma, irresistibly, 'surely you do not intend to recommend that the human species goes naked – as apes go naked!'

Mr Elton became a little confused under his companion's sparkling gaze and had begun an exposition more as Emma had expected, along the lines of the virtue of nakedness as a symbol for spiritual purity which has no need of disguise, although not – to Emma's thinking – with much clarity of thought, when he was rescued from chasms of misunderstanding and schisms of theological interpretations by the arrival of Mrs Elton.

Until this moment she had been crouched among the cherubs, uttering cries of admiration which occasionally gave way to an unrepressed sob of bitter frustration and envy. But the splendid train she sported at her back was unfortunately edged with loose, swinging tassels which the babies – in particular, the hearty Frank – could not be restrained from clutching and pulling as if they were attached to bells. Mrs Elton retreated therefore and arrived at her husband's side in a discomposed and saddened state of mind.

'I have interrupted your conversation, Mr E.!' she cried and added, with a look at Emma, 'your very deep and serious conversation, as I saw.'

As Emma knew pretty well that she was far too busy detaching herself from sticky fingers to see any such thing and therefore only 'saw' it in her mind's eye as the thing she feared (Mrs Knightley of Hartfield and Donwell was always a rival to her for her husband's admiration), Emma felt quite justified in a little defensive sally:

'Not deep at all, my dear Mrs Elton, I assure you – in fact, you might more accurately call it *shallow*, since we discoursed on the subject of nakedness!'

Mrs Elton's face at this word was all Emma could have wished and inspired Mr Elton to mutter 'Adam and Eve' several times in an ascending order of intensity and, when this did not change his wife's expression of shock, out came the word 'symbol!', repeated quite half a dozen times.

'Well, I do declare, Mr Elton may have been talking in symbolic terms,' contributed Emma with a cheerful smile. 'Symbols are very much in his line – I have often heard him use the word on Sunday and I remember poor Mrs Goddard once asking me why Mr Elton was so keen to talk of such a very loud and unnatural musical instrument. She talked of course of the "cymbal" for, although running an excellent school, even *her* understanding during sermons can sometimes fall short of Mr Elton's learning. But I did not talk in symbols just now; I was talking of these babies and how the floor reminded me of a ceiling painted with cherubs; it was then Mr Elton introduced the theme of nakedness – but I am boring you!'

Mrs Elton, who was not looking bored but cross, gave Emma a sharp look and pronounced, 'Dear Mrs Knightley, you and I must be paired together as the only married ladies who are not in the state of motherhood.'

She had chosen her barb well; to be paired with Mrs Elton in such a vulgar way – or in any way at all – depressed all Emma's levity into a silent contemplation of the scene. Let the Eltons carry the conversation!

'I have often noticed – in my experience at the baptismal font,' began Mr Elton, 'that no one baby is any different from any other. I am quite at a loss to put child to parent. Perhaps one of you ladies has a better-schooled eye?'

Emma owned this (but only to herself) a reasonable comment and wondered whether she could solve his problem. There were four very small babies in the room – Mrs Weston's, Frank Churchill's, Harriet Martin's and Isabella's – and several others belonging to Isabella and Mrs Weston, only slightly larger. They were all pink-cheeked, round-faced babies, all fair, all blue-eyed or at least without dark eyes. She thought, perhaps, her own nephews and nieces the handsomer, with higher brows and more slender noses, but that could have been merely the result of the partisan role of aunt.

'I must agree with you,' she said to Mr Elton, 'they are identical; it makes one long for a strain of somewhere else. Italy or France,' she added, recalling Mr Tidmarsh's dark good looks.

Before Mrs Elton could express the dissension Emma intended to provoke, it became clear that the babies were being removed by their nurses and that they would soon lead off to dinner.

Mrs Weston, advancing to where they sat, her cheeks flushed, her look radiant – Emma could hardly believe it was the same woman who had seemed old to her fifteen years ago – cried, 'You are so tolerant! I could not forego the pleasure to see my friends – their children – dear Isabella so soon to depart – but now we will sit down – Can you credit it, we will be sixteen, even though I could not persuade Mr Woodhouse nor Miss Bates to attend and I have only included Henry and John of the children! Our little dining-room will be quite stretched to the limits! Tell me, dear Emma,' as they stood she took her old pupil to one side, 'I hope you do not take offence at my inviting the Martins but Mr Knightley encouraged me and they go, of course, to the Coles' – although old Mrs Martin will never stir outside her kitchen.'

There was no need for Emma to answer because Mrs Weston was off again, more excited than Emma had ever seen her and in a moment on Mr Knightley's arm who was to lead her into dinner.

'And may I have the honour of giving you my arm?' Mr Weston's friendly face was in front of Emma as, one by one, with all the ceremony due to such a large party, they proceeded, with the very few steps necessary in such a moderate-sized house, from parlour to dining-room.

The sixteen sat round the table, previously considered scarcely large enough for twelve, were: Mr and Mrs Weston, the two Mr and Mrs Knightleys, John and Henry Knightley, Mr and Mrs Elton, Mr and Mrs Cole and four Martins – Mr and Mrs Martin, Miss Elizabeth Martin and her younger sister Miss Louisa Martin. The conviviality was considerable, exceeding that which might have been if they were in less close proximity, and the noise level was extreme; so that although a lady might hear a gentleman's boom with reasonable clarity, a gentleman must bend even closer than he sat already, if he were to catch a lady's quieter tones.

Mr Weston's placement, done with self-conscious gravity and many quick looks at his wife, who had to shake or nod her head a few times, put Mr Knightley opposite Emma and between Mrs Weston and Harriet Martin. Since Mrs Weston was much occupied by watching for the general good, Mr Knightley could only talk to Harriet who was looking the very picture of health and dressed in a most elegant blue gown that Emma would never have credited her for choosing – her taste, during the time of their friendship, at least, running to over-flowered pinks and shiny rosettes. It was vexing that she, Emma, knew that a blue gown was always Knightley's favourite and even more vexing to see the way he leant towards his pretty neighbour.

'Mrs Martin must have a very soft voice,' she commented to Mr Robert Martin who sat at her left side.

'She does,' he agreed, with every indication of complacency at a quality that a more disinterested observer would have grasped at once that Mrs Knightley was noting down as a fault. 'She lacks confidence,' he continued, 'I tell her so; I tell her to speak up and make her meaning plain, but she says she does not wish to.'

'Perhaps she does not have any meaning she wishes to make plain,' said Emma, trying to take the savagery out of her voice with a light trill of laughter.

'She looks too much to the importance of others, I tell her so. She cannot disagree. I believe she was born incapable of disagreement.'

'Oh,' was all Emma could think of to comment on this piece of information which rang true enough to her experience of Harriet. What she wanted to ask was how the excellent, sensible Mr Martin could be so very content, as he certainly showed every sign of being, living his life with such a flaccid creature – quite like living with a pretty sea anemone who floats this way and that with the waves – but then she remembered a conversation she had had with Mr Knightley before their marriage in which she had extolled the agreeable qualities of Harriet as just those to please any man in the world, however sensible. Now she saw evidence of the rightness of her judgement not only in the handsome man beside her, quite besotted by his wife, but also by the handsome man opposite her now leaning back a little with a look of insufferable smugness as Mrs Martin positively chortled at some of his wit, showing in the process all her pearly white teeth.

'Ugh!' groaned Emma, just about grinding her own pearly molars.

'You spoke?' inquired Mr Martin.

'Nothing of consequence. Tell me, how does your piano-forte do?' It seemed this instrument was their subject in common.

'Very well. My sister, Miss Elizabeth Martin, has a real talent, so I am told. She plays for us most evenings – with all the runs and extravaganzas anyone could wish. My mother prefers simple songs, however, and since none of us can produce a decent note we invite the shepherd in once the lambing season is over. He does a creditable "Soldier's Lament".' He paused to look at Emma who in her new resolution not to stare across the table was fixing him with an intense regard.

'Although if we have need of "The Yellow-haired Lad-die",' continued Mr Martin, 'Mrs Martin's absolute favour-ite, we must call on Mr Knightley to perform. But then I need not tell Mrs Knightley about her Mr Knightley's musical talent.'

He need. Emma's hazel eyes flew wide in astonishment. Mr Knightley sing – she would have been as surprised if she had been told that Knightley's horse stood on its hind legs and produced a rendering of 'See the Conquering Hero!'. Knightley sing! She had never heard him open his mouth at Hartfield or Donwell in all her years of consciousness. It was true that she knew he had some sort of ear because his voice was firm enough in church but she had never considered he would perform a solo and particularly not 'The Yellow-haired Laddie'. If anyone had asked her she would have said conclusively it was not in his nature.

As Emma writhed under such thoughts and the cause of it all ate his mutton with contented demeanour, Mr Martin asked Mrs Knightley about her friend, Mrs Tidmarsh. 'Did she plan to visit? Did she sing as well as play the harp?'

Emma answered, but distractedly, and eventually Mr Martin gave in to the neighbour on his other side, Mrs Elton, who had been trying for the last ten minutes to attract his notice with various little gasps and shrieks. This allowed Emma to indulge all her talents for fancy with such success that by the time the mutton had been cleared from the table and the apple dumplings brought in their stead, she had become convinced that the only reason that Mr Knightley would have lowered himself to the silly sentiment of 'The Yellow-haired Laddie' (she had never heard the song but she assumed it to be silly and sentimental) was because he had been inspired by the kind of romantic passion, wild, deep, uncontrollable, that he had never shown to her (nor, perhaps, felt for her) and that could only be expressed in song.

'Oh, that were a deep sigh, indeed!' Mr Weston beamed on Emma. 'I hope an expression of satisfaction not of want!'

The question remaining – Emma turned unseeing eyes on Mr Weston's complacency, everyone except her seemed complacent tonight – was whether it was Miss Elizabeth Martin, Miss Louisa Martin or Harriet Martin who had inspired such sentiments in Mr Knightley's bosom? The answer was in front of her – plain for all to see! He loved Harriet Martin!

'The apples are our own, you know. I do believe we have the airiest store chamber in Highbury—'

'Yes!' exclaimed Emma. Now she understood it all. Against all his sense of dignity, the direction of his marriage vows, his duty, religion and friendship (to Mr Martin) he loved Harriet! He loved her for her gentle charms, her softness, her agreeing nature, her skills in the home – doubtless he was offered warm cakes lightly dusted with her own hand; he loved her because her money had saved his brother's honour – because she made nothing of it – because she lived near his beloved Donwell and tended the gardens and let the apples hang till winter and walked beside the river – and took his wet clothes and dried them

– and was always cheerful and admiring and thought him a god among men, although of course in her eyes all men were gods—

'Will you take a glass of wine?' inquired Mr Weston who had moved from apples to baby Frank without one word of encouragement, nor missing one—

'No!' cried Emma with such a chilling look that Mr Weston shrank and eyed the bottle of wine in his hand as if he had picked up poison by mistake. For the reason above all why Mr Knightley loved Harriet – so Emma knew without the possibility of doubt as her eyes were drawn irresistibly to her one-time friend's creamy bosom, scarcely disguised by an expensive piece of lace – was because she was a mother! A pretty, nay beautiful, good, obedient, loving, sweet-natured, hard-working mother! Overcome with agitation, Emma fell back in her chair.

'You are not well—' Mr Weston bent over her anxiously. 'The heat – the proximity – so many—'

'I am very well!' Emma sat up straight with an imperious look of disdain meant for the lady across the table but received by Mr Knightley whose attention had been caught by his wife's falling backwards and then her sudden return to the upright. The disdain surprised him and, noticing Robert Martin, about to try his turn at conversation, he assumed, to his disappointment (but little real surprise), it was meant for that gentleman. Nevertheless he smiled at Emma, admiring, at least, her air of animation which added so much more to her beauty than the languor that had come over her too often recently.

He smiles at me, thought Emma, but he loves another! However, even in her excitable, imagining state, this did not seem quite true to her – too much like a Gothic novel, she decided. It struck her that, although she had hit on this love, on Knightley's part it was still unconscious. He did not know his own feelings; this would explain why such

an honourable man could let such love form in his breast:
he did not recognise it; he still thought he looked on, and
admired, Harriet as the wife of his tenant, his ex-tenant,
his friend – that, in all honesty, must be the word – and
not as someone to inspire deeper emotions. In this lack of
self-knowledge lay hope, Emma, mind racing, told herself,
because what is unacknowledged may pass and leave no
trace while the acknowledged can never be altogether
eradicated; it must always leave a memory. Therefore her
first, instinctive wish for confrontation, questions, reproach,
must not be indulged. She must make believe she saw
nothing, understood nothing; in that way Mr Knightley's
emotions might return to her unchanged.

There remained only one further matter; but this was
almost too painful to consider: the sense she had, on
observing Knightley's attentions to Harriet, that he saw
her as a woman, whereas he treated her, Emma, despite
being eighteen months married, as the child he had always
known. She had not been able to arouse a passionate side
of his nature – Ah, it was too much!

'May I?' Mr Weston was offering Emma his arm as the
assembly rose to leave the room; dinner was ended – a
dinner that for everyone, with the exception of Emma,
had passed with a high degree of enjoyment.

Emma's most crushing blow – that Harriet, silly little
Harriet – could arouse a manly ardour in Mr Knightley
where she could not – contradicted the view put forward by
Mr Frank Churchill, and at least partly believed by Emma till
now, that she had married a man whose nature was sensible
rather than passionate. A friend would have advised her
that an accurate view of Mr Knightley's character might
have been better formed by close application to the subject
rather than allowing a man demented with sadness and
guilt to plant seeds of doubt and a dinner-time imagining
to override years of closeness. But jealousy is a fierce,

unreasoning master and as Emma entered the parlour, head held high, she had never felt more convinced by anything in her life, that Mr Knightley harboured the very strongest feelings for Harriet Martin.

But the rest of the evening must be got through; they would not be kept late, Mrs Weston promised – old friends need not impress their hosts by staying beyond their usual hour – but they must have a little music, a hand or two of cards. So first Emma must sit down at the pianoforte and play with good humour and then listen to Miss Elizabeth Martin.

This she did with curiosity, for as Mr Knightley's accompanist, Miss Martin must arouse new interest, and she noticed, with uncharitable pleasure, that although Miss Martin, a pretty dark-eyed girl, played with great musicality and a nice touch, her technique showed a decided lack of elegance.

'Mr Martin confides in me that they are to have a music teacher come from London to his sister once a week,' said Knightley, seating himself at his wife's side. 'Mrs Goddard could not provide anyone to raise her to the level she deserves.'

Emma nodded at the justness of the case; it was the lack of a good teacher that explained her lack of elegance. She smiled a little. The sound of her husband's voice, his close presence at her side had an immediately soothing effect; her horrible fears could not be totally dispelled – she must believe still in his feeling for Harriet – but he was also hers – she could feel it in his attentiveness, in the tender expression on his face, in his every word, his breath – Yet, as Elizabeth Martin drew to a close, she could not resist a sidelong question, 'You do not sing tonight?'

'Sing?!'

'You are surprised. But I hear in Abbey-Mill Farm, you sing, whenever requested, "The Yellow-haired Laddie".'

Mr Knightley's brow cleared; he laughed. 'I learnt it as a child – it was my mother's favourite and old Mrs Martin's too – they persuade me into it now and again – I would never do it in public. But Mrs Martin is such a good creature and swears that that song does her more good than any tonic.'

'Your mother's favourite! I never knew—'

'You were not born,' he smiled.

'You never told me.'

'It is a silly song. Emma, my dear – what is the matter?'

'Nothing.'

'Always nothing,' Mr Knightley sighed to himself.

'I am sorry.' They sat for a moment without speaking. The piano was closed, the tables set up for cards. Mr John Knightley and Isabella were talking together and came over to where Emma and Knightley sat so silent amid the gaiety.

'We would like to take the carriage early,' said John Knightley.

'Ah, brother,' Mr Knightley roused himself to a smile, 'you revert to old habits of early departure!'

'I am of the same mind,' said Isabella.

'Mrs Weston understands, we have all the trials of our removal ahead of us on the morrow.'

Emma smiled at her sister. 'Let us all go together.'

But that could not be; the Westons would be offended and the horses could hardly pull such a carriage-load for there were still Henry and John to be taken back, although the other children and maids were long gone.

So another hour must be passed. Yet it did not pass as sadly as Emma expected for Mrs Cole made much of her and Mrs Weston told her she had never seen her look finer, although a little too thin – but that must be still the effects of London – and everybody seemed to be laid out to be charming and to make her feel important and loved;

and, more consoling than all this, Mr Knightley never left her side for a moment and, when they sat together in the darkness of the carriage, he took her hand gently.

'My dear – I have been too busy – that separation in London – Isabella's family at Hartfield – may I suggest, when the weather has warmed, we make a trip to the sea, for a week, perhaps even two.'

The sea! The dark waves with their white curling tips, the shiny pebbles thrown this way and that, the wild seagulls in a streaky sky! 'Oh, yes. I should love that above all things!'

28 ∫

Hartfield settled down quickly after the John Knightleys' departure. Mr Knightley was out of the house most days, Mr Woodhouse and Miss Bates were as comfortable in each other's company as ever – like a pair of twins who mirror each other in every outlook and attitude – and Emma, once her housekeeping was done, spent the rest of her day in avoiding the piano and her sewing, in the usual round of visits – to people with whom she felt little in common – in charitable work of which she did more than usual until Vicarage Lane grew quite accustomed to her brisk step and her businesslike dispensing of comfort – and in a new activity: reading to improve her mind.

The first time Mr Knightley found Emma engrossed in Dr Johnson he commented with his usual shrewdness, 'So Mrs Tidmarsh has prevailed where Miss Taylor failed.' But he was not ill-humoured and looked over the list that Philomena Tidmarsh had compiled, after taking advice from Dugobair, with real interest. 'I had the estate to manage from such a young age – I left any serious reading to John. You must teach me, Emma.'

'Do not make fun of me!' she was indignant; but Knightley protested he did not, and was regretful that his responsibilities had cut short his education. This threw a new light on him for Emma who had always felt his inferior in every way, except in lively wit, not that she produced much of that at the present time. 'Perhaps we could read aloud together?' she suggested, a little doubtfully and, although that had not yet taken place, it was a happy prospect which, with the plan to visit the sea as soon as the weather warmed – perhaps in late May – gave Emma a tolerable sense of hope that she and Knightley might, after all, deal well enough. Perfect happiness she no longer dared expect but a closeness, a linking of their two spirits, was altogether necessary to her.

She wrote to Mrs Tidmarsh, in somewhat disguised tones, about this need she sensed in the human make-up (she did not mention herself) to complete oneself by joining to another. Mrs Tidmarsh replied in terms that showed she perfectly understood her friend referred to herself by advising her to read Mary Wollstonecraft's *A Vindication of the Rights of Woman*. 'However, my dearest Emma,' she continued, 'I no longer have a copy and, since I can fairly assume that such a volume will be neither available among the books at Hartfield, nor in the larger area of Highbury nor, quite possibly, in the whole county of Surrey, it may be best that you take comfort in the fact that you, at least, have joined your life to a man whose attitude to women is as humane and rational as any attitude could be when held by a person of the other sex.'

Emma had smiled to herself; it pleased her when Philomena spoke approvingly of Mr Knightley – even though the next sentence might end with nearly as complimentary a reference to Mr Martin. She did not wish Mrs Tidmarsh to be a source of contention between Mr Knightley and herself.

'My dear!' she wrote, 'You would not credit it, but Mr Knightley and I are to study Doctor Johnson together. We will have quite a schoolroom here soon. Even Miss Bates let go her beloved Times newspaper – to which she is addicted with a passion – to look through Dryden's *Dunciad*.'

But this letter was not answered for nearly a week – a long week to Emma – and when a letter came it was from the Reverend Dugobair Tidmarsh.

My stepmother has asked that I should write – she has been ill – the old trouble – for a week now – she improves but slowly and I am more anxious than I have ever been. She does not know that I write this – she merely wished me to make a few vague excuses for the want of a letter. But I feel it my duty to ask you now, that which you had so kindly offered before you left London – in short, that she could come and stay with you in a week's time – perhaps two – and, in the good health of the countryside, in your company, out of the noise and dirt of London, away from her duties and obligations, regain her health. As Virgil writes, "Fortunatus est ille deos qui novit agrestis" – Fortunate is the man who has come to know the gods of the countryside.'

There was no possibility of refusing such a request, Emma knew it at once. She could not make such a friend of Philomena that she discussed with her the most private thoughts of her heart, and yet confine her to the pages of a letter. She must come; she would ask Knightley at once – although, indeed, she expected no great objection from him – he did not know of Mrs Tidmarsh's foundling background and perhaps would not care if he did. Mr Woodhouse might worry – a stranger in the house was something that had never occurred at Hartfield; but Emma had learnt that an early application to Miss Bates resulted in a gradual introduction of any subject he might have found discomposing, over chess (Miss Bates still had not vanquished him, although it was assuredly within her grasp) or cards, so that the change, or whatever it might be, came to him when it was already part of his thinking. Emma would tell Miss Bates that there would be two visitors in a fortnight's time – for Mr Tidmarsh mentioned his hopes to accompany his stepmother and he might stay a night or two – and by the time they arrived Mr Woodhouse would be as comfortable with the idea as if it were Isabella or John Knightley returned, but without their noisy children!

So Emma decided and so it turned out. The date was fixed, Mr Knightley was amenable, Mr Woodhouse only properly expectant and Emma, reviewing the room that Mrs Tidmarsh would inhabit, decided just a few days before her visitors would arrive, on a special visit to Ford's so that she might replace the muslin at the window and enliven the armchair with a piece of new chintz.

The day was dry, her spirits so gay that they could not even be dampened by finding Mrs Elton, with Mrs Cole at her side, engaged in doing just what she was about to do – turning over materials with the object of brightening up the furnishings of a spare bedroom.

'Mrs Knightley!' Both ladies looked on Emma with the greatest show of delight but Mrs Elton spoke first. 'You have found me before I found you because I have a letter for you in my reticule. You will never guess why we are in Ford's!'

'To look over new chintzes, I should say,' replied Emma, 'if I may judge by the rolls of cloth in front of you.'

'But why do we look?' She was arch, her eyes winking with excitement. 'You will not guess, perhaps, unless I give you a clue?'

'Yes, give Mrs Knightley a clue,' echoed Mrs Cole, apparently in equal excitement.

Mrs Elton tipped her head on one side in thinking mode; she put a mittened finger to her chin. 'It is for a bedchamber,' she eventually said with great deliberation, as from one whose words portend falling stars or moons with horns, 'which is not – usually – used.'

'Ah,' Emma was grave, as if bemused, although she knew only one happening (or potential happening) that turned Mrs Elton into quite such a lamentable being – 'A bedchamber? Unused, you say? Perhaps it suffers from mice?'

'Oh, no!' – Mrs Elton, shocked.

'Or draughts!'

'Certainly not!' – Mrs Elton, aghast.

'But you must expect visitors— ?'

Mrs Elton clapped her hands and Mrs Cole jumped up and down – or would have done if she had not been so solidly based.

'I have it!' Emma paused, stared triumphant into the two eager faces – 'Mr Elton is entertaining the bishop!'

'The bishop?!' Both ladies spoke the word as if it were 'Napoleon'. And it was true that the bishop of the area was a red-faced man who rode his horse about like a doctor and enjoyed his snuff and his port more than anything in this world and – as he had once confided in Emma when she had the misfortune to spend a dinner at his side – in the next world too.

'Not the bishop,' said Emma.

'Give her another clue, Augusta, dear,' said Mrs Cole. 'Perhaps,' she lowered her voice to a whisper, 'a pig could come into it, a baby pig.'

But Mrs Elton had had enough of the game, and handed over a paper to Emma with a certain dignity. 'It is the Sucklings. They come in three or four days' time. Since we are so cramped for space at the Vicarage, Mrs Cole is to give a dinner – a ball indeed. Here is the invitation.'

'Ah!' cried Emma, relenting, for she was happy that day. 'I am so glad. But will you be able to accommodate two more guests for I have visitors arriving from London not long before?'

This coincidence, working on Mrs Elton's competitive sense, restored all her liveliness and, once she had ascertained they were a young widow and an even younger man who was, moreover, a London clergyman, she was all smiles. Mr and Mrs Suckling (in her view) would be in no way replaced as the starring guests but Mrs Tidmarsh and her stepson would make very acceptable additional guests.

Mrs Cole began to count numbers on her fingers, Mrs Elton had the chintz she had chosen parcelled up and soon the bell at the door rang as the two cheerful ladies left the shop, and Emma could make her modest preparations for seeing her guests comfortable in peaceful solitude.

Nevertheless, on her return to Hartfield, she could not resist a note to Mrs Tidmarsh on the subject of the proposed ball.

My dear – I have committed you to gaiety which, I now realise, you may not have the strength or inclination to attend: the Sucklings – of whom I have written to you – seem truly to be expected at the Vicarage and a ball given by the Coles (you remember I wrote of them too) – you are invited but do not be anxious; bring a feather or two for your coiffure but, if you are not well enough, we will make you happy staying quiet at Hartfield—

By return of post came Mrs Tidmarsh's answer:

I am as strong as a lion! Three days of country air and I will be able to stand up for every dance – you must not credit all Dugobair's fears – remember, he lost one mother at an impressionable age – I am packing all my feathers which means my trunk may almost fly on its own – for a harpist is always the very queen of ostriches.

Undoubtedly this ball was to be the greatest, even on Highbury's calendar, for several years. The resources of Ford's being deemed inadequate for such a celebration, materials were brought by every post from London; local seamstresses had never been so busy and fashion plates and pattern-books were exchanged between houses as if they were circulating libraries. Emma, herself not uninfected by the atmosphere, decided on gold satin with a violet velvet trimming, which she judged as far from anything Harriet Martin would choose as possible. Even Miss Bates, who, by some remarkable sleight of hand, had persuaded Mr Woodhouse that it was his duty to attend the ball, and who was normally an unassuming dresser (as indeed was appropriate to her situation) was discovered by Emma returning from Ford's with a parcel which was revealed, not without maidenly blushes from Miss Bates, to contain strips of plum brocade which Mrs Ford had kept below the counter and which Miss Bates intended to affix to her black silk.

'Where do you intend to affix it?' inquired Emma, somewhat bemused – and indeed charitably concerned that Miss Bates should not make a fool of herself (and therefore Mr Woodhouse, for they were sure to be affixed to each other) in front of the Sucklings; it was extraordinary how even Emma, despite her stern views on Mrs Elton's vulgarity, had begun to believe, by sheer virtue of Mrs Elton repeating it so often, that Mrs Suckling really did aspire to a notion of high fashion that might put Highbury to shame.

Miss Bates was vague as to what portion of her dress should be adorned by the brocade. 'Perhaps the bodice,' she suggested eventually.

Emma looked at Miss Bates' small, flat chest and thought

it best not drawn attention to. 'Perhaps panels might look better – in the skirt.'

'Or a train?' Miss Bates gave a strange self-conscious smile.

'Oh, I don't think a train,' said Emma firmly. 'To wear a train, you must have a head-dress and I hardly expect you to wear a head-dress.'

'Quite. Quite.' Miss Bates became in a flurry, although there seemed no reason for it, and left the room with murmurs of Mr Woodhouse which left the plum brocade still unaccounted for. Probably, Emma thought to herself, Miss Bates would think better of the whole idea and put the material safely away in her drawer.

Preparations for the ball and preparations for her visitors left Emma little time for politics or philosophy; but, on the day that the Tidmarshes were expected, she laid a book or two on the little table in the parlour.

Mr Knightley, who had stayed in to greet the guests, noted it and gave Emma an indulgent smile which she understood and did not altogether appreciate. 'My reading is not abandoned, you see!' she said, half humorously, half defensively.

'You have put them there as a symbol,' said Mr Knightley. 'As another might lay out her sewing.'

'Or as a man might lay down his hunting crop,' added Emma, although hardly knowing what she meant since Knightley never had followed the hounds.

The discussion could not continue, however, for it was interrupted by the easily recognisable sound of the wheels of James's carriage – it had been sent to London – entering the driveway at its usual steady pace.

Emma flew out, Mr Knightley stood at the door and Miss Bates, peering out at the noise, went to inform Mr Woodhouse.

'My word!' exclaimed Mr Knightley, who was not usually so involuntary.

'I think – I think,' Emma stared at the object, like a great golden ploughshare, protruding out of the carriage, 'they have brought the harp!'

The carriage stopped; James climbed down – servants were summoned – harp, cases, Mrs Tidmarsh and the Reverend Dugobair Tidmarsh had arrived.

'Oh, my dear!'

'My dear!' The ladies kissed; the men shook hands; the guests came into the hallway where they were introduced to Mr Woodhouse (on a stick) and Miss Bates (twittering behind him); and Emma looked at her friend. It was a shock – or, at very least, a surprise.

It is a well attested truth that a person may give a very different impression according to the habitat in which they are viewed: a gardener in his garden will take on the rustic charm and ease which he will lack in a concert hall; a queen will appear grander in her palace than she will beside her coach if the wheel comes off; a jockey will be a large man on his mount, a midget among his peers outside the profession. Philomena Tidmarsh, in London, had seemed to Emma a fine, elegant-looking woman, with her eagle features, black hair and predilection for striking mixes of colour in her dress and jewellery, but here, now, standing in the beautiful simplicity of Hartfield's hallway, silhouetted against the window, through which trees, lightly clad in their spring green, waved in a gentle breeze, she looked, not merely striking – but – Emma sought for the word as her friend's purple and orange turbaned head swayed over Mr Woodhouse, and found it: she looked outlandish!

'My dear,' Mr Knightley nudged her arm, 'your guests must be tired.'

'Not at all!' cried Philomena, 'or, let us say, I am perfectly exhausted and perfectly exhilarated all at the same time!'

'You should rest, my dear,' Mr Tidmarsh took his stepmother's arm.

At least Mr Tidmarsh appeared perfectly quiet and gentlemanly in his clergyman's black; indeed, the only change that transference to the country had made in him was to show him as far more handsome than Emma had recalled. He was, with his darkness and lean figure, quite like a romantic hero, Emma thought, although not at all the sort of looks she herself admired. She gave Knightley a quick look; he was bearing up well under Mrs Tidmarsh's effusions.

She was explaining that her recent indisposition had made it impossible for her to play her harp but that she could not bring herself to leave it aside any longer and, moreover, had always previously found it most efficacious in restoring her health and spirits – not just because of the exercise it engendered but because of the soothing nature of its music.

Mr Knightley assured her of the harp's welcome; he, personally, had so much admired her playing at Christmas in London. There only remained the question of where it should stand.

'I am sure any corner will serve!' cried Philomena.

But this could hardly be the truth; draughts must be avoided for Mrs Tidmarsh's health, sun must be avoided for the health of the harp, and Mr Woodhouse, who had retired to his favourite chair with the look of an animal who felt safe in his lair, was curiously adamant that any free corner in the parlour would not do for one reason or another.

The arrival, the welcome, the warm feelings on all sides were in grave danger of being dispelled when Emma felt a pluck on her sleeve.

'Yes, Miss Bates?'

She whispered, 'I wonder – my rooms – empty – dry – sun hardly makes its appearance before two—'

It was decided! James should be found before he had time to unharness the horses and the harp should be transported into Highbury where it could be visited by its owner on a daily basis.

Good humour was general. Mr Woodhouse lost his beleaguered look and offered poor Mrs Tidmarsh a basin of gruel – her illness was in her favour once he had established she had suffered from nothing infectious. Mr Knightley and Mr Tidmarsh went off immediately on a walk – they would follow the carriage into town and see the harp to safe harbour, Miss Bates tucked the rug round Mr Woodhouse (a comfort after such a disturbance, even on a warm day) and Emma ordered coffee and cakes for her friend.

'All this and coffee too!' cried Mrs Tidmarsh when it came, and she looked at Mrs Knightley. 'I have never been so happy to be anywhere in my life!'

Such unaffected gratitude and warmth of feeling must do much to counteract the adverse effects of an appearance and a personality which for a while, with sinking heart, Emma had thought more appropriate for the stage than Hartfield's quiet country life.

29

Emma's fears that she had invited a garish cuckoo into her nest lessened quickly and in a day or two had quite disappeared. Mrs Tidmarsh was very unlike any other lady in Highbury, in looks and manner – that would not change and for that her hostess should have been prepared since it was the very reason she had felt drawn to her. But the particularly exaggerated dress of her arrival had not been repeated on the days that followed, nor that high-pitched level of excitement. Poor Mrs Tidmarsh, without experience of the English countryside, dressed and acted out of nervousness and a wish to impress; indeed she admitted it to Emma. Once she had been shown her room – which she admired excessively, saying it made her feel like a shepherdess – and was assured the harp caused no problems, she settled down into a much easier pitch. Besides, for the first two days she was so tired from the journey that she descended very little from her room and, when she did, won the heart of Mr Woodhouse by a willingness to take any of his health-giving potions, not excluding the noxious gruel.

'I tip it into the poor geranium,' she confided in Emma, as they sat in the drawing-room, on the third afternoon of the visit, 'that way I do not disappoint your dear, kind-hearted father and do not kill myself.'

'I wonder that no one has thought of that before,' replied Emma, determined not to be shocked.

'It is just as well for the geranium that no one has,' laughed Philomena. 'Now, tomorrow, I must catch up with Dugobair and become a tourist. I feel quite strong enough. May I meet your old friend, Mrs Weston?'

Emma reassured her this was only too easy as Mrs Weston had far too many responsibilities to be ever away from her home.

This surprised Mrs Tidmarsh considerably and she began further questions about the ladies of Highbury. She showed a great interest in Mrs Goddard's school. 'The pupils pay, you say?'

'Oh, yes. Mr Martin's wife—' Emma paused and then went bravely on – 'Harriet Martin attended the school and so did his sister, Elizabeth, and one further sister, Louisa, is still there, I believe. You will know that the Martins have come into quite a bit of money—' another gulp – 'or rather Mrs Martin. They are building a dining-room.'

'A dining-room!' exclaimed Mrs Tidmarsh disapprovingly, clearly not appreciating the significance of such an essential to social life. 'If I came into money, I would not spend it on something as dull as a dining-room; it is always the dreariest room in the house – at St Peter's I never enter the room from one bishop's visit to the next!'

'What would you build?' asked Emma.

'A turret! With winding stone stairs and battlements. I should fly a flag—'

'Oh, Philomena!'

'Do you remember I once informed you I was writing a novel—'

'I am not sure—'

'I stopped. I started. I stopped. And now I have started again. It is to have a heroine who is as brave as Jeanne d'Arc and as beautiful as Desdemona.'

'Oh.'

'Do you not like the sound of it?'

'Oh yes. It is just that I thought you would write something more – more serious—'

'Serious! You do not think Shakespeare combined with an admirable French heroine—'

'The French are our enemies,' tried Emma, timidly, feeling out of her depth.

'The war has ended—'

'Only very recently. But I had thought you might write about people who are closer to our lives – more real—'

'You are quite in the right of it. I must not waste my intelligence on sentimental rubbish. Out of the mouths of babes and sucklings – on which subject, is it true, as I have been informed, that the ball is deferred?'

'Only till Friday.'

'But Dugobair may miss it.'

'No, indeed. He has promised Mr Knightley to return.'

'They are very thick, your husband and my dear vicar.'

'Yes. They are. I am glad of it. I believe they give each other great pleasure,' Emma smiled at the picture of these two gentlemen, so unlike, and so happy in each other's company. 'They instruct each other, one in the art of countryside management and the other in classical learning.' Indeed, as she finished speaking, she saw the two of them riding up the driveway side by side and, as if in illustration of her description, as they entered the hallway, she heard Mr Tidmarsh proclaim in his clever, quick way, 'Naturam expellas furca, tamen usque recurret,' followed by Mr Knightley's good-humoured plea, 'Translate, if you please, sir.' On which Mr Tidmarsh laughed and pronounced, 'You may drive out nature with a pitchfork but she is constantly running back.' 'Oh, I can see why John made a friend of you!' cried Knightley.

They came into the drawing-room, tousled and hearty,

with even Mr Tidmarsh's sallow cheeks coloured by sun and wind.

Together they removed to Emma's special round table where they were joined by Mr Woodhouse and Miss Bates. Afternoon cups of tea had become an institution – both Tidmarshes were thought far too under-nourished by Mr Woodhouse – and, as Emma presided over the teapot and sugar tongs, her heart swelled with pride at the scene of cheerfulness for which she could not fail to take principal credit.

'We looked in at Abbey-Mill Farm earlier,' said Mr Knightley. 'Mr Tidmarsh was keen to renew his acquaintance with Mr Martin.'

'It was my acquaintance,' objected Mrs Tidmarsh gaily. 'My cowardly son did not join us at Miss Eliza O'Neill's performance on the excuse of pressing parish business. Now, Mrs Knightley – you have grown all of a sudden very silent – support me in my remembrance. Is it not true that Mr Tidmarsh declined the honour of an evening with Mr Martin – although I believe it was Miss O'Neill he avoided rather than your friend!'

Since Emma made no answer, Mr Knightley, after casting her an inquiring look, took up the point. 'Mr Tidmarsh met Robert Martin, I understand, on an earlier occasion – the occasion on which Mrs Martin was staying in my brother's house.'

'To be sure. I had quite forgot. Pretty little Harriet Wilson, I met her with Isabella. I must be allowed to visit them very soon. Tomorrow, perhaps. I thought Mr Martin such an honest, upright man, it will be a pleasure to see how he makes out in the way of marriage. Emma, may we forego Mrs Weston one more day, and go for the gentleman-farmer?'

But Emma seemed to need all her concentration for a sugar lump that would not be separated from its fellows and fell back off the tongs time and time again, until her face was quite heated. On this occasion, Mr Tidmarsh took up the conversation. 'I have never seen such a charming pastoral, though they knock walls about just now. Mrs Martin even persuaded Miss Elizabeth Martin to play a tune to show off their new pianoforte. Though her modesty forbade her more than a few bars, I was struck by her talent.'

'Praise from my son indeed,' commented Mrs Tidmarsh.

'We are sorry Mr Tidmarsh must take his leave from us so soon,' Mr Woodhouse offered, keen to be a part of the general benignity.

Mr Tidmarsh bowed; Mr Knightley comforted Mr Woodhouse by informing him that their guest would return; Miss Bates allowed that no one would wish to miss the Sucklings' Ball (as the Coles' dinner was termed); Mrs Tidmarsh smiled at Miss Bates and said that the last ball she had been to was on the eve of the Battle of Waterloo; and only Emma was quiet, the glow that had been around her when they first sat down, dimmed. Gradually her spirits revived, her voice was heard again, but more as if she made an effort than as a natural effusion of happiness.

The next morning, Mr Tidmarsh left early to catch the post-chaise and Mrs Tidmarsh returned to her theme of an early visit to the Martins. Somewhat to her surprise, Emma remained unconvinced that this should take precedence over a visit to Randalls; she insisted that Mrs Weston deserved their attention first and that a visit to Randalls could be combined with a visit to the harp, languishing unplayed in Miss Bates' rooms; moreover, they could reach all these objectives on foot which, with a rest in between, would do her dear friend good – whereas Abbey-Mill Farm was way beyond Highbury and the carriage would have to be ordered, perhaps difficult as James was suffering from gout. 'Besides,' here Emma lifted her voice and smiled at Mrs Tidmarsh, 'if we did go, we would certainly not find Mr Martin at home in bright weather like this and that, I cannot help believing, my dear Philomena, would seriously diminish your pleasure in the visit!'

Overwhelmed by such a high tide of good reasons to give up a project which was more a whim than an absolute need, Mrs Tidmarsh deferred to her friend and, by eleven in the morning, the two ladies were halfway along the path to Randalls. Philomena breathed deeply of the mild air – particularly so for April – and felt sure she smelled the sharp sweetness of eucalyptus. 'Ah! How that reminds me of a house Mr Tidmarsh and I inhabited in France – a long summer of study and music – it was the last before we returned to London and he fell ill. My dear, never forget the blessings of a happy marriage.'

'But I thought – or perhaps it is a consequence of the decease of Mr Tidmarsh— ?'

'You are delicate, my dear Emma. I will not marry again, that is true. I do not believe, as is said, marriages are made in heaven. If an equal partnership were possible – if affection could go hand in hand with respect and friendship – but I must not lecture you – you who are living the very situation that I describe?' She paused expectantly – the question mark like the Damoclean sword over Emma's head.

'It is true,' began Emma, 'that Mr Knightley and I, owing to our long association – I have known him as long as I can remember – do not have a marriage based on a sudden,' she hesitated, but the word must be said, 'passion—'

'Ah!' Mrs Tidmarsh drew in a breath.

'He has always been my guide in what is right; his upright nature, goodness—'

'—upright nature, goodness—' repeated Mrs Tidmarsh.

'—have shown me the way of right behaviour since I was a child—'

'But you are no longer a child?'

'No. No. I am not—'

'And therein lies a lack – a lack that leads away from perfection—'

'He is not used to confiding in me. Why should he be?' Emma had stopped walking, and unconscious of her actions, dug a hole in the gravel with her toe, making it quite damp and dirty in the process.

'A lack of openness,' suggested Mrs Tidmarsh, placing her gloved hand (in maroon leather with gold buttons) on Emma's arm.

Emma looked at the glove askance, but did not see it. How had she said so much to this stranger at her side? How could she be so disloyal to her beloved Knightley as to discuss his faults without use of thumbscrew or rack? A tear came into her eye and she turned an appealing look to Mrs Tidmarsh.

'I understand,' Mrs Tidmarsh bowed her head, 'Your silence tells me all; I see you regret your confidence – the feeling does you credit – but do not fear, the subject is closed. I am a clam – Mr Knightley is as perfectly virtuous as his name. We shall walk on.'

They walked on; the sun continued to shine; Emma's tear dried and her little act of betrayal began to seem less important. By the time they reached the front of the house, bounded by yellow daffodils like a ribbon round a bandbox, the two bonnets nodded cheerily together like any two gossips on a village square.

'I saw you approaching from the nursery window!' Mrs Weston was at the door, her lack of elegance – for she had been supervising the babies' bathing, if the dampness of the front of her dress were proper indication – made up for by the warmth of her welcome. 'Mrs Tidmarsh – for I know all about you – will have to forgive my lack of formality; with three babies under two years of age it is impossible to aspire to proper appearances. Come in, come in!'

They did so – Emma most happily and Mrs Tidmarsh

with curiosity for she had never been in a home which so combined a high level of gentility with human nature in the raw. She expanded on this to Emma on their continuing their walk to Highbury after half an hour of bustle and childish cries and tantrums.

'Little Frank Churchill is a noisy baby, certainly,' laughed Emma.

'Little, you call him – he seemed a giant!'

'His father is a tall, well-made man – but narrow rather than broad.'

'Ah, the runaway father – here is a story out of romance! Has any more been heard of him? I remember when we talked in London, you told me he had gone to Europe.'

'He is thought to be in England once more – he was seen at Enscombe, the large Churchill estate that he is to inherit.'

'And his frame of mind? From all that you told me, he is an example of a most passionate man!'

Emma blushed and was glad to find them entering Highbury. Had she really described Frank Churchill to Philomena in such terms, such intimate terms? 'Now,' she said briskly, 'we will find your harp directly; you will be glad to sit down quietly, I have no doubt.'

Faced with her instrument, Mrs Tidmarsh became a different person, Emma thought, as she watched her caress the gold wood surround and lightly ripple the strings. She seemed – how could she phrase it? – complete, perhaps that was the word. And, as she sat in the little room, with its desolate air of unuse, she wondered whether Mrs Tidmarsh's need for a husband was supplanted by her need for her harp. It was an original idea to her – for in the musical area, Mrs Tidmarsh was modest and did not allow herself any special talent. Yet as her long fingers, released from maroon and gold, tried a few gentle runs, Emma, sitting idly, felt convinced that if Mrs Tidmarsh were ever to be described as passionate, it would be a passion directed not to a person, certainly not to a man, a husband, but to her harp.

'You have slept!' Mrs Tidmarsh stood over Emma in mock accusation – 'and, while you slept, a knock came on the door, and a young man's head came round. Just for a minute, and then he was gone. A very handsome young man!'

Emma sat up straight. She had been asleep – and dreaming, of the sea, she thought, though the image receded fast enough with Philomena energetic in front of her. 'You are supposed to be the one who lacks health!' she smiled.

'So you are not interested in my visitor?'

'A young man, you say?'

'He pronounced, "I heard such music!", closed the door again and disappeared. I looked out of the window but only saw a parade of burly countryfolk – what can they eat to reach such a size? – and that is when I woke you.'

'You are a siren,' said Emma, 'drawing the soul out of the young men of Highbury – although I cannot think but that you have imagined the "handsome" part, unless it were Mr Elton. Was he very pompous-looking, as if his sermons were printed in good black ink once a week?'

'Not at all! So it must remain a mystery. I shall tell Dugobair I am the Siren of Highbury – he will be most amused, although in truth it is depressing to think I could not keep you awake, my dear!'

'I believe it is an inherited family trait,' smiled Emma, 'quite impossible to resist.'

'You refer to your dear sister, Isabella. However, you do not have the excuse of a house full of children to wear you down.'

'I am shamed. But come, we must return to Hartfield. I do have some household duties and in the country we keep to our dinner hours as if we were on board one of His Majesty's ships of the line!'

It had been a most companionable day. Emma allowed Merry to dress her hair before dinner with a most smiling visage for her little mirror. Mr Knightley found her thus and showed his pleasure by sitting down to watch the performance.

'You are not sorry, after all, to have Mrs Tidmarsh in our midst?' he said.

'I am not sorry,' she agreed. 'Her conversation is stimulating to my mind; it takes me from damp sheets and lardy cakes.'

'Oh, Emma! Can your husband not do that for you?' he smiled.

'He can when he is here but a husband must be out and about.'

'And have you progressed further with Mr Pope and Dr Johnson?'

Emma admitted that she had not; but she had listened to Mrs Tidmarsh playing and that had been most uplifting; it did not, after all, seem necessary to mention the soporific effect. Mr Knightley expressed himself keen to share this experience and, with good humour showing on both their faces, they descended, arm in arm, to the drawing-room.

30

It is remarkable how often the adage, on the face of it quite unlikely to be true – that there must be a lull before a storm – is borne out by events in real life. The particularly happy evening that was spent at Hartfield – Mr Woodhouse charmed by Mrs Tidmarsh who treated him like a man of wisdom and discernment so that he responded with as much gallantry as to be near flirtation (Miss Bates with her nose just a little out of joint); Mr and Mrs Knightley in sympathy with each other and their surroundings so that they drew the curtains on their four-poster with careful hand – all this was violently broken into at three or four in the morning when a loud rapping was heard at the back door, accompanied by cries of 'Fetch Mr Knightley! Fetch Mr Knightley!'

There was a scurrying of servants both outside the house and within; Mr Knightley's horse was produced from the stable, wisps of straw still adhering to its mane and its tail tied up inelegantly in a piece of twine; Mr Knightley produced himself, nightshirt tucked into trousers, hair on end, jacket buttoned up wrong. There was a fire at Donwell Abbey! Mr Martin had sent to Hartfield. Men with buckets were wanted; James should follow and anyone else who had a horse or a strong pair of legs.

The word 'fire' spread through the house; everybody,

except Mr Woodhouse who still slept sound, was at his window. It was a dry, starry night but a wind blew, rattling the panes. A maid thought she saw a red sky in the direction of Donwell but Sterne, monumental in her night-time robe, clipped the silly girl around the ear and said she always did see everything through rose-coloured spectacles. If a glow was visible from Hartfield, then the situation was dire indeed.

Emma, standing trembling at an upper window, was joined by Philomena. Together, their long dark hair trailing over their pale peignoirs, they stared into the innocence of velvet sky.

'If it were not for the wind,' murmured Emma.

'And I have not even seen the Abbey yet!' cried Mrs Tidmarsh.

Miss Bates, looking very strange with thin greyish plaits like rats' tails and a selection of threadbare woollen shawls thrown one over the other – despite the circumstances Emma noticed this pitiful lack of nightwear and determined to give her material to make some – joined them with pressing offers of hot drinks.

'I cannot sleep again, it is certain,' said Emma. 'Not till Mr Knightley returns and we hear the worst – if it is the worst!'

'Can we not be of use!' cried Mrs Tidmarsh.

'No. It would not do at all. Mr Knightley would not want it.' Emma was firm. 'I shall dress and wait in my parlour. But I cannot allow you to lose your sleep, my dear Philomena. You must return to bed.' Eventually Emma's wishes prevailed and she was able to sit all on her own, waiting and wondering.

About three hours later when light was showing in the sky, Mr Knightley returned. One look at his face was enough for Emma. She clasped his hand, 'You saved it!'

'We saved it – oh, my dear – it could have so easily – the whole house—'

'Sit down, let me get you a glass—'

'I will tell you first – the relief – The fire had started in the very centre of the house, in the fireplace indeed it seems, but then it fell out into the room, looked for further fuel and found Jane Churchill's pianoforte—'

'The pianoforte!' exclaimed Emma.

'How everything to do with that poor woman does seem to end in tragedy! The piano is now scarcely more than a few strings – If it had not been for the proximity of the river and a chain of willing hands wielding every sort of container – I saw Mrs Martin with a saucepan—'

'Harriet there!'

'All the Martins were in the chain – we needed every hand—'

'Oh.'

'Were it not for so many hands, Jane Churchill's piano would have been the match to burn down the whole of Donwell Abbey. At one point I feared it. But, it is saved! Only the room in which the piano stood is damaged, as much by water as flame.' He turned to Emma, noted her stricken face. 'My dear, you are exhausted.'

'And how was the fire begun?' Emma's voice was low. Two images were in front of her, both imagined; in one, Harriet Martin, golden curls tumbling, bosom heaving, strove heroically beside Mr Knightley (the saucepan, being an unheroic object, had disappeared from the scene); in the other, Frank Churchill brought out a tinder-box and, with a wild gleam in his dilated eyes, struck a red spark.

'By no metaphysical agency. Perhaps a tramp – some person warned the shepherd of a fire.' Mr Knightley glanced with seeming casualness at Emma. 'Mr Martin tells me you advised him of the possibility of an intruder last year. He blames himself for inattention, although it is not his business. An empty house must always stand at risk of a vagabond. But we must not talk more. As you may perceive by my blackened face, I am in great need of water for a purpose other than anti-inflammatory! Come, my dear. We have had a lucky escape. Whoever was guilty had at least the sense to give a warning. Now, do not stand any longer looking so unhappy; I tell you, the news is so much better than it might have been, that I am almost cheerful!'

The fire was over. Jane Churchill's piano, some old panelling and certain exhausted persons in the Highbury and Donwell area (although their exhaustion somewhat compensated by the advantage of a good story, for the flames grew higher at every telling) were the only sufferers.

At Hartfield there remained the task of informing Mr Woodhouse who had given evidence of a level of deafness, not previously recognised, by remaining unaroused until his chocolate was brought in to him by a maid whose eyes shone with the heavy duty – much impressed on her – of not giving her master any account of the night-time alarms and excursions; she compensated for this by pulling back the curtains with such energy that poor Mr Woodhouse was almost blinded by the brilliant April light.

Miss Bates volunteered for the task of informing him, and Emma was glad enough to acquiesce; she was pale, she was listless and, when Mr Knightley kissed her before departing to review the damage at Donwell by light of day, she could scarcely manage a farewell smile. It was impossible for her not to believe that Frank Churchill had returned to his old haunt, and finding the pianoforte – such an emblem of the violent love and high secrecy of his engagement to Jane Fairfax – had been unable to restrain himself and set light to it, in the process risking the building in which it stood. Emma felt this must be so and – yet again – castigated herself for not divulging the whole story to Knightley, and – yet again – allowed him to ride away, into a spring morning fit for kings (she noticed it as an added twist to her sorrow) without saying one word more than, 'Take care, the structure may be affected', at which he laughed indulgently. 'Not a bit of it; the structure of Donwell Abbey has been sound for three hundred years and will not be rocked by a little bit of a blaze!' He took her chin between his fingers, 'Promise me you will rest this morning and perhaps we'll have James take out the carriage later and you can see for yourself.'

He left – firm stride – clatter of horse's hoofs. Emma, for Philomena kept to her room, wandered the house, evading her father and Miss Bates. If Frank Churchill had started the fire – of which she remained utterly convinced – then what might he not do next? Might he not in his wildness – after all these months past, still wild – take his fury out on his little son? No, that could not be possible! For a father to injure his son was unthinkable! Yet she could not help remembering the woeful accusation he had shouted when she had mentioned the baby, 'Murderer!' he had cried. What if the months abroad, travelling, without fixed abode or responsibilities, had deranged his mind still further?

At some moments, Emma gave in utterly to her fears and became paler than a ghost and uttered little cries of distress; at others, berating herself for giving in to her old enemy, an over-active imagination – she did not need that now, she was too sensible – she read Pope and Dr Johnson; at other times she managed to compose herself, sit down and, looking out at the sunny garden, assure herself that nothing cruel and horrible could come out of such a harmonious scene.

It was during one of these calmer moments that she saw two gentlemen riding up the driveway. One she recognised easily enough as the burly figure of Mr Weston, sitting his horse as he did his chair with easy confidence; the other was a slimmer figure, a young man, she estimated, and not known to her.

She turned to tidy herself and found Philomena just descended. 'I hear the fire was overcome without damage to anything but the art of making music,' she cried gaily. 'And now I see we have visitors. My dear, how did I ever allow you to persuade me that life is dull in the country!'

'It is Mr Weston,' murmured Emma, 'his companion is unknown to me—' she paused.

The servant had opened the front door and the two gentlemen could be heard asking for her in loud, cheerful voices – Mr Weston and someone with a lighter voice who pronounced himself, quite audible to the two ladies in the drawing-room, 'to be nearly as pleased to be back at Hartfield as he had been to be at Randalls'.

'What is it, dear Emma?' asked Philomena, seeing her friend's face of amazement.

'It is – Frank Churchill,' she said.

'Frank Churchill? Ah, the tragic widower – the wicked runaway! My dear, it is better than a play!' she dropped her voice to a whisper, as the gentlemen entered the room.

'Mrs Knightley!'

'My dear Mrs Knightley!'

It was Frank Churchill – but a Frank Churchill very far from Emma's imaginings or the desolate figure she had last seen under the willow trees along Donwell River. This was a handsome, clean-shaven, clear-eyed young gentleman, nearly a replica of the Frank Churchill she had first met two years ago – were it not for the few lines that creased the sides of his mouth.

Introductions must be made but, while the ladies studied formality with curtsies and invitations to take a seat, Mr Churchill was irrepressible. Even in a stranger's presence, he did not curtail his tongue – 'I am back! I am back where I belong! Better still, I am forgiven for my shameful flight –

although if you could know how I have suffered – but we will not talk of that – I have seen my son. I can say, without any possibility of contradiction, that he is the finest boy I ever did see!'

Mr Weston looked on indulgently as Frank talked on thus – quite forgiven indeed, it was easy to see. Round the room he went, admiring everything, filled with happiness, joy, satisfaction—

Emma watched this performance, almost too astonished to speak, beyond a few necessary murmurs. One thought came continually: could this Frank Churchill – this gentleman who was all easy affability – possibly be the person who started a fire in Donwell Abbey? It seemed out of the question; and yet the coincidence of his presence was too great for her not to suspect him still.

'You are quiet, Mrs Knightley,' said Mr Churchill, coming up for the first time closer to her, although avoiding her gaze.

'Poor Mrs Knightley was up half the night,' contributed Mrs Tidmarsh.

'Ah, yes. Yes. The fire.' The words came out of Frank's own mouth and he did not give ground.

'You have heard what was burnt?' asked Emma, trying to still the tremble in her voice.

'We did,' answered Mr Weston, as Frank was silent. 'Poor Jane's pianoforte.'

'It is so,' Emma agreed and watched Frank bow his head. As they all seemed to wait for him to speak, he raised his head again and, gazing with clear eyes at Emma, pronounced clearly, 'It is the last of her, the very last.'

'Not a bit of it! Dear boy, not a bit!' Mr Weston interrupted. 'We must not forget little Frank! What is a box of rosewood compared to a living soul!'

But Emma had received the message from Frank; she had seen it in his eyes. He was the incendiary; he had risked Donwell Abbey out of some indulgent whim to destroy the memory of Jane Fairfax! She understood it all! As self-centred as ever, he had gambled with another's property to satisfy himself! And, to make it even worse, far from feeling shame – the fear, the danger they had all felt last night – his eyes had expressed a kind of pride. The look had almost been boastful! It was all Emma could do to restrain herself from unmasking him then and there – but this was made impossible by the entrance of Mr Woodhouse and Miss Bates who had been informed of their visitors.

The emotions of good Miss Bates on setting eyes once more on the husband of her beloved niece could be imagined only by one who, like Isabella before her, had taken to heart the parable of the Prodigal Son. Reproach for Frank Churchill's long, painful absence was never likely in a woman of Miss Bates' disposition, but her humble welcome, her downcast eyes so filled with tears that if she had raised them she would have hardly told Mr Churchill from Mr Weston, informed all who witnessed it that she had now surpassed the testament and disowned any belief that Frank Churchill had ever failed in the most upright, nay, virtuous behaviour.

'So good,' she murmured ecstatically, 'to return at just this moment, so right, so proper' – although why it was right and proper for Frank to return now rather than months earlier was not clear to anyone.

'Now, Miss Bates,' Mr Weston took her hands, 'you need not be so overcome. Now that we have him, we shall hold him for a good while. But he does have one favour to ask of you – my dear lady, a favour is not for crying over—'

'Such a kind, soft heart,' commented Mr Woodhouse who had been more of a spectator than usual – too many events for him to do more than hold his shawl closer.

'You see, Randalls, as you will readily understand,' began Frank, 'is full to the brim – these children have nurses and the nurses have maids – I have never seen so many women in one place—'

'Go on, Frank, do not proceed down a side track—' In an aside to the ladies, 'He is very emotional, poor boy!'

'In short, dear Miss Bates,' said Frank, quite gaily, 'may I take up lodgings in your rooms at Highbury?'

It being entirely unlikely that Miss Bates would say no – although she could not get to the 'yes' beyond 'honoured' and 'proud' – the matter was soon settled and it was only Mrs Tidmarsh's intervention that held up final arrangements for a little longer.

'My harp?' she pronounced the word with a glittering look at Mr Churchill which Emma happened to catch before the lady's lashes closed modestly over it.

'A harp?' Mr Churchill gazed about the room. 'I do not see a harp.' But Emma, senses acute to every nuance of his manner, saw that the innocence of any knowledge of a harp was feigned and that the quick look he directed at Mrs Tidmarsh was playful. It did not take much more perspicuity to realise that the young, handsome man who had peered round the door of Miss Bates' room while Mrs Tidmarsh plucked and she, Emma, dozed, had been Mr Frank Churchill. Amongst so much else, in particular the fire, it did not seem of great importance to Emma, however, except insofar as it made it certain that Churchill had arrived in the area the night before and not that morning as he had made Mr Weston believe.

Meanwhile, all was settled in the affairs of the harp. Mrs Tidmarsh would preserve visiting rights: Mr Churchill would undertake to be away every day between one and three o'clock; Mrs Tidmarsh would be undisturbed. There was nothing for Mrs Knightley to add. Now the gentlemen must be on their way.

All was flutter and flurry as everyone, save Mr Wood-house, proceeded to the driveway, but the horses must make their way there from the stables and Mr Weston took Mrs Tidmarsh and Miss Bates inside again away from a chill breeze.

'Emma!' Mr Churchill stood close to her.

'Mrs Knightley—' Emma, looking stern, moved as if to follow the others and then changed her mind. 'I shall inform Mr Knightley that it was you who lit the fire at Donwell. You cannot deny it. Do not even try to deny it! I can see it in your face, in your eyes! You are not even sorry for it!'

He was immediately all dejection and emotion. 'No, please – all these good people—' he waved his hand at the house – 'my name – please – it is over now, what I was, before – I am reformed – I am straight—'

'How can you dare say that when only last night you risked my husband's home!' – an indignant whisper.

'Look at me – think what I was! – how far down the road to ruin – Would you condemn me to that again? If you knew how I have struggled to bring myself to where I am now! But it is in your power – If Mr Knightley knows, he will certainly tell others – he is not as you and I – he does not understand the emotions to which we are subject – Oh, Emma, I beg you, not for myself but for the sake of Mr and Mrs Weston, for Miss Bates who has seen so much misery and is now made so happy to believe me a hero again – most of all, for the sake of little Frank – should he be condemned to a father who is accused of arson? Oh, dear Emma, I implore you!' Here he tried to take her hand and, although she took it out of reach, she did not move away.

'I admit it – it was a moment of madness! My sufferings all came back to me when I saw the piano – it was madness but the harm is slight – Would you make it the reason to undo all my prospects? Oh, Emma – I plead with you—'

She said nothing.

'You will be silent?' he continued, a little more confident.

'At least for a few days – until I have established my good intentions—'

Emma nodded, spoke low, 'I will. You have convinced me that others will suffer – Mr and Mrs Weston, your son – others, innocent—'

'Oh, thank you! Thank you!' Now she could not restrain him from taking her hand and covering it with kisses. 'Oh, even in gratitude he is intemperate!' Emma thought incoherently, and was much relieved to hear the horses come stamping and steaming round the corner. It was fortunate that there was enough reason for agitation to explain her flushed cheeks and uneven breath to those inside the house who now came out to join them.

31

Mr Knightley's reaction on being informed over dinner of Mr Churchill's reappearance, was succinct, 'He must have heard of the Sucklings' Ball.'

'I conceive,' said Mrs Tidmarsh, 'that you do not have the very highest opinion of Mr Churchill.'

Mr Knightley bowed but would not be drawn further; this may have been in deference to the sensibilities of Miss Bates, who wore the starry-eyed look of young love, a demeanour viewed with some disapprobation by Mr Woodhouse who felt able, after Mr Knightley's comment, to pronounce with, it is true, many regrets that he should have to say it, 'That young man was never quite the right thing when it came to shutting doors. I cannot help but recall a time when poor Emma was forced to walk behind him into every room so that she might shut the door after him.'

'Oh, Mr Woodhouse!' cried Miss Bates. 'That were a terrible fault indeed, although I may be allowed to call it a weakness. Perhaps he has learnt better habits during his travels on the Continent.'

'I fear,' joined in Mrs Tidmarsh, 'there are far less doors on the Continent so the possibility of his improving his closing skills by constant practice is not high.'

'Less doors!' cried Mr Woodhouse. 'What a savage place the Continent must be!'

'On the other hand, although there are less doors,' continued Mrs Tidmarsh, 'there are also less draughts.'

'Less draughts,' repeated Mr Woodhouse, unsure what this imported.

'The climate is less draughty. Perhaps that is why Mr Churchill found himself so comfortable there.'

But at this Emma decided Mrs Tidmarsh's gentle mockery of her father had gone too far. Besides, she would have preferred any subject for dinner conversation than Frank Churchill. She could not understand why Mr Knightley had not immediately made a connection between Frank Churchill's arrival and the fire at Donwell, and the prolongation of their discussion as to his being 'quite the thing' or 'not quite the thing' grated on her sensibility. These were enough reasons for her to change the subject. 'At what time may we expect Mr Tidmarsh to arrive?' she inquired.

'Pray, do not look in this direction,' cried Mrs Tidmarsh who had been in high good humour all day. 'Tomorrow, I make certain, but the time will depend on his parishioners; I have no doubt, left to himself, he would be here for breakfast, he is so taken by life in the country and – if I may presume to meddle in areas traditional for one who wears widow's weeds – he has found a more particular interest,' she smiled at Mr Knightley, 'a little outside the bounds of Hartfield.'

Emma looked for enlightenment to Mr Knightley and he smiled too. 'I suspect you talk of his shared interest in music with Miss Elizabeth Martin.'

'You term it that!'

Mr Knightley turned to Emma. 'Miss Martin has at last found a fitting companion for her playing. Mr Tidmarsh possesses a fine tenor voice and an enviable repertoire of unknown songs. We may have reason to test both if visiting Abbey-Mill, after we have seen the fire damage at Donwell.'

Although Knightley looked at her interrogatively, Emma could see that, as always, he had made this plan without any thought of consulting her wishes beforehand. As always, she must follow where he led, an even more galling realisation when the direction he took was to Abbey-Mill. It was on the tip of her tongue to show her bitterness by crying, 'I wonder you do not take up abode at Abbey-Mill Farm!' But she was stopped by good sense and also the thought that, but for her father – her father, not his – they would be living, if not at Abbey-Mill, at Donwell Abbey which, leaving out of the reckoning the charms of Mrs Robert Martin, Mr Knightley might like even more.

Dissatisfaction, once taking hold, grows tentacles as fast as an octopus. It seemed to Emma that evening, as she sat among those she held most dear, that every subject caused anxiety or pain. Yet she had no recourse to fight her feelings for he whose understanding she had most respected all her life was now her husband and had become a part of her dissatisfactions.

Outdoing even his stepmother's speculations, the eager Mr Tidmarsh arrived even before breakfast. He had written a poem, he said, to pass the journey which was in the form of an invocation and opened,

> O Persephone
> O Spring-time goddess
> Who casts your cloak of flowers
> Upon the grass
> Look with favour upon youth
> And happiness that love—

Here Philomena interrupted with a meaning look at Emma and the comment that it sounded as if it had been translated. 'Could you not speak more from the heart, Dugobair, dear?'

Mr Tidmarsh seemed surprised at this but not offended; his was not a nature to take offence since all information or comment, critical or otherwise – whether on tea-making or Italian sonnets – was taken in as material for his fertile mind. 'From the heart, you say. I had assumed a poem could not be written other than from the heart – a poem of this sort, at any rate – a celebration of the perfection of an early morning's ride in the spring – but perhaps you are right. I am too influenced by the Latin writers, by Ovid—'

While he considered the proper poetic forms to express sentiment, plans were made and the carriage brought round, so that the party could make an early start for Donwell. Despite the unseasonable warmth in the air, Mr Woodhouse declined the invitation and accepted, with much tender gratitude, Miss Bates' decision to stay with him. She deserved this gratitude, for her wistfulness, as she stood at the door to wave them off – the two ladies and Dugobair in the carriage and Mr Knightley on horseback – was pathetic in the extreme.

'I believe Miss Bates would make a fine social butterfly in different circumstances,' said Mrs Tidmarsh meditatively.

'She was always used to be glad of any invitation that came her way,' Emma commented indifferently. Why had Knightley not been pleased to join them in the carriage? was her thought.

Meanwhile Mr Tidmarsh was scribbling on a scrap of paper not more than two inches square.

'You write a very *small* poem now!' said Mrs Tidmarsh.

'It is not the quantity of words which leads to success, but the quality.'

'Surely there is a minimum. Emma, give us your view, you have been reading deeply these last few weeks – how many words to make a poem? A hundred? Fifty?'

'Obscurus fio. Horace would understand your accusation.'

'I believe,' said Emma, having an inspiration of memory,

'that Pope said, "'Every poet is a fool but not every fool a poet."'

'Bravo!' cried Mrs Tidmarsh and, seeing Mr Knightley riding not far from the window, called out, 'Did you know what a learned lady you have married?' She withdrew her head again. 'Although I could wish it from a writer whose views on our sex were more kindly.'

'But you recommended I read Mr Pope,' protested Emma.

'For his wit and general cultivation he is necessary but not for his views.'

In such rattling style, the journey past Randalls, Highbury and into Donwell itself, was soon accomplished. As they entered the driveway of the Abbey, Knightley came to them again and again to point out to Mrs Tidmarsh this aspect here, that magnificent old tree there, and soon they must stop and descend so that they might walk from the last bend in the drive and have an uninterrupted view as the house arose in front of them. This they did; and, indeed, Mr Knightley's pride in his old family home (Emma had never been so conscious of it) was fully justified by its mellow golden stone in the spring sun, its accumulation of courtyards and stone-carved windows, its patchwork of stone roofs, some gently sloping and some steep as pointed hats and its tall chimneys, either clustered in charming patterns or standing alone, twisted, like a maypole, sharp-edged or straight and true.

'I am in love!' cried Mrs Tidmarsh, 'I am in love with a house! It is like an edifice out of a fairy tale. Oh Emma, how can you bear to live away from it!'

Emma did not answer. There was no use; both Mr and Mrs Tidmarsh talked incessantly. Mr Knightley opened the heavy front door and, cold and damp as it was, they flew around in raptures over the 'romantic atmosphere', the 'unassuming elegance', the 'glorious sense of generations

of Knightleys who had each added their own loving touch'
– this from Mrs Tidmarsh.

Mr Knightley smiled and Emma wondered if he wished
she would say such things. But she had known the house
too long to be surprised by anything about it. It was just
Donwell Abbey – Mr Knightley's home – perhaps some
time in the future little Henry Knightley's home. Emma
sighed.

Mr Knightley caught this sigh and thinking it arose from
sadness at the sight that now lay in front of them, took his
wife's hand. 'It is not so bad. As you see, the remains of the
pianoforte have been taken and now we must await warmer
weather to open the windows and dry out the water.'

It was sad sight enough; but Emma could not help
remembering that the last time she had been in the room
was in her search for Frank Churchill and that it was on
her orders that the piano had been placed there.

'May we come in? Mr Knightley! If you please!'

Voices were heard calling from outside the house. Leaving his guests to rummage further afield, Mr Knightley
returned to the front door where, judging by the amount
of noises, he found a large group of would-be sightseers.

Emma waited and was prepared enough to appear calm
when Mr Knightley was followed by Mr Robert Martin, Mrs
Robert Martin, Miss Elizabeth Martin, Miss Louisa Martin,
Mr Weston, Mr Frank Churchill, and Mrs Elton – the last,
seemingly in a fever of excitement which showed by her
exclaiming, 'What a tragedy! What a tragedy!' every second
or two without altering a look of glee which lit up her face.

'We were walking by,' said Mr Martin, more calmly to
Emma, 'and Mrs Elton saw the door open.'

'What a tragedy!' parroted Mrs Elton, patting and then
knocking the soaked panelling. 'It will never recover, of
course. Never be the same. The only thing to do will be
to replace. What a tragedy!'

'New things can be very fine,' began Harriet Martin. 'I prefer new things—'

'There is no need to replace the panelling at all,' said Emma sharply. 'Over the last three hundred years, Donwell Abbey has withstood far worse—'

'Civil war, pillage, rapine, death, storm and disaster!' pronounced Philomena Tidmarsh, appearing from an inner room with a dramatic flourish which would have made Miss O'Neill proud but startled Harriet extremely. (Emma noticed it with satisfaction – and surprise because she had already forgotten the first impression Mrs Tidmarsh made on the unwary.)

Before introductions could be effected between Mrs Tidmarsh and Harriet Martin and the Misses Martin who had not yet met Emma's dramatic visitor, Mr Tidmarsh sprang from a recess or even, as it seemed, out of the very panel Mrs Elton had knocked on so disapprovingly. Indeed she gave a little scream and jumped aside.

'My apologies!' He bowed but could not repress the question he had prepared for Mr Knightley: 'Would I be correct in my surmise that the Knightley family came into this house after Henry VIII had relocated our religious orders?'

'Now, Dugobair, I will not have history when we have so many interesting people present from this century,' Philomena turned to Mrs Elton. 'Do you not find that the study of history so often comes between the practice of living?'

Mrs Elton, goggling somewhat, was spared the need for a reply by Mr Knightley at last effecting introductions and Mrs Tidmarsh being removed to quiz Harriet while Mr Tidmarsh, face alight with emotions quite unrelated to anything dead or buried, had spotted Elizabeth Martin and gravitated to her side. He then, Emma noted with surprise, fell silent; this did, above all, suggest admiration.

The four other gentlemen, meanwhile, had repaired to the burnt-out fireplace where they stood discussing the likelihood of the chimney being injured from the inside. Emma could hardly believe her ears when she heard Churchill's ringing voice inquire of Knightley, 'And do you have any idea of how the fire was started?'

'We have our suspicions,' replied Knightley, as polite as ever, although his expression indicated to Emma a tension whose cause she did not dare examine.

'I collect you suspect a deliberate act by an intruder,' pursued Mr Weston.

'We do.' Knightley's tone was clipped, as if to discourage further conjecture.

For Churchill to instigate such a discussion – doing so, moreover, in the presence of someone to whom he had admitted his guilt – so disconcerted Emma that she turned to Mrs Elton who stood at her side and said quite forcibly, 'I suppose a few flames, a little water must be conceived as less of a tragedy than if the ceiling had fallen in!'

Mrs Elton could not but take this as a reference to the unfortunate collapse of a part of the Suckling home, the much-vaunted Maple Grove. She wished to riposte – it was an insult, she divined, and should have a riposte – but her mind refused to produce suitable words. Eventually, while Emma stared – her thoughts of course on the fireplace – Mrs Elton cried shrilly, 'A fire is a tragedy, a falling down is an Act of God!'

Her vigorous tone attracted the attention of the men at the fireplace who broke apart and came back to the centre of the room. In the general movement that followed Emma found herself drawn aside by Frank Churchill who immediately whispered, 'You are shocked, I can see it in your face. But how else should I behave? A reformed man must show an interest in a friend's troubles.'

'You are shameless!' hissed Emma, and had moved

to leave him when, catching the most unwelcome sight of Harriet Martin in high-spirited conversation with Mr Knightley, she faced Frank again. 'You need not look happy!'

'You wish me to wear sackcloth and ashes and go about with a long face? But I was always taught that saints were cheerful people!'

'However you may change, Frank Churchill, you will never be a saint!' This time she did leave his side for the party was gathering together for the purposes of a walk round the grounds.

'Oh, how Mrs Suckling will regret her continual delay,' cried Mrs Elton, 'when I tell her what a splendid tour she has missed!'

'We may all regret her delay,' said Emma, picturing her golden satin which she expected to have delivered on the following day. Never vain of her looks – which in itself might be taken for pride since she took for granted a natural superiority – this dress and how she would look in it had been taken much more seriously than any garment before. She was determined to shine at the Sucklings' Ball!

'You refer to the ball!' said Mrs Elton, with great satisfaction. 'I do not worry about the delay since Mrs Cole pronounced in Mr Elton's hearing that an evening such as she planned might tax the great Creator himself; and Mr Elton, in his most ringing voice, gave it the "Amen!"'

'You talk of the ball,' Mrs Tidmarsh joined them, 'I should have been most disappointed if it had been put off. I have brought with me a costume I wore in theatricals when I played that great heroine of Britannia, Boadicea. Unfortunately Mr Tidmarsh, who cannot like any show, forbade me the helmet, but I can still promise you a dashing and unusual effect – I have made substitute for the helmet with feathers!'

Mrs Elton was saved from the need for an appropriate

comment – although her raised brow and pursed lip suggested that she might not altogether share Mrs Tidmarsh's
enthusiasm for her costume – by the party moving out to
the garden.

32 ∫

It is a feature of walks taken in company that two may walk happily side by side where three or more will never find their situation even tolerably comfortable. Three do not fit easily on to paths; the wind and sky disperses the voice into the sky so that those on either side of him or her in the middle must lean across to hear each other; the differences in their stride irritate; progress is interrupted by a continual falling back and facing forward, all in order to overcome the unalterable fact that they are not a partnership of two!

For this reason, a large group, intent on serious ambulatory exercise – rather than standing around in walking mode – will always form up into pairs. Out of such a coupling – sometimes conjoined by a conscious will, sometimes only by the chance of who stood next to each at the time of departure – an interesting result may emerge. There is nothing so conducive to intimate conversation than a lively step and a face at your side rather than staring directly at you, as so often at table or in a drawing-room. The body enjoys a sense of freedom which it imparts to the head and the tongue; words are passed while skipping round a stone, holding back a branch, or scrambling down the steps to a ha-ha which would never be spoken in the sedate confines of the front parlour.

If anyone had ever made a study of the whereabouts of

those young people (or even not so young) when they first come to an understanding, or, at least, an attraction, later leading to marriage, a brisk walk on a fine spring day would outdo every other location.

The company setting out from Donwell on just such a fine day, was immediately decreased in size by Harriet saying she must return to her baby directly and, Louisa Martin volunteering to accompany her, they set off by the quickest path. Already pairs were forming – Dugobair had Miss Martin firmly on his arm and, not apparently aware of the compass, had wandered off towards the unused and unromantic stable before being recalled by Mr Knightley.

Mrs Elton, with a determination that would have been admirable in a captain at the masthead, a limpet on a rock, or a ferret in a hole, had attached herself to her host, deserving her place, as she must have felt, by her stream of laudatory cries – 'What a tragedy!' had been replaced by, 'What perfection!'

Hampered as he was by this ever-praising encumbrance, Mr Knightley managed to lead off his party on the most scenic route to his favourite avenue of limes. Behind him came Emma on Mr Weston's arm, with Mr Martin taking only a few paces in attendance and then falling out with the excuse – which Emma accepted as perfectly right and proper – that a man like him (rich or not) should not have time to spend walking in a gentleman's garden which he already knew as well as the back of his hand. Besides, she was comfortable with Mr Weston; there would be no surprises from him, no hissed words of passion – only good nature and, if that sometimes passed the bounds of good sense, then she was used to allow for it.

'Come up, Frank!' he was calling over his shoulder now. Who had picked whom (if that was how it happened) was not known by Emma but it must be instantly clear to anyone with eyes or ears was that Mr Churchill and Mrs

Tidmarsh, bringing up the rear, had immediately struck up a most cordial understanding. Her voice could be heard declaiming a line or two of poetry and his – somewhat to Emma's surprise, since she had never thought of Frank as educated in literature – completing the verse. There was much laughter and, whenever she turned her head, a view of Mrs Tidmarsh's most expansive hand gestures.

'They do not mean to catch up with us,' Mr Weston acknowledged the obvious, with some disappointment. 'I suppose Mrs Tidmarsh has travelled abroad a good deal. It is that, no doubt, that gives them so immediate a sympathy.'

Emma might have argued with him since she had her suspicions that Mr Churchill had spent far less time abroad than he pretended but, at that moment, words, sounding very like French, wafted forward to them. 'Yes,' she admitted, 'that does sound remarkably like the French language they are speaking.'

Mr Weston sighed. 'Frank has always had an excellent ear – for music or for language. I believe his appreciation of poor Jane was entirely due to the excellence of his ear and the excellence of her playing.'

'Ah,' commented Emma for want of real agreement. 'Have you heard yet from old Mr Churchill now that Frank has – has returned? He must be most relieved he is safe.'

'Indeed. Just so. Although the poor old gentleman's health has suffered greatly since his wife died—'

'—And his nephew disappeared,' Emma could not prevent herself from interposing.

'That too.' Mr Weston looked a little discomposed before returning to his more satisfactory train of thought. 'I have visited him once since he set up in Richmond and could hardly credit he is but half a dozen years older than myself; yet I have a child younger than Frank's, younger than my own grandson, indeed. I do wonder whether it is not poor Mr Churchill's age, or age in appearance,

and decrepitude which makes him a little hard on dear
Frank—'

'A little hard?'

'He has not altogether forgiven Frank for leaving the
baby.'

'But surely his distress, his agony of mind, after a dear
wife's decease, were reason enough— ?'

'Mr Churchill does not seem to place as much emphasis
on Frank's agony of mind as we do—'

The last words of this sentence, delivered with a discern-
ible air of disquiet, were almost drowned by a bellow of
hearty male laughter as Frank and Philomena caught up
by a pace or two.

'As we do,' repeated Emma by way of encouragement
for she could see that Mr Weston had something more
to add.

'We do. Indeed we do. But Mr Churchill, poor old man,
perhaps entering an early dotage, he suggested that Frank's
behaviour during his marriage did not follow the path of
perfect – perfect rectitude.'

'Mr Churchill means, I suppose,' said Emma, torn uncom-
fortably between an urge to hear the worst of Frank and
a strange, unaccountable urge to defend him, 'that Frank
would not be in Yorkshire as much as was convenient for
him, for them. But surely a young man can be allowed
to spend time in London; and his wife should, instead of
complaining or languishing, follow him!'

'Just so. That is exactly my thought. I said as much to
Mr Churchill. To blame Frank for Jane's lack of health, is
like blaming the cook for a bad oyster. I said that to Mr
Churchill too but he was not receptive, not receptive at all.
I fear he could not quite take in my likening poor Jane to
an oyster, although I thought it rather apt – her being so
secret, so lacking in candour – although, now I come back
to it, the saying is about a *clam*, is it not? So I was not

altogether straight.' At this witticism it was his turn to give a hearty bellow of male laughter which reminded Emma with sudden force that Mr Weston and Frank were natural father and son and must share some traits in common.

'Did Mr Churchill say more?'

'Ah, you are thinking me a heartless sort of man to make a joke about poor Jane Fairfax. You are right. Let us change the subject; it is too lovely a day for dreariness and woe, for an old man half out of his wits. He suggested, would you believe it, that Frank had taken up with another woman in London and if that doesn't prove the old gentleman is off his head then I'm living on St Helena!'

This remark, delivered with another guffaw, carried Mr Weston forward at suddenly increased speed – and left Emma standing, stricken, horrified. The words fitted in too closely with what she recalled of Frank's self-accusations muttered and screamed by the river. She could not remember what he had said with any exactitude except that he laid some of the blame for Jane's dying to his own account. It was too dreadful to contemplate! Almost unbelievable! That someone so in love that he had married a young lady without portion and with the pitiful Bates's as closest relatives, should lose those feelings so quickly. Yet she must also remember Mrs Campbell's hints – and think, too, that he had just risked a venerable old house for the whim of burning up a pianoforte that brought him sad memories. What sort of man was this!

'Who is this stopping and standing like Patience on a Monument!'

Although Emma had begun walking again, she had been too slow to catch the speeding Mr Weston who had been snatched up by Mrs Elton while Mr Knightley dropped back a pace, and now she was overtaken by Frank who had just spoken, on one side, and Mrs Tidmarsh on the other.

'My dear,' cried the latter. 'You told me Mr Churchill was

handsome and rich but you never told me he was amusing! It is so seldom one finds amusing men; it is because they get no practice – unlike ladies, whose principal education is how to entertain members of the opposite sex. Men, I believe, are quite happy to be strong and silent and even go in fear of being thought "lightweight" if they make a witticism. Am I not right, Mr Churchill, are you not in danger of being called lightweight?'

'I am too rich for anyone to dare call me lightweight!' exclaimed Frank.

'There you are! Perfect! How many men would risk such a statement! He is a perfect – I do believe he may even be a woman in disguise!'

It was impossible for Frank to let that pass and Emma found herself caught between an ever-rising level of sallies which fired across her so that she felt like a schooner caught between two gunships. It was a relief when she saw Mr Knightley turn and, on seeing her situation, come back to her and take her on his arm. Letting the laughing duo go ahead, they fell back. The peacefulness was very soothing to Emma's troubled spirit.

'It is good to walk here, with you on my arm,' Mr Knightley spoke after a pause. Emma glanced at his face, he was not thinking of Frank or Mr Weston or Philomena or any other trying or disagreeable person. His head was high, his eyes looking ahead, around, lighting on trees, just opening to flower, on a bird trilling above their heads, on the sky streaking now with silver, on the lime tree avenue in front of him.

'Oh, I wish we lived here!' cried Emma, feeling it with all her heart. It seemed to her, all of a sudden, that her cloudiness of spirit, all that came between her and Knightley, would be dispelled if they could live together in the ambience of Donwell – his home, his family's home for generations.

'My dear,' his face was even brighter. 'Do you truly feel that? You have never said so before – I hoped—'

'I do. I do' – she was fervent. 'We could be free here – be ourselves here!'

His face closed a little as if he distrusted such wild words. 'I am myself wherever I am with you,' he said eventually, calmly.

'Oh, yes!' – a bitter tone entered Emma's voice; for his calmness was inimical to her enthusiasm. 'You are always yourself!'

'Emma!' – an appeal.

'No. No. We are not quarrelling!' But why were tears pricking at her eyes? Was she some silly girl dreaming of a hero to sweep her off her feet? It was too ridiculous, emotion arising out of the horrible things that she had been forced to think about Frank. She and Knightley were not part of that kind of ugliness; they were kind and loving to each other.

'Knightley,' she laid her hand on his arm.

'I wish you would call me George.'

'But—' His voice had been husky, strange.

'But you will not,' a smile was forced, 'as you told me that day in the garden when I told you of my love, that you never would.' He had seen Mr Weston and Mrs Elton stopping and turning; they had reached the avenue, the object of their walk. Miss Martin and Mr Tidmarsh already stood under the small bright leaves, looking upwards like star-gazers. Mrs Tidmarsh and Frank, still jocular, stood in the middle of the avenue. They must all convene.

'I shall call you George when we move in to Donwell!' cried Emma, inspired by she knew not what.

Knightley had just time to give her a look filled with emotion, entreaty, longing – all the qualities that she had decided not to expect from him – when they were engulfed in a wave of *esprit de corps*.

It is a second rule of a walk taken in company, that those who participate feel a particular sense of camaraderie. The feeling is as strong as the walk is long, so as much feeling cannot be engendered in the distance from the Abbey to the lime tree avenue as would be aroused in a party who cross from Land's End to John O'Groat's or follow the path that led Hannibal across the Alps; but the atmosphere, nevertheless, in that spring-time green, with bodies warmed by the exercise and the sun and faces and minds cooled by the freshness of the air, tended towards a collective sense of self-congratulation, of a disinclination to disperse their separate ways.

This is a contradictory sort of behaviour since each has passed their time, as described, earlier making sure that they walked in pairs, but now, at the end, they suddenly deem it absolutely necessary to talk to everybody else. So Dugobair, having submitted to Mrs Elton taking over Elizabeth Martin (which she did with many insinuations as to the reason for the heightened beauty of her looks), advanced on Emma and Mr Knightley.

'You brought me here last week,' he addressed the latter, 'but I did not perceive its charms as clearly as I do today.'

'I believe there is a particular reason,' Knightley smiled. And Emma had the pleasure of seeing that a grown gentleman may blush as well as a young lady.

But now Mr Churchill and Mrs Tidmarsh returned to them, with Mr Weston not far behind. 'Mrs Weston will be sending out the Bow Street Runners!' he cried. 'I must make haste – I have Mrs Elton with me but there is room for another—'

Involuntarily, Emma looked at Frank; this should be him – she wanted him gone; she willed him to go. But Mrs Tidmarsh interjected, 'Oh, we cannot let him go so soon – can we, my dear Mrs Knightley? There is room enough for four in our carriage, is there not?'

Emma could not deny it, although the thought of sitting so close to a man of whom she had learnt to think so badly, of whom she was still trying to teach herself to believe the worst, was in the extreme distasteful. Whether Frank read her expression she could not tell, but he now cried, 'But surely we planned to gather at Abbey-Mill Farm! Did not Mrs Martin suggest it? I am sure she did!' Seeing Elizabeth and Mrs Elton approaching, he applied to her, 'Are we not expected by your sister to call?'

Elizabeth looked confused, willing to please at least one of the party, unwilling to displease any – in this she shared the characteristic of her sister – but clearly with no knowledge of an expected visit.

'We must return home, at least—' Emma spoke firmly. The last thing she intended was to sit watching Mr Knightley lost in admiration as Harriet played the busy mother and housewife. Her heart still retained a reflected glow of that look Knightley had given her when she had expressed a desire to live at Donwell; it was a fragile flame and would not stand Harriet's strong attractions. Oh, how far she had sunk! thought Emma in parenthesis, when she could be thinking of Harriet Martin as a real rival to herself!

But the argument was not over about who should go where, with whom and when. Emma remained adamant for Hartfield, Mr Weston for Randalls, Mr Churchill for Abbey-Mill, but Miss Martin merely gave her time to trying not to look at Mr Tidmarsh with too much attention, an activity he was also engaged in, although with much less success; Mrs Elton took first one side and then the other, each time with an equal assurance of her making the right choice; Mrs Tidmarsh laughed and looked at the sky and said, 'On such a day as this it hardly matters where one goes!' – a point of view which earned her a vexed frown, quickly disguised, from Emma; and Mr Knightley who had the authority to make a decision, stood by, silent.

Eventually, he did move, to take Emma's arm, 'I will have the carriage come to the nearest part of the lane.'

She nodded; it was her wish; but where would he go? He was on horseback – free and independent. She could almost believe that the horse had been chosen for just that reason.

'I have things to do here. I shall stay.' He answered her thoughts and her pride made her refrain from asking whether he might not just take refreshment at Abbey-Mill.

Knightley left; the carriage appeared; Mr Weston and Mrs Elton escorted Elizabeth Martin to Abbey-Mill where their carriage waited and – as Emma had dreaded – she, the two Tidmarshes and Frank Churchill were together in the carriage.

The top was opened under Frank's exhortations and with Emma's agreement for, at least, it lessened the sense of intimacy, and soon James was making as much speed as his careful nature allowed, while Frank recommended new horses, a different way of harnessing and eventually likened their progress to a funeral procession.

It was a merry ride for three out of the four occupants, and even Emma's spirits rose as she watched the much-loved environments of Donwell and Highbury pass by. Soon came the turning to Randalls.

'Shall we take you up, Frank, or do you prefer to walk?' asked Emma politely.

'I live in Highbury, you know – in the lovely Bates' apartments,' he joked.

'At least you have my harp for company,' smiled Mrs Tidmarsh.

'But I thought you ate at Randalls,' said Emma.

'Indeed I do, when I can find enough leftovers from the nursery! I do believe those babies eat more than a grown male – but I had thought you could bear my company another half-hour and I would come to Hartfield – I may walk back to Randalls from there.'

He was insistent; Emma could do nothing more without making her feelings too distinct. Mr Churchill stayed.

33

'So Mr Churchill came back with you and stayed,' was almost the first sentence from Mr Knightley when he returned later to Hartfield.

'On no invitation from me,' said Emma who was very concerned with straightening her sash, twisting and turning in front of her bedroom glass.

'You know I do not consider him a man of rectitude, yet you continue to show him all signs of your greatest affection. Private conversations.'

'That is too much, Mr Knightley! You are not looking with eyes to see.'

'No?' he had his gravest face on, the one that before their marriage when he had been more teacher than lover, had often sparked Emma into rebellion.

'No!' Why should she say more? An image of his cantering away in the direction of Abbey-Mill was in front of her eyes.

Mr Knightley bowed and gave her his arm so that they could descend to dinner.

That repast was made lively by the good spirits of Mrs Tidmarsh who so engaged Mr Woodhouse with a mixture of cajolery and good sense – or at least that which he would see as good sense for it included pronouncements on the danger of marriage, leaving home, altering the status quo, mixing with your inferiors and over-indulging in rich sauces – that he, whose anxieties usually lent a constraint to the proceedings, was reduced to nothing but a series of tranquil nods. Miss Bates was equally silent, though she looked much; Mr Tidmarsh spoke twice, both times in heartfelt tones, but since on the first occasion he used the Latin language and on the second the Greek, with, moreover, no translation following (a thing he usually remembered to do and which showed an abstraction of spirit), his contribution to the conversation was decidedly minor. Mr Knightley did talk a little, in his usual measured tones, about a case of cattle-thieving that had come before him in his role as local magistrate; the thief had facilitated his escape by setting light to a barn which, although only partly filled with hay given the time of year, burned merrily enough for some hours.

'And what will be his sentence?' asked Emma, in trepidation.

'It is not yet pronounced; but damage to property is a most serious offence. He will be lucky if he is only to be transported to Botany Bay.'

At this point Mrs Tidmarsh began a laughing reference to the benefits of forced travel which, having been elaborated in all detail, were then most thoroughly denied for the benefit of Mr Woodhouse.

The subject, therefore, of fires and damage to property, was not revived, and a connection to the destruction of Jane's pianoforte at the Abbey, which Emma had dreaded, not forthcoming.

The evening, however, did not pass entirely without further reason for her discomfort. She was in her bedroom preparing for sleep when Mr Knightley, jacket off, came to her.

'I believe that you have a duty to warn your friend against Mr Churchill,' he began without preamble. 'She is clever, she has been married, but she is a lady almost on her own – for, much as I appreciate her stepson, he is not educated in the matters of the world. Mrs Tidmarsh comes on Frank Churchill without the understanding of his nature that we have—'

'But our understandings differ—' began Emma; why, she knew not, since she had every reason to believe that she knew far worse of Mr Churchill than anyone in Highbury – except for Mr Weston, who did not believe it.

'I once had occasion to call Mrs Tidmarsh a flirt,' continued Mr Knightley, standing four-square on his still booted feet. 'It may be only that on her side; she may be as light as he – but, I repeat, as her hostess and friend I feel it your duty to give her warning!'

His pronouncement over – like a judge in a court, he was so solemn, Emma thought – he seemed prepared to leave for his room without any reaction from Emma. She could not let this be.

'Philomena is a lady of sound good sense who has seen far more of the world than I – and probably than you also. How could I presume to warn her?'

'I have given you my opinion.' Mr Knightley kissed her hand, a brief touch of his lips, and was gone.

At eleven the next morning Emma and Mrs Tidmarsh found themselves together in the upstairs parlour reading lines to each other from Shakespeare's *Romeo and Juliet*. At the line 'Call me but love and I'll be new baptiz'd . . .' Emma put down the book and moved closer to her friend. 'I must warn you. It is my duty. I have seen your feelings for Mr Churchill, your pleasure in his company—'

'My dear!' interrupted Philomena with a startled look of amusement.

'Please – it will not take a moment – you must forgive the presumption – but there are things he has done, things

I know or suspect that make him hardly eligible for society!'
She stopped, with a gasp. Was this indeed true?

'That is serious indeed. May I ask what are these things?
Such an accusation cannot be fired wildly without reason
or it becomes slander.'

'Slander?' inquired Emma, rather put off her stride. 'Yes.
Yes. But for the sake of Mr Weston, his father, I cannot
reveal all I know – or suspect—'

'This "suspect"? What does "suspect" mean? People
always use the word "suspect" when they are not certain and
a man's reputation must not be ruined without certainty.'

Emma had never seen Philomena so severe. The interview was not proceeding at all as she had expected; it
seemed she must say more, however unwillingly. 'He was
not kind to his wife,' she said.

'Ah!' Now Mrs Tidmarsh smiled again. 'He was not kind
to his wife. My dear Emma, if that is it, I believe you utterly.
A man like Frank Churchill will never be kind to his wife,
particularly if she is as docile, sensitive and poor as I gather
Jane Churchill was – and, moreover, doted on him without
reserve. I must tell you, my sweet Emma, my innocent
Emma, that, as a very young bride married to a much older
man, I met young gentlemen like Mr Churchill – married
young gentlemen – sadly often. Remember, I was sixteen
when Mr Tidmarsh chose me and he was nearly fifty. The
difference was extreme. My looks were gentler then, very
attractive to the opposite sex – I had not such a tart tongue.
Men looked at me and thought me captured by a Bluebeard,
they wished to take me in their arms and comfort me. I met
many gentlemen like that, both here and on the Continent
– married young gentlemen, just like Frank Churchill, who
loved their wives dearly but who did not have the stamina
to stay at home.'

'That is shocking!' cried Emma.

'Yes. It is. The Franks of this world love strongly, very

strongly, I do not deny them that, but it is a shallow sort of love which does not hold them rooted. I called Frank "amusing" yesterday. Do you remember?'

'That you find him amusing is obvious.'

'He is amusing; he amuses me; I enjoy his company, his youth, his handsome face and charming manners – he is, after all, five or six years younger than I, indeed he is my son's age, to be sure – but I can see also that he very likely is a scoundrel.'

'A scoundrel!' echoed Emma. If Mrs Tidmarsh thought that, then she need give no further warning.

'So you have no need to worry. If I dance every dance with Frank at the Sucklings' Ball – if that should ever take place, which I begin to doubt,' here she gave Emma a cheerful smile, 'if I danced every dance with Frank, took sherbet in the garden with him and drove home with him alone in a closed carriage, it would still mean that I found him amusing but knew him to be a scoundrel!'

On this note their conversation on the subject of Mr Churchill was closed. Emma was made fairly easy and was able to inform Mr Knightley, somewhat coldly, that she had delivered his warning to Mrs Tidmarsh who had received it as something of which she was already apprised.

'She likes him because he is amusing,' Emma asserted. To which Mr Knightley responded in an ironic tone, 'I had thought Mrs Tidmarsh too clever to be satisfied with what is merely "amusing".'

The days that followed were rendered flat by the arrival of a letter from Mrs Elton – delivered by Mr Elton in person – regretting that, owing to her own indisposition, she had had to put off the Sucklings for a fortnight but with the news that two weeks on Friday was fixed for the ball. Mrs Cole had assured her that the weather being that much finer in the month of May – as it would be by then – would make it possible to open the doors to the terrace which would ensure greater space and dignity to the proceedings.

Unfortunately this was read out in the hearing of Mr Woodhouse who could hardly believe his ears and held up all conversation for some time with his admonitions to Mr Elton on opening doors to a garden sure to be damp. Mr Elton was so concerned with describing the depths of Mrs Elton's affliction which combined headache, heartburn, sore throat, difficulty with breathing, that it eventually diverted Mr Woodhouse from the subject of doors. Such symptoms in one generally known throughout Highbury as stronger than a dray-horse so surprised Emma that, after Mr Elton had removed himself from the house with a parting shot of, '—her pain so intense that we could not receive the Sucklings, however much they might plead—' she turned to Philomena with the comment, 'I do suspect it is the Sucklings who have cancelled and Mrs Elton's dreadful illness is entirely because she cannot bear the shame of admitting she has been spurned yet again.'

'I believe you have hit on it, my dear. Although I am sorry to see you grown cynical. For my part, I worry our gowns will be quite out of style before this ball takes place! I shall be happy enough, however, for I have vowed to neglect my harp no longer and practise each day for at least three hours. God-given talents must never be spurned.'

Mrs Tidmarsh was as good as her word in the days that followed, and disappeared every day, by foot, to Highbury whence she returned with every symptom of hard musical exercise, and retired to her room for a rest before dinner. Mr Tidmarsh returned once more by post to London – after promising to be back again well before the Sucklings' Ball (although nobody believed that was his reason for returning) and Mr Knightley was, in his usual way, daily from the house.

Since Miss Bates was as assiduous for Mr Woodhouse's

happiness as ever, Emma was left much to her own devices, and finding her self-respect in need of raising – she could hardly remember the days when she held a very good opinion of herself – she spent many hours in taking succour to the cottagers. The poorest members of the Highbury community were surprised by such sudden eager attention from Mrs Knightley but agreed among themselves that marriage had made her a listless benefactress, although her poor humour did nothing to alter the taste of her potato and mutton soup or the feel of the flannel cloth she brought. The older women gossiped that after one year and six months of marriage – it was the only sort of arithmetic they had mastered – and her such a particularly healthy young lady and Mr Knightley so much older (even if he did not look it) – it was no wonder she seemed wan. 'Why, any one of us would have popped two little 'uns before she's even got herself one!'

The not unsympathetic looks of these simple women perhaps conveyed some of their judgement to its subject for, as Emma wandered home on a day that, despite the month of May only just being broached, was almost too hot, she found herself, for the first time, questioning whether her childlessness was due to some internal deficit in her or whether her own lack of enthusiasm and the difficulties that had arisen between her and Mr Knightley (which she could not see clearly and therefore could see no end to) were acting as a natural control. She did not know and had no one to ask. Nor, except that she did not want to live with a sense of failure in any area, did she feel any increase in her desire to be a mother. Consciously picturing Mrs Weston and Isabella, both lost to her under a welter of progeny (and unconsciously seeing the glories of Harriet Martin's triumphant maternal beauty), she could not think the world needed her to increase and multiply. On the other hand, the cottagers' looks were pitying and had become more pitying in her imagination as she reached the Hartfield drive. Perhaps, odious idea, they considered her like Mrs Elton who wore her childlessness as if she feared God had taken the trouble to strike her barren – Oh such pompous self-pity!

With such uncomfortable thoughts Emma hesitated to open her own front door. The only good thing, she gave a wry smile, was that she had not even considered the problem of Frank Churchill for at least fifteen minutes.

'Emma! My dear!'

She turned to Mr Knightley's voice. He was standing by the bench which ran round the large beech tree at the bottom of the garden. He had obviously just risen and stood expectantly. As she went to him, her heart, which sometimes seemed to know things she forgot, beat happy and quick.

Over the bright grass tripped Mrs Knightley, her gown pale as she entered under the shadows of the tree, her cheeks rosy, as Mr Knightley, carried away by her beauty, the warm air, or whatever thoughts he had been turning over in his head as he sat on the old wooden bench, enfolded her in his arms.

Peace, perfect peace! They sat and Emma laid her head on his shoulder. If only they could lie like this at night – but then – Ah, there were too many thoughts—

'I have been at Donwell Abbey today,' said Mr Knightley, 'to meet Mrs Hodges and Harry; they have come back in some distress.'

'Mrs Hodges? Harry?' murmured Emma, hardly wanting a conversation about such dull-sounding people.

'My housekeeper and her son who I turned off when I came to Hartfield.'

'I remember. You found them another post.'

'Yes. That is just it. Mr Williams, their employer, has decamped without warning – with money owing them.

They ask me whether they can live at Donwell or in a cottage for just the price of their keep.'

'Have you answered them?' Emma sat up and stared at the dappling light dancing all around.

'I wished to ask you first for your view. Emma—?' He broke off but the appeal in his eye told the story. He wanted there to be a way for them to move back into Donwell – eighteen months was enough for him. He wanted his own house, his own servants, his own life. Emma understood him. Yet she looked away – how the light jigged and bobbed! She pictured Donwell, that venerable old house, the room in which they would sleep, the great four-poster, the dark panelling, the long corridors outside, the echoing dining hall with its portraits of Knightleys from centuries before, the old-fashioned kitchen and housekeeper's room where she would sit with Mrs Hodges – not an easy woman, as few are who have looked after a bachelor for years. She saw the simple shape of Hartfield beyond the shrubberies, its clear lines, quite like a doll's house, its regular, large windows that let light in at every time of the day. She had lived her whole life there, its simple, unpretentious elegance was part of her, needed no thought.

'Donwell is in need of a great deal of attention,' she said slowly.

'It is – the damp, the fire.' He hastened on from that, 'it is becoming a sad place.'

'Oh, Knightley – I know I said the other day—' she paused. He would not ask her direct, it was all up to her. She could almost wish that they had gone to Donwell straight away after their marriage. Perhaps everything would have been different. Yet now, to go there now, to be with him alone in that vast gloomy house – Abbey – with the echoes of so much history – to be with him there in the estrangement that was so often between them – to have no one else between them as they sat at either end of that long oak table – she could not do it! It would be too miserable, too lonely—

'I fear dear papa would never consent to leaving Hartfield.' Now she had admitted she knew what was in his mind.

'I had thought – Miss Bates—'

'Oh, Miss Bates!' – everything was in Emma's voice.

'I see.' Knightley stood. Turned away from her.

'But you should take on Mrs Hodges and Harry. It will safeguard the house from any further – intruders.'

'Intruders. Yes. I will take your advice.' Their conversation was at an end. They left the garden and entered the house where Mr Knightley took a cup of coffee and soon after left. Later a message came that they should proceed into dinner without waiting for him as he would be back late. However, Emma found he had left a folded paper for her in her upstairs parlour; it was an invitation from Mrs Martin to attend dinner at Abbey-Mill Farm, 'to inaugurate the dining parlour just completed'.

Ah, thought Emma, for the Martins everything is new, bright and fresh; they can look forward to an increase in happiness every moment of the day. Knowing Mr Knightley would not countenance a refusal to such an event, she sat down at her desk immediately and wrote a most gracious acceptance on behalf of herself, Mr Knightley, Mrs Philomena Tidmarsh and the Reverend Dugobair Tidmarsh. At least she could be content that it would give nothing but pleasure to the latter.

34

'Not a lofty room. The proportions are of the very smallest parlour at Maple Grove!' Mrs Elton's voice could be heard pronouncing, as the party from Hartfield were shown through the front part of Abbey-Mill to its recent extension. The carrying power suggested its owner had recovered remarkably in the space of a day from such a severe indisposition as her 'Mr E.' had described.

'Your surmise was correct.' Philomena nudged Emma.

'You are too critical, my dear.' Mr Elton's voice came now. 'The Martins have no wish to aspire to the architectural distinction and amplitude of your dear sister's abode. This room will charmingly fill their – er – smaller needs. Is that not so, Mrs Martin?'

Harriet Martin tried to suggest she thought it a very large room – a church hall of a room – without disagreeing with her guests – a task quite beyond even her powers of amiability so that, after a few false starts of, 'We are so pleased—' leading nowhere, Robert Martin continued with, in Emma's view, polite restraint but nevertheless firmness, 'We consider the room perfect.' Then the attention could be turned to the new visitors.

Harriet came up in a rush of nervous excitement. 'We are so very honoured – I scarcely dared hope – Without Mr Knightley's encouragement—'

These were the very words to make Emma, whose determination to like and admire had been encouraged by Mrs
Elton's insufferable conceit, nearly forget her resolution.
Hiding her discomfort, she turned to the large picture
window and remarked with hard-fought-for good humour,
'You have a most delightful vista.' Indeed the late-afternoon
sun glowed over the apple trees which were carpeted
around with pale fallen petals and beyond, she could just
discern the river and the trees that hid Donwell Abbey.

'Yes. It is quite delightful.' Harriet was grateful and was
soon joined by Mr Martin and old Mrs Martin so that
they stood in a row surveying the view. Behind them the
Eltons could be heard finding new ways of diminishing the
proportions of the room, but the Martins did not listen. It
was Mrs Knightley's approbation they most wanted. Mr
Knightley had already seen and commended.

'It is the way up to Donwell,' recommenced Harriet timidly as Mrs Knightley's silence became a little pronounced.

Emma turned round and stated with a finality which
overcame the Eltons' imprecations, 'Your room is a great
success, Harriet, I congratulate you!'

'Oh, thank you, thank you!' She gazed about her, saw the
awkwardness of people standing in a room that had nothing
but one table and eleven chairs – somewhat unmatched, as
Emma noticed. 'We must dine at once, I fear, for such a
large party will hardly squeeze into any other room.'

'I think Mrs Martin will not stop with one room,' said Mrs
Tidmarsh to Robert Martin beside whom she was standing.
Mr Martin laughed, 'It is her money so she may do as she
pleases.'

The words, spoken quietly enough, happened to fall into
a silence as people found their places at table; no one
could fail to hear. Harriet blushed deeply, the two Martin
sisters blushed lightly, old Mrs Martin who was supervising
dishes burnt her finger, although only at seeing Harriet's

discomfiture; Mr and Mrs Elton exchanged glances in which the word 'vulgar' was writ in the air between them, Mr Knightley stared ahead with a stoic impassivity and Emma, seated first, stared at her plate as if its poorly executed decoration of a rose in bloom held the answer to the meaning of the universe. Only Mr Tidmarsh and Elizabeth Martin, finding chairs together as if by right, showed no signs of any emotion beyond perfect happiness.

As is so often the case, a disturbing happening such as this was followed by an exuberance of conversation which set off the dinner to a great beginning. The food, though inelegant, was fresh and plentiful and the view from the window remained delightful, as Emma, who was sitting opposite it, continually remarked.

Mrs Elton, seated by Mrs Tidmarsh, remained in critical mood. 'I wonder they did not invite Mr Churchill to make up the numbers – but I suppose that a table meant for eight that already holds eleven can hardly be expected to fit twelve! Mrs Suckling never sits down less than fourteen. It is her lucky number, she says, but I say everything at Maple Grove is lucky.'

'Perhaps they sat down one short of fourteen at table on the evening the ceiling fell in on them?' suggested Emma, who had heard the conversation from the other side of the table.

'Oh, Mrs Knightley!' cried Mrs Elton, whose most salient characteristic was an unwavering confidence when anyone else would have felt foolish, 'the falling ceiling – and wall – was not a question of lucky or unlucky, as I explained to you before, that was an Act of God. The luck was that they all got out safe and sound without a scratch – and Mr Suckling with the sauce-boat aloft in his hand. That was so lucky as to be almost a miracle!'

Admitting herself defeated, Emma listened instead to Dugobair Tidmarsh, who was explaining to Elizabeth the biblical use of numbers as applied to generations. 'You are so very much cleverer,' he said, 'than my parishioners who, even after a full hour's sermon on the subject, still cannot answer the simplest quiz I put to test them. They remained quite bewildered by the inspiring line, "And all the days of Methuselah were nine hundred sixty and nine years: and he died". I fear St Peter's is very cold and it dulls their senses.' The subject of the proper temperature for churches – neither too warm so that the worshippers might doze in their comfort, nor too cold so that their brains no longer functioned – then kept them very animated for long enough for Emma to lose interest as to whether they found agreement, although she was perfectly certain they would.

She turned, therefore, to Mr Martin who was sat on her other side and was informing Mr Elton that they were expecting Mr Churchill after dinner when they were planning some musical entertainment. So Frank's absence, the chief virtue of the evening as far as Emma was concerned, would not be for much longer.

'We will be very squeezed in the parlour, I fear,' Harriet was saying to Mr Knightley, but the rest of the sentence – a sentence which caused Mr Knightley to smile (how Emma disliked that smile!) – Emma could not catch. Up till now, she had managed to resist thinking about Harriet who, quite properly, had placed her principal guest on her own right. They were not in her eye-line but on the same side of the table, so there could be no repetition of that terrible evening at the Westons' but, from now on – after that smile she had caught as his face turned – she could not stop herself from trying to catch their every word, entirely commonplace as any she did hear, turned out to be.

Dinner, however, was not long-drawn-out since old Mrs Martin was used to serving busy, active people and had no idea of prolonging a meal for conversation. Soon they were in the parlour and Elizabeth at the piano while chairs brought from the now-christened extension were fitted into every other corner. Meanwhile, almost unannounced, Frank was among them and sitting close to Philomena.

Emma looked at Mr Knightley. Was it worth asking that they leave early and send the carriage back for the Tidmarshes? She did indeed whisper it, as Elizabeth began to play and Dugobair raised his voice in what sounded very like an ode of his own making; 'O dark lady whose voice is like music, whose fingers are whiter than any key and who holds the key to my heart—'

'We must give the Martins fifteen minutes more,' he returned.

So they sat quietly and listened to what indeed was a most touching concert, although Mrs Elton was heard to say with her usual clarity of diction, 'I do dislike this modern music extremely, it is so painful to an ear as educated as mine!', and Frank and Philomena began to be very amusing together. Emma had time to look at her friend and think that the cleverness and independence of manner which she had so admired did not look so clever when conjoined with Frank Churchill. Ten minutes had passed when Dugobair stood down and Churchill took his place. It was all done so quickly that Emma could not now take her leave without appearing impolite.

She must therefore listen to Churchill singing, with all self-consciousness for the heroic posture, 'The Soldier's Lament' and 'Robin Adair'. His light tenor as she knew from before was agreeable enough, but his complacency as to his good impression on his audience, beyond bounds.

'Shall we go now?' whispered Emma – too late, yet again.

'And now I shall sing a special favourite of our hostess.' Taking up the even more strutting pose of a coxcomb (or so Emma thought, and was quite certain Mr Knightley felt the same, if not more so), Frank struck up with 'The Yellow-haired Laddie'.

How had he known? It was an insult – a challenge, for he sang the song as a mockery, with a smile on his lips and the words emphasised so that the sentiment became ridiculous.

'He makes it ridiculous,' hissed Emma to Mr Knightley.

'He makes himself ridiculous,' replied Knightley.

But at last Frank too stood down to such approbation from Mrs Elton that her hands seemed like cymbals. Emma stood; Mr Churchill bowed, smirking for the applause; Mr Knightley stood.

'You are not going!' cried Frank. 'You cannot be offended that I have stolen your song!'

'I own no song,' said Mr Knightley quietly, although there was a bustle now of Harriet ordering tea and Elizabeth being besought by Dugobair to return to the piano. 'You are superior to us all, Miss Martin.'

Above it all, Frank raised his voice, 'I have heard Mr Knightley has a fine singing voice, although it has not been my good fortune to hear it. Perhaps he may be persuaded?'

'I am afraid we must leave,' said Knightley, but since he would not deign to lie with an excuse, his words did not have much force.

'Mr Knightley sing!' cried Mrs Elton. 'That would be a joy indeed. May I ask if you are a bass? I am sure you are a bass!' Eagerly, she scanned his face as if the sign of the bass note were there instead of an excellent straight nose.

'Baritone, ma'am,' said Knightley.

'Mr Knightley has the most perfect baritone in the world,' said old Mrs Martin coming into the room from one of her forays.

'Perfect baritone, is it!' exclaimed Frank Churchill, with a jeering face, and Emma, pink and pale by turns, thought she heard a laugh from Philomena, although when she turned, her face showed nothing more than polite expectancy.

'What do you like to sing, Mr Knightley?' asked Mr Tidmarsh, who seldom felt atmospheres and was genuinely interested in what his admirable new friend would choose. 'Elizabeth will play for you.'

'As she has before,' said Mrs Martin proudly.

'I never sing in public,' said Knightley shortly, looking for Emma so that they might leave.

'I never thought to see a Knightley show the white feather,' said Frank Churchill to the one nearest to him who happened to be Robert Martin, who moved away at once. But his tone was only a pretence of confidentiality and was perfectly audible, in the little parlour, to Mr Knightley and to almost everyone else.

'Do, please, Mr Knightley, let others hear your voice!' cried Harriet, and just at that moment, Mr Knightley took a step towards the pianoforte.

'Just one,' said Knightley, looking at Elizabeth who came to him at once.

'Capital!' cried Mr Elton.

'*Cara sposa*, be seated!' ordered Mrs Elton, the Italian in her rising to the music. They all took seats – Mr Churchill with such a look of smugness that a cat would envy.

Mr Knightley and Elizabeth conferred; a place was found in her book. Knightley took up a position where his eyes, as Emma could see, rested on the view over the river which the small window in the parlour also overlooked. 'I shall sing,' he said, "Oh the Hours I Have Passed in the Arms of My Dear".'

There came an inelegant snort from Mr Churchill and an elegant 'Bravo!' from Mrs Tidmarsh; and the piano took the tune.

Emma, whiter than the mist stealing over the river, clenched her fists so hard that the nails cut into her palms.

She had never seen Knightley look more romantic, more handsome, but how would his voice be? Surely he would not have answered Frank's silly challenge unless he was sure of his powers?

She had not long to wait. Mr Knightley opened his mouth and the only fear that remained about his musical ability was that the beauty of his singing would make the tears roll down her cheeks. His voice was indeed perfect, strong, warm, clear; Frank's light tenor seemed insipid by comparison, as shallow as the man himself.

'If only', thought Emma, and now the room was utterly still as everybody listened – even Frank kept quiet – 'if only I could be certain that he had decided to perform before Harriet asked him to!'

The song finished. Dugobair roused himself first. 'It is pity you are a gentleman, or you could have been a singer.'

Mr Knightley smiled and put Emma on his arm. He took the compliments that accompanied their departure modestly. 'I sing once a year,' he said, 'but when I was eighteen, nineteen, twenty, I took it very seriously. As I fell away from my best, I grew to dislike the sound of my voice.'

'That is often the case with talented musicians,' agreed Mrs Tidmarsh. After all, the party was breaking up and they would all travel to Hartfield together.

Churchill was off, particularly quick to leave, making as excuse his ride back by horse and the darkening sky.

The carriage came – more thanks – more politeness – farewells – and through it all Mr Knightley's voice, so melodic, so moving, sang in Emma's head.

The journey to Hartfield which Emma might have wished to spend alone with this new husband she had discovered, was passed by Mr Tidmarsh closely questioning Mr Knightley on his musical education and discovering that, for light relief, Mr Knightley had always had a particular fondness for Irish airs, one of which he had sung that night. Emma said nothing; Mrs Tidmarsh said very little which, for her, was less than nothing; and so they arrived back just as the sky finally became black.

To their surprise Mr Woodhouse met them in lively form. 'You should not have stirred. I have often told you that home is the most agreeable place, have I not? And tonight, by stirring yourselves, you have missed a visit from Mr John Knightley!'

Mr Woodhouse was triumphant; Mr and Mrs Knightley were duly sorrowful; and Mr Tidmarsh and Mrs Tidmarsh were politely regretful.

35

Tea was brought in, biscuits too, because the Martins would not know about biscuits as thin as wafers – and no one could go to bed until Mr Woodhouse had told them every detail of Mr John Knightley's news which amounted, in Emma's view, to very little, beyond the happy assurances of close-fitting windows and doors and a cook who made excellent egg puddings. However, he did let slip that John had brought a letter from Isabella for Emma and from that moment she longed to be quietly in her room. A sister's voice – a sister, moreover, who, with fewer natural resources of mind or spirit, had faced far greater difficulties than she, Emma, was ever likely to – must be just the accent to put her own troubles in proportion. Mr Knightley would not go bankrupt, was never ill-humoured and loved her to at least some degree – as a sensible, affectionate older brother perhaps; Frank Churchill would – must – leave Highbury sooner rather than later; at some time she and Knightley would remove to Donwell; it was inevitable, as inevitable, she thought with a lowering of spirits, as her choosing to become Mrs Knightley; – but of her own feelings she did not wish to take account.

At last the party broke up and Emma immediately took a candle and the letter to her upstairs parlour.

My dearest Emma, John's visit gives me the excuse to write; I shall find the time for a long letter, knowing he will be away for a day or two and I can catch up with my tasks. I am lucky, perhaps, that the house is so small, for now that I have only three servants – although the maid of all works does enough for three on her own – I am lucky in that too – there is never a moment when I am not called on for some duty or another. But, and I thank God for it, the children here are all very well and healthy – you would hardly recognise the baby, she is so round. I cannot speak about my dear Henry and John who, as you know, have already been a month away at school – thanks to your Mr Knightley's generosity. I know it was time that they learnt independence from their mamma – John tells me this every day – but I cannot but suffer under such a separation, my only consolation is that the two boys are together and I rely on one to tell me if the other has any illness or unhappiness. You, dear Emma, cannot conceive of the torture endured by a mother when her first babies—

here Emma thought of the tough rumbustiousness of her nephews with a smile—

are away from you, in another's care; it is a constant misery and, since I must keep merry for the other children during the day, I cry myself to sleep every night. Ah, there are some advantages to the childless state! Happier to relate is my dear husband's dedication and sweet temper—

Emma raised an eyebrow at this descripton of her sardonic brother-in-law. Can he have changed so much?

You would scarcely believe what a help to me he is with

the children, when his work permits. He was even up in the night with the baby – I could not wish for anyone to endure what he has endured over the last months and I cannot but record that his nature, although always excellent, has now become almost saintly. Mrs Campbell who was here the other evening – my dear John even allows me a visitor more than once a fortnight – remarked on the change at once. 'You have a saint for a husband, I see!' she commented – or something to that effect, when he brought in the tea things as I had let the maid out for an hour. 'I only wish my poor Jane had married such a gentleman, instead of the person she did!' She was referring of course to Mr Churchill and I, naturally enough, mentioned to her that he was now lodging at Highbury. At which her face – I said to John afterwards that I wished the subject had never arisen, it gave her such pain that I was fearful of apoplexy.

It transpired that, although Mrs Campbell had always known Frank had not been kind to a lady she loved almost as a daughter, and she had her suspicions of worse – she had recently visited old Mr Churchill – he is not expected to live long, she reported – who told her that Mr Frank Churchill – of course I never knew him as you did – that Frank Churchill – too shocking almost to write down in a Christian home full of little children – spent his time in London with a woman already married (Mr Churchill did not divulge her name) who added to the two children she already had with her husband – a lax man by all accounts – by the sum of a pair of twin boys which she did not bother to disguise (although she had no intention of leaving her husband) belonged to Mr Churchill.

At this Emma must put aside the letter for a moment such was her shocked surprise. But in a moment it was taken up again and her eyes racing over the pages.

This birth, a month or so premature, took place just a week before his poor wife also gave birth. No one knows if she was aware of the situation but it seems only too likely that the woman's boast of two husbands at the same time and now two children at the same time – reached her – perhaps by the Godless woman herself. Is it not a terrible story? Even though my heart is as soft where children are concerned as it is hard on such immorality, I could scarcely blame myself for crying, 'Thank God!' when Mrs Campbell concluded this sorry tale by the information that the twin boys – welcomed by the immoral husband as his heirs since both previous children were girls – have since died. There is some justice, I said, adding, as I thought of their innocence – they may be cherubs in heaven.

I then told Mrs Campbell of your reports of Jane's son, his good health and energy; that cheered. But she would come back to the father, to Frank Churchill. I believe she was seriously worried that he would do more damage among the ladies of Highbury! He is so charming, she said, so handsome, so amusing. I made no comment at this for it seemed she was debating to say something further. What is it? I asked. Old Mr Churchill promised me to secrecy but I cannot feel he is right; and if it is known, it will make Frank Churchill seem far less charming, handsome and amusing. Surely a knowledge of his behaviour – and Mr Churchill has not forbade you that – I said, should take those attributes from him? 'But there is something even more decisive.' 'What?' says I. She took a breath. 'The knowledge that old Mr Churchill has entirely cut his wicked nephew from his will! Once that is known, his charm, his looks and his wit will be very much less obvious.' Oh Emma! I could say nothing to her, but bow my head. He has brought it on himself – yet what a punishment! To be lifted to the heights of a great house and an estate and then thrown down, on to nothing – as I understand it, literally nothing! I could almost feel sorry for him, with my dear John's experiences so recent – except then I think of his poor wife – not just penurious, but dead.

What a world we live in! What a world for my poor children to grow up in! I think of Highbury as a kind of Arcadia but even paradise had its snake! So beware, my dearest, and if you feel it necessary to pass on the news of the alteration in Frank Churchill's circumstances – if, for example, someone is thinking him too charming – then, remember, he does not know his disinheritance himself yet. He does not come near Mr Churchill who has done so much for him and who is approaching the end of his life, so Mr Churchill does not inform him. As Mrs Campbell says, what conceit and arrogance he must possess, that he could not consider the possibility of this when he cannot bother to pay the smallest attention to a man who has been, for most of his life, his *father!* Mrs Campbell was so very upset after our conversation that I persuaded her to some of papa's gruel which she pronounced 'very interesting' and assured me that even a spoonful was enough to set her to rights. She described it as 'better than hartshorn' which I found strange but put it down to her emotional condition.

The letter did not even end here; however the name of Frank Churchill, Emma could see from a quick scanning, did not figure again. It seemed that Frank Churchill was far, far worse than her wildest imaginings. The only mitigation she could see was the genuine distress she had seen in him when he was hiding at Donwell the previous year. Obviously sorrow, of which she still believed him capable, had been compounded by a heavy load of guilt. No wonder he had been mad, no wonder he had fled; it showed, at least, that he was not so hardened in his immorality that he could not feel. He *had* felt. When he had clutched at her, held her on the banks of the river so that she could feel the warmth of his body, the strong beating of his heart, he had been a man filled with desperate misery. But that did not exonerate his guilt for his past ill treatment of Jane nor for his present neglect of old Mr Churchill.

Mrs Campbell was right; the punishment fitted the crime. Frank Churchill, poor, might have a chance of salvation.

Emma looked up. She had sat long at her desk; she was cold, the small fire out; yet Mr Knightley had not come to her. Her head was too filled now with the news imparted in the letter to understand why he should be leaving her like this. Was he ashamed at having sung at the request from Harriet? She could think no more.

She proceeded into her bedroom and was unsurprised to see that the bed stood empty. Knightley must already have gone to his room – without even bidding her good-night. She held the letter still; she could not wake him with it and yet he would leave early— On the other hand, he already thought so ill of Frank that it would hardly change his opinion. Poor Westons! thought Emma, her thoughts still disordered as she prepared herself for bed. She would do without Merry who was too curious a girl. How would the Westons bear such a disgrace to their heroic Frank! She could not think of that either. As she lay in bed, she began to wish that Mrs Campbell had not called on Isabella and that Isabella had not broken her usual rule of talking about nothing but her children. Ignorance, or at least partial ignorance – for she knew Frank Churchill was not good – would have been easier. Her last idea, as she found a sleep more troubled than restorative, was that she should consider giving Philomena the news of Mr Churchill's changed financial prospects as soon as she found her alone on the morrow; at least she could test out Mrs

Campbell's view that a man's power to amuse is graded in accordance with the size of his income.

Unfortunately for the chances of this plan, Emma slept late and Philomena left early for Highbury. Instead Emma found herself in the company of Dugobair who was reading the Bible – the Old Testament, as Emma soon discovered – in the drawing-room. Now and again he could not restrain a line or two bursting from him, after which he started in surprise at these words filling the room – quite as if they had nothing to do with him – and then, assuming responsibility, apologised profusely. It was after he had cried, 'My father hath chastised you with whips, but I will chastise you with scorpions!' that she felt moved to introduce the subject of Frank, and of Philomena's attitude towards him. She could think of no cleverer way – for her head ached that morning – than to set off quite plainly with a question.

'How do you think Philomena likes Frank Churchill?' – a blush came over her cheeks.

'How?' repeated Dugobair, head over the First Book of Kings, Chapter 12. But the echo of her words came back to him before she managed a repetition and he answered, quick and intelligent: 'My stepmother has many virtues – she is clever, an excellent musician, an inspiring teacher, an energetic friend – but she does not *like* men.'

'What?' exclaimed Emma, taken aback.

'That is what you asked, is it not? Whether my mother likes Frank?'

'Yes – I—'

'My answer is just, although I speak of her attitude to all men, not just Mr Churchill. Philomena may enjoy a man's company if he makes her gay; if he is handsome enough he appeals to her eye, as a picture might; if he seeks her out, she will not repulse him. But she will not *like* him. She makes, perhaps, a small exception for me – she is truly fond of me, I believe – but I am outside the normal race of man,

I am her stepson; besides, my awkwardness with the world makes her think me not quite masculine.' He gave Emma a fixed look. 'In this she is wrong. But so far it has not been necessary to disabuse her.'

'Oh!' said Emma, quite amazed at the crispness of Dugobair's analysis – he who usually seemed so remote from a knowledge of the basely human.

'So you see she cannot *like* Frank Churchill – or at least no more than she likes a well-trimmed bonnet or a string of amber beads. Have you not wondered why my mother, a young good-looking woman, has never married again?'

'It has not been so long since your father's death – and her very deep attachment—'

'Deep attachment!' Mr Tidmarsh shut the Bible with a clap. 'Will you be shocked with the truth?'

'The truth can never be shocking,' said Emma virtuously, although curiosity inspired this encouragement and she suspected she might be very shocked indeed.

'The first Reverend Tidmarsh, my father, God rest his soul – although I do not feel sanguine on that subject – married Philomena when she was scarcely sixteen. As you know, he plucked her from the Foundling Hospital; he called her "a lily among weeds". He married her; he taught her music; he took her to France, Italy, Switzerland. She was his – his plaything—'

'Oh!' said Emma faintly.

'—his servant, his mistress, his slave. He was her master. I was at school in England but whenever they returned, I saw how it was. He had bought her. She had no other life, no escape – he used her – no, I will say no more – his friends – no – let us just say, she was not happy. She learnt how to please him – every evening she played him to sleep with her harp – she learnt much from him – he was a brilliant man but he never allowed her to be anything but a poor foundling girl. She could not love him, she could not even like him; but she lived with him for ten years. You understand now. Philomena cannot *like* men – it is not in her nature as it was made for her by my father. I took refuge from him in books, in learning, Philomena had no real escape. When he died, she vowed never to marry again. Have I answered you?'

'Yes. Indeed, yes. I had not meant—'

'You did not want so much of an explanation. Philomena tells me I am long-winded. That is why she prefers women – ladies, like yourself. She says ladies speak so much more to the point – sensible ladies, that is, such as she sees you to be. She is very fond of you; but then you know that; you will have felt that. She *likes* you and she amuses herself with handsome Frank Churchill. I must stop. I have said enough.'

He had. Out of all that shocked and amazed Emma, she held on to one most important piece of information. Philomena had vowed never to marry again. In that case she need not tell her anything more about Frank. She could let events unravel naturally, without a hand from her. It was a relief and worth, on the whole, the sense of unease she had felt when Dugobair had protested how Philomena *liked* her. She was not sure she wanted to be liked with quite such intensity as was conveyed by his remark that Philomena had other female acquaintances whom she *liked* in the same way.

These thoughts made her increasingly uncomfortable sitting in the same room with Dugobair, bent once more over his Bible. So when he next uttered, 'There is death in the pot', followed soon after by, 'They found no more of her than the skull, and the feet, and the palms of her hands—', she did not wait for his apology but, muttering 'Parsley butter', fled from the room.

36 ∫

A student interested in the workings and perversities of fate and chance would not have been surprised that the event most often anticipated in Highbury over a period of nearly two years, took place at a time when expectation was at its lowest. The first Emma heard of it was when Merry, sent early to the shops, returned with face even redder than usual and cap strings undone.

'They have come! They have come! The Sucklings have come!' she panted out, standing in Emma's bedroom, for all the world as if King George himself was in Highbury.

She had seen them, she avowed, at Ford's; they had stopped to ask the way, blocking the whole street with a barouche-landau and a coach, although there were only two of them, without the servants.

'Surely you mean the Crown?' inquired Emma to regulate the wild flow. 'Everybody who passes through Highbury asks the way at the Crown. You mean they sent their servant into the Crown?'

'Begging your pardon, ma'am,' Merry puffed out a little for she knew she was in the right; furthermore, she was conscious of having been in just the right place at the right time. 'I was in Ford's myself, as you sent me for the trimming—'

'Yes. Yes.'

'—when Mr Suckling himself came in to ask the way to the Vicarage—'

Now Emma felt a great need to ask more – about his appearance, his behaviour, his importance, but Merry was determined to prove without doubt her absolute rightness. 'He was standing so near to me I could have touched him and when he'd got the directions – himself, not a servant – he bought a pair of York Tan gloves!' she ended on a note of triumph.

'York Tans!' exclaimed Emma. Well, Mr Suckling certainly knew how to make himself liked in Highbury. To buy a pair of gloves before he had taken more than two paces in the town! It was remarkable.

'Then a lady's voice called him from the coach,' continued Merry on a lower note since she knew her mistress well enough to see she was a perfect captive to her report. 'A jolly-sounding voice – not haughty like—'

This was a further surprise to Emma who had fixed on Mrs Selina Suckling as the most odious of creatures – any sister of Mrs Elton had to be that and the owner of Maple Grove must be far, far worse. She had, in her mind's picture, a tall bony lady with a nose as long as Philomena's but hawk-like rather than elegantly straight. She had endowed her with a vulgar, conceited manner, an overbearing nature and total self-confidence – all these things most usually expressed in a very ugly and haughty voice.

Despite it not being the thing to question a servant about a gentleman or lady, she could not resist the temptation. 'But how can you be certain it was Mrs Suckling if you did not see her!'

'Well, Mr Suckling called her "dearest heart", if that is reason enough,' said Merry, returning to her sulkiness.

'Thank you; I believe my hair is quite tidy enough for breakfast,' said Emma, sharply. 'And we will doubtless see the Sucklings for ourselves soon enough.'

'They will be breakfasting at the Vicarage now,' said Merry, recovering her excitement. 'They must have put up somewhere near last night to arrive so very early—'

'Thank you, Merry.'

Emma descended and of course nothing else but the Sucklings was talked of throughout breakfast which was attended by all those at Hartfield, including Mr Knightley, who had returned from his early ride to Donwell.

'I wonder that poor Mrs Elton had time to put on her best morning-gown with such long-expected visitors arriving so suddenly!' exclaimed Miss Bates, charitably concerned.

'It is most thoughtless of Mrs Suckling, most selfish,' said Mr Woodhouse. 'And York Tans, you say, just like that, over the counter, no forethought. They sound a most impulsive couple. Not at all what I should have expected. Poor Mrs Elton; she will be wishing they had not arrived if it goes on like this.'

'Surprise can scarcely be continued,' pointed out Emma.

'The ladies will be very pleased,' said Mr Knightley, looking at Emma properly for the first time that morning because he had previously been so taken up with bacon and kidneys. 'Emma will be able to wear that elegant dress I have seen in the wardrobe but not on her person.'

His smile, for some strange reason, made Emma's eyes fill with tears which must be blinked away hastily before anyone noticed.

'And at last my feathers can fly out of their wrappings!' cried Philomena.

Only Mr Tidmarsh, who had laid his large Bible carefully on a side table before taking an ample portion of ham and porridge (sitting strangely side by side on the same plate so that Emma suspected he thought the porridge was potato), seemed unmoved by the arrival of the inhabitants of Maple Grove. His face wore, indeed, a more than usually bewildered air and, eventually, after he had listened to a good fifteen minutes of conversation in which every sentence included the world 'Suckling', he asked politely, 'May I ask who are these Sucklings? I believe I have not had the honour of making their acquaintance in Highbury but I can see I am sadly out of luck. They must be remarkable people to hold your attention for so long. Miss Bates, I cannot help noticing, has not even finished her milk pudding.'

Mr Knightley laughed heartily at this. 'Do not make yourself unhappy, Dugobair. None of us know the Sucklings, although Mrs Elton has spoken of nothing else since her arrival here. Her power over us is so great that we would probably rather meet the Sucklings – although we all presume them to be quite vulgar and stupid – than anyone in England. Our interest, that you have noted so accurately, merely points to the strength of curiosity – which may yet become one of the deadly sins!'

'You are too hard on us, Mr Knightley!' cried Mrs Tidmarsh. 'It is the ball, Dugobair; you knew all about it a week ago. Until the Sucklings came, the Coles could not give their ball!'

'But surely the Coles may give a ball any time they please – with or without the Sucklings?' inquired Mr Tidmarsh innocently.

'A ball must have a reason, a *raison d'être* as the French would say. The Sucklings are the *"raison de danse"*.'

'It is very agreeable to see everyone so happy,' said Mr Woodhouse, 'I have never known a breakfast more sociable. I do declare it is more like a dinner, when I am always amazed by the way that even the quietest young ladies will put themselves out to speak – even venture opinions.'

'Oh, papa!' It was in this kindly-old-gentleman role that Emma could always love her father best. 'We must thank the Sucklings for this then, that they have turned a breakfast into a dinner.'

'And soon,' added Mr Tidmarsh, with his eye jealously

guarding his Bible from the servants clearing dishes, 'if I have understood the matter right, they will turn a dinner into a dance!'

After this summary of the beneficial effects of the Sucklings' advent, breakfast was concluded.

Emma, watching Mr Tidmarsh depart speedily with the good book cradled in both arms, and desirous of addressing Mr Knightley, commented, 'Mr Tidmarsh is most attached to that Bible.'

Knightley stopped beside her, looked into her face, 'It is from the Donwell library. A great old book. It has been in the family for generations.'

'I see.' Emma lowered her eyes, although she laid her arm on his sleeve. 'I wonder you let it out of the Abbey.'

'I like it to be read – and by such a one as Mr Tidmarsh.'

They began to walk together out of the dining-room and into the hall. Emma, feeling a sudden urge to cast herself into Knightley's arms – followed almost immediately by a wish to escape to the kitchen, upstairs, to the drawing-room – stayed quietly at his side. They were alone together in the hall but not private enough for Emma to say what was in her mind, 'Why did you not come to me last night?'

'I am glad you will have a ball to amuse you,' said Mr Knightley. 'You have not been in spirits lately.' It was a statement where she would have preferred a question.

So they parted.

It was inevitable that many of Highbury's worthiest inhabitants felt the necessity to take a walk – or a ride – into town that day. Emma and Philomena, one in urgent need of exchanging the trimming bought mistakenly by Merry (quite the wrong shade of sage) and the other determined to conquer an awkward rill on her harp (she was sure Frank would be outside his rooms early on such another fine day), set off arm in arm. They were soon joined by

Miss Bates, breathlessly exclaiming her need for a particular cherry twist with which she would mend Mr Woodhouse's favourite waistcoat.

'Can I not purchase it for you?' inquired Emma. 'I shall myself be in Ford's.'

'Oh dear me no! I have the colour fixed quite in my head. I could not trouble you—'

'You certainly cannot pass over your head to Mrs Knightley,' laughed Mrs Tidmarsh. 'I suspect we shall find Highbury remarkably full of life today.'

Indeed it was so. They had hardly reached the main street before Mr and Mrs Cole could be seen proceeding towards the Crown with excessively genial expressions.

'Mrs Knightley! Mrs Tidmarsh! Miss Bates!' Mr Cole hailed them from a distance. 'You have heard the news, of course! Mr and Mrs Suckling in town before the cock crowed thrice! Ha! We have already a note for dinner so that we may make plans for our ball – although in truth the plans have been in place for these many months!'

All this was said, or rather shouted, before the two parties had managed to close the gap. The moment they were near enough for the semblance of a confidential whisper, Mrs Cole took over from her husband, 'Poor dear Augusta – she was found in her rubbed yellow dress with an apron over it and her hair quite undressed. It is a terrible thing when you are caught out by your sister in an unladylike attire merely because you are an excessively conscientious housekeeper. She wrote me she was quite mortified!'

'We are off to the Crown,' continued Mr Cole. 'May I give at least two of you ladies an arm?'

The three ladies began explaining the reasons for their hastening into Highbury but Mr Cole – made forcefully gallant, perhaps, by his satisfaction in knowing he would in a day or two have the honour of looking after them in his own house – soon had Mrs Tidmarsh on one arm,

Emma on the other and Mrs Cole lined up with Miss Bates behind. 'Whatever your occupations, you cannot forego a quick inspection of the two carriages in which the owners of Maple Grove travelled. I must say it is a notion that amazed Mrs Cole and I. A carriage for each person. We wondered whether this is done in the best circles? Mrs Knightley, we told ourselves, would be assured to know of such a notion – if it were fashionable, that is!' – with which he turned inquiringly to Emma.

'The only reason I can suggest for such a separation is that Mr and Mrs Suckling do not enjoy each other's company over a long period,' replied Emma.

Mr Cole looked a little taken aback by this pronouncement which had a distinctly critical ring, but Mrs Tidmarsh laughed immoderately – a reaction explained when Emma saw Frank Churchill crossing the street towards them.

'Off to spy on the famous Sucklings' equipage!' was his happy cry. And soon he had taken Miss Bates and Mrs Cole on either arm and fallen in behind them.

Emma was beginning to feel distinctly ridiculous – even more so when, on arrival at the Crown, she found Mrs Goddard stopped with a string of pupils and saw Mr Weston approaching on his horse at a brisk trot. Dignity fought with curiosity and Emma found herself gathered with her friends in the inner courtyard, inspecting the modes of conveyance chosen by the owners of Maple Grove which – since she had never shown the slightest interest in discerning the peculiarities of one carriage from another in all her life up to that point – proved that Suckling fever was sweeping away even the most engrained habits of mind.

'They are fine enough carriages,' pronounced Frank generally, with the air of a man most fitted for judgement. 'But I always hold you cannot tell the quality of a carriage till you have the horses harnessed and are spanking down the turnpike. A carriage without horses is like a harp without a player.'

'So true! Absolutely!' Mr Cole relished the wit while Frank bowed to Mrs Tidmarsh and Mr Weston tapped the barouche-landau assessingly with his riding crop.

'But there are certainly two of them,' Miss Bates suggested timidly.

'Most definitely two,' agreed Mrs Cole, which was followed by a satisfying level of shared assurance that the two large objects shining brightly in front of them were indeed two carriages, to be more exact a barouche-landau and a chaise.

'Notwithstanding we see them standing here, I still find myself surprised that they should feel the need for two,' Mrs Cole frowned in illustration of her puzzlement.

'Perhaps they felt two would be useful since Mr and Mrs Elton do not possess one at all?' suggested Miss Bates and, finding many eyes turned her way and many minds engaged on estimating the possible truth of her statement, retreated nervously to the entrance to the courtyard.

Emma, too, had begun to think of leaving and was following Miss Bates when a magnificently large shadow was cast across the arched brightness of the street followed by a magnificently large gentleman. Seeing his way blocked by two ladies, and the courtyard quite filled with people as if for a party, he stopped and made noises of surprised affability; although these were mostly of one syllable and would not have been recognised by Dr Johnson as worthy for inclusion in his so-called English Dictionary, being of the 'Huh! Ho! Eh! Ah!' variety, amongst them was eventually pronounced the word 'Suckling', the hat removed and a wide bow made – wider than it was deep since his huge girth made folding-over an anatomical impossibility.

Emma, being nearest, understood what was not at once clear to the rest of the assembly. Here stood Mr Suckling in person – he of the York Tan gloves, of the collapsing house – his fortitude in keeping hold of the gravy-boat now, perhaps, explained. Mr Suckling might be the grandest of gentlemen, in his sister-in-law's eyes; he was also quite certainly the largest.

'A giant of a man!' as Mrs Tidmarsh laughed to Frank Churchill when, after such loud expressions of goodwill that the horses in the stable began to think the hunt was in town and stamped their feet excitedly, the Crown courtyard party broke up and the various groups set off for their various destinations. Sage thread, cherry twist and the difficult rill unaccountably forgotten, Emma, Miss Bates, Mrs Tidmarsh and Frank Churchill – the latter two arm in arm – turned their steps in the direction of Randalls so that they might share with Mrs. Weston all the details of their meeting with Mr Suckling. Mr Weston, on horseback, cantered ahead to inform his wife of their arrival. 'We want no rubbed yellow dress and apron in our house!' he cried.

Emma, walking with Miss Bates, listened to everything said around her, the anticipation of the ball now definitely set for two days hence, the repeated theme of Mr Suckling's size and obliging manner, so unexpected, calling forth all Philomena and Frank's store of wit, but she, herself, was silent. It was, in fact, a real pain for her to walk in such close proximity to a man about whom she knew such disgusting things. For the sake of the Westons, she must not divulge the truth of Frank's nature, but she would do all in her power to avoid his company. So resolved, when they reached the turning to Randalls, she unhooked her arm from Miss Bates and, murmuring excuses, instructed them as firmly as possible to go on without her. They went – their high spirits needing further social outlet – but not before Mr Churchill had tried to take Mrs Knightley's hand in farewell – and seen the hand snatched from him. They all saw it indeed, saw Emma's confusion and flushed face but no one, not even Mrs Tidmarsh, who usually did not follow the rule of ignoring awkwardness, made any comment.

'I wish he would go!' thought Emma as she hurried along her solitary path, with the image of questioning eyes in front of her. 'I wish he would take ship and go – go to Madagascar!' she thought, identifying the furthest-distant point she had ever heard of.

37

All Highbury's attention was now focused on the weather; not that they had suddenly become especially interested in the growth of the wheat, turnips or spring corn, but that they wished this summer sun and mildness to last through the night of the Sucklings' Ball.

Mr and Mrs Perry, Dr Hughes and Mrs Hughes, Mr and Mrs Ottway, Miss Ottway, Miss Caroline, Mr George, Mr Arthur, Mr William Cox, Miss Ann Cox – all had been invited, all talked of carriages, shawls and satins. At Abbey-Mill, Randalls and Hartfield, the conversation was much the same, with particular intensity at Hartfield where Mr Woodhouse's decision as to whether he would attend or not depended entirely on the glass, the moon, and the rising damp. It was understood that those at the Vicarage believed that the weather would stay fair and, in order to bolster confidence in the Coles who, as hosts, bore a heavy responsibility for the comfort of their guests and had therefore ordered a fire in every room – 'which will send us all to the devil' as Mrs Elton was reported to have commented – spent all their time with Mr and Mrs Cole. This, at least, was the reason given for no further appearance by Mr Suckling, nor any sighting at all of Mrs Suckling. 'A man of his size would not wish to stay long in the confin'd space of the Vicarage,' as Mr Weston explained to anyone who cared to listen. It seemed that the ball must open the Suckling season for which the Crown meeting had been a false start.

Emma looked forward to the ball with a mixture of excitement and dread. The excitement was natural in a young lady who had a new dress to show off and so seldom was given the opportunity to dance in elegant circumstances (she had quite disavowed her previous estimation of the Coles as 'tradespeople' and 'vulgar'). The dread arose out of a sensation, founded on nothing rational, but very strong all the same, that the ball would be a climax for many of her anxieties – about Frank, about Harriet, about Knightley.

'My dear – you are so lovely – I have never seen you so lovely.'

Mr Knightley stood behind her as she surveyed herself in the long glass. The golden satin dress, with its violet trimmings, caught the bright lights in her hair, turned her skin whiter, made her smooth tight waist smaller. She could not but acknowledge she was beautiful and was glad of it. She leant forward to pick up her string of pearls.

'I have something for you.' Knightley opened an engraved box and held it out to her. 'Our marriage was such a simple affair, so quick; but I would not have you any less impressive than Mrs Suckling,' he smiled a little.

A necklace of three diamond stars gleamed on a bed of blue velvet. 'There are single diamonds for your ears. They have not been worn since my mother died twenty-five years ago.'

As Emma did not speak but only looked, in truth, quite bewildered by the jewels, he lifted the necklace out and held it round Emma's neck. 'Remember,' he whispered, 'you are my wife and I am proud of you.'

Clasping the necklace, he lightly kissed her cheek and left the room.

Emma sat down, heart racing. What had he meant? There

had been a portentousness in his words, 'Remember, you are my wife,' and choosing this night after more than eighteen months of marriage to give her these diamonds whose existence she had not even suspected! What did it mean? She could not make it out and yet it increased her nervous anticipation.

The gathering in Hartfield's drawing-room, before the arrival of James with the carriage, had a theatrical air most unusual in that quiet country household. Only Mr Woodhouse, seated in his habitual place for he had decided to enjoy cards with Mrs Goddard rather than suffer the ball, presented an unchanged appearance. Mrs Tidmarsh and her stepson were already there when Emma descended. True to her word, Philomena was dressed as Boadicea in all but the feathers on her head which were dyed purple and were so tall as to nearly reach the ceiling. The purple matched her long velvet tunic which was topped with brass chain-mail. This had already caught the attention of Mr Woodhouse, who was so captivated by his guest (as a slave might have been tied to her chariot) that even this excess of costume was transformed under his admiring gaze. 'See, Emma dear, Mrs Tidmarsh wears so many necklaces that it almost covers her dress! Is that not a fashion as yet unarrived in Highbury!'

Emma agreed that such generosity of decoration was unknown in Surry and could say no more, for Philomena had seen the stars on her friend's breast and could not contain her appreciative exclamations. 'Who would wear more than one necklace if the one was such as that!'

So then Mr Knightley must explain their origin and Mr Woodhouse needed so much reassurance that they were not a new acquisition – although where he found this idea no one could understand – that Miss Bates was able to sidle in quite unnoticed. It was only Mr Tidmarsh's polite welcome, 'You are very fine, Miss Bates,' that made them turn.

'Who is that come in?' asked Mr Woodhouse, a little querulous with so much to confuse the calm of his
drawing-room.

'It is Miss Bates, papa,' Emma bent to her father, 'dressed
up to go to the ball.'

'Oh dear – I am sure – Oh dear – Mr Woodhouse – Mrs
Goddard here—' began Miss Bates, for her old friend was
already present. If she hoped by her usual fluster to distract
attention from her costume, it was not to be.

'Magnificent!' Mr Knightley bowed gallantly.

'I do declare, a bird of paradise!' cried Mrs Tidmarsh and
for certain there was a little silver feather on the top of Miss
Bates' turban.

'Oh dear – may I be of assistance – Mr Woodhouse – so
kind – perhaps I should not go – so far – so long—'

Emma could not help smiling a little at this since Miss
Bates had shown an extraordinary determination to attend
the ball – whether Mr Woodhouse came or not. 'You cannot
waste your brocade panels,' she advised. 'There will be
never be such an opportunity to give them an airing.'

'So good to me – dear Mrs Knightley – if you are certain
– Mr Woodhouse comfortable—'

It was certain that Mr Woodhouse could not be comfortable until he and Mrs Goddard were settled quietly at the
card table so the party proceeded to the carriage. Here
there was a small delay when it became clear that the
ladies' dresses and, in particular, Mrs Tidmarsh's head-dress,
needed more space than was available.

'We should have begged for Mr Suckling's barouche-
landau!' cried Philomena. 'I would have loved to sit in the
open and nod my feathers to Highbury! Come, Miss Bates,
admit it, you would have liked to show yourself off to the
crowd at the Crown!'

Luckily – as Emma thought – this was not possible and
the problem of space was solved by Mr Knightley and Mr

Tidmarsh electing to walk the distance. 'All your prayers have been answered,' said Mr Knightley, 'it is the finest evening imaginable. We pedestrians will have the best of the bargain.'

So it was that Emma descended from the carriage with no husband at her elbow, and the three ladies entered the Coles' house without a gentleman between them.

'We will wait to be announced,' said Emma, in decided tones, as they stood in the hallway quite surrounded by bowing servants, which made apparent the formality of the occasion. She needed Mr Knightley and Mr Tidmarsh to give a semblance of dignity to their party. They sat therefore in the hall; but the few minutes they had to wait before the arrival of their escorts proved even more painful to Emma than if she had entered the ballroom with Miss Bates looking like an over-upholstered *chaise-longue* on one side and Philomena looking like a Parisian actress on the other. For in a moment, the Westons had arrived and with them Frank Churchill who, smiling in the way a man does when he knows he is the handsomest and wittiest gentleman in the company, came straight to Emma and whispered in her ear, 'So your husband leaves you like a wallflower to wait around for him. Be careful someone does not ask you where to put his cloak!'

Emma felt anger heat her up like an oven; the only release would have been to hit him with her fan or kick or stamp on his toes. Since none of these were possibilities open to a well-bred lady, she hissed, 'You are a fool and a scoundrel!'

He met this with laughter even more infuriating and the comment, 'What *passion* for my little pleasantry!'

Perhaps fortunately for Emma's reputation, Mrs Tidmarsh joined them and it was agreed on Mr Churchill's offering his services so that they should go in together.

'The most amusing man in the room,' whispered Philomena to Emma, behind her fan, as they left.

'You will wait for Mr Knightley I have no doubt,' said Mrs Weston as Emma stood to greet her friends, 'but perhaps we may take in Miss Bates.'

'Oh no, – I do not think – Mrs Knightley on her own . . .' began Miss Bates, her words tailing away as she moved off on Mr Weston's other arm.

So Emma had a moment longer to compose herself and to feel all the joy of seeing Mr Knightley's arrival, tall, straight, kindly, a true gentleman.

'What is it, Emma?' he said at once. 'You seem upset.'

'No. No. Nothing.'

'Was that the Westons and Mr Churchill I saw in front of us?'

'Yes. They took Mrs Tidmarsh and Miss Bates.'

'I am glad you waited.'

'I would do no less. But where is Mr Tidmarsh?'

'He has seen the Martins' carriage and hovers like a dragonfly over water for Elizabeth. I believe we shall have an announcement there soon.'

'She will make an excellent vicar's wife,' said Emma as they began to move along. Now there were the Coxes to be nodded to and Emma's train to be lifted in one of her hands.

'I can guess exactly what you are thinking,' said Mr Knightley, just before they joined the company.

'Oh, what!' exclaimed Emma and her colour, which had just subsided, rose again. Could he have divined that Frank Churchill filled her thoughts?

'You are thinking that at long last we are going to have all our curiosity satisfied and will feast our eyes on the remarkable Mrs Selina Suckling.'

Emma need only nod agreement, for here was the welcoming party, a bustle of Coles and Eltons, the huge Mr Suckling and somewhere among them a sturdy little woman, with no pretensions to looks or elegance, who must be, who could be, no other – except she looked so little the part – than the haughty owner of Maple Grove, the arbiter of taste and fortune, the scion of Bristol and Bath, the toast of the Gloucestershire countryside, the lady whose prospective disappointment in the Knightleys' wedding arrangements had led her sister to call it 'a most pitiful business' (the words had been repeated by her maid in Ford's and therefore heard by all of Highbury) – this lady now, round features as undistinguished and cheerful as a seller of buns on a London street, stood in front of them. Or rather she moved immediately towards Emma and Mr Knightley and, in a high, rather squeaky voice, began with unaffected words of delight in, at last, meeting her 'dear sister's dearest friends'. Such an assumption, so far from the truth, might have caused Emma to adopt a hauteur of which she was perfectly capable. But this Selina Suckling was so modest, so ordinary, so humble even, that it would have been like trampling on a sparrow.

'Yes. We have expected your arrival over many months,' Emma smiled.

'Indeed. Perhaps you heard, our house suffered a partial collapse. I tell Mr Suckling it is the land. The land is soft and yet holds the water. Maple Grove is very ill-sited, I fear.'

'Maple Grove ill-sited!' exclaimed Emma, who been taught by Mrs Elton to believe her sister's house was the nearest thing to heaven on earth.

'Oh, yes!' bellowed the giant Mr Suckling, overhearing the end of the conversation. 'I tell Mrs Suckling we should rename the house Maple Grave. But she insists it a morbid joke! Maple Grave, eh! Grave instead of Grove!'

'We could have lost our lives – or the lives of our dear children,' began Mrs Suckling again, when her husband's pleasure at his witticism had diminished somewhat. 'My father, you know, was in the building trade so I know—'

'Mrs Knightley, Mr Knightley,' interrupted Mrs Elton

with shrill determination, 'Mr Cole wishes to escort you over to the drinks table—'

Emma obeyed; Mr Knightley took her arm again; they had seen Mrs Suckling and for a moment Emma had forgotten Mr Churchill in the pleasure of discovering that the Mrs Selina Suckling who had, through the medium of her sister, entered Highbury as a despot could now, in her own person, be counted as nearer in spirit to Miss Bates.

'We must begin the dancing,' said Mr Cole to Mr Knightley. 'I have engaged musicians, you know, from London. But if everybody stands around like this, we will never get more than half a dozen sets.'

'I suppose you must arouse your guests of honour to their duty,' suggested Mr Knightley tolerantly.

'Yes. Yes. It is a fix. I told Mrs Cole it would be a fix. You see, neither Mrs Suckling nor my dear wife dance any more; they plead shortness of breath.'

'And Mr Suckling?' inquired Emma, smiling. 'He certainly has the figure to make "A Trip to Highgate" all on his own.'

'If only the guests would finish arriving and we could start,' worried Mr Cole, looking towards where his wife, the Eltons and the Sucklings still held their ground by the door.

'Ah, the Martins have come up now,' said Mr Knightley.

Emma drew herself up and followed the direction of his gaze. There stood Harriet, silly, ignorant, sweet, spineless, Harriet who she had once patronised, encouraged, dropped and who was now rich, a mother and perhaps an object of her husband's admiration. How happy she would have been to see her dressed vulgarly, with foolish pretension, with the tassels, lace and brocade that made Mrs Elton so easy to despise! But Augusta Elton had few claims on good looks and Harriet was in the golden blush of her greatest beauty; she might become overblown in time but now Emma saw a sylph of silver and blue gauze, as elegant and tasteful as anything she could imagine and, by her newly educated, London experience, very fashionable and very expensive.

'Harriet looks – looks . . .' Emma was brave but Mr Knightley's expression was veiled to her; she could not tell what he thought and she let her words die away.

The line was now in the process of formation: Mr Cole was to lead off with Mrs Elton; Mr Suckling, it transpired, still wanted a partner. It became sadly clear to Emma that her fate was to dance the first set she had enjoyed for two years with a man who was more like a ship set on its stern than a human being. Her eyes implored escape from Mr Knightley but the ship was bowing in front of her (as far as he was able), and Knightley only said with a smile, 'Mrs Knightley and I will have the next. Pray, do not mind me, sir, I shall sit out or, if my feet insist on movement, find them another partner.'

The music, harpsichord, violin and cello, struck up and there were ten couples standing up. Emma, as keen to see what took place with the watchers as the dancers, saw Knightley join the Martins, kiss Harriet's hand (or had she imagined that?), saw Mr Tidmarsh gesticulate at Elizabeth who laughed, saw Mr Martin, a little uncomfortable in his tails, saw, as she changed places again, Mr Churchill dancing down the line with one of the Miss Coxes and Mrs Tidmarsh standing up with Mr Weston. She saw much but heard little, for either the shrill tones of the musicians or the heavy breath – gasping and wheezing and panting – of her partner, from whom perspiration flew like the spray from the prow of a ship, blocked her ears to any outside sounds.

It gave her a sense of remoteness which accorded with her earlier sense of dread.

'I have always admired the light step of a young lady,' croaked Mr Suckling in a slower passage.

Emma smiled politely. She could hear him but it meant nothing. The dance continued. The dance finished. Mr Suckling had survived, although his face was almost the colour of Miss Bates' brocade panels.

'Mrs Knightley returned safe and sound,' Mr Suckling handed Emma back before producing a large handkerchief and retiring behind a pillar.

'Mrs Knightley is such a graceful dancer!' exclaimed Harriet.

'I would love a glass of wine,' said Emma, fanning herself.

'I do declare I could not take even the smallest glass of wine,' said Harriet.

'A glass of wine and not even the smallest glass of wine,' said Knightley, lifting off two glasses from a passing waiter's tray.

'And may a mother dance?' asked Emma.

'I am afraid I have never learnt to dance.' Mr Martin joined the conversation, his face so shaved and washed as almost to dispose of his usual handsomeness.

'I remember Mr Knightley had the pleasure of standing up with Mrs Martin at our last Highbury ball,' said Emma, determined to turn the knife in her own wound.

'And would you like to stand up with me, my dear?' Knightley took her hand, held it.

'Yes,' said Emma.

A happy dance; a rest; a dance with Mr Weston; a dance with Mr Cole; Emma began to feel that the evening, which seemed to swing from difficulty to pleasure, was settling on the right side when the last dance before supper was announced and with it appeared Frank Churchill. He bowed; his blue eyes, a little inflamed, looked into hers and asked for the honour of this dance, 'Mr Beveridge's Maggot'.

'I am promised to Mr Knightley,' said Emma.

'That is odd; I am quite taken aback by that.'

'I have only danced once with Mr Knightley.'

'Of course I would understand that you would want to dance more than once with your husband; I do not dispute that; it is not my business as a mere friend – even as an *intimate* friend – to dispute that.'

'You are not my intimate friend!' Emma's heart pounded, although why he should feel such a danger in a drawing-room, surrounded by all her friends, she could not tell!

'Ah, that may be so; it is for you to say. But the reason you cannot stand up with your husband is because Mr Knightley has just led Harriet Martin to the head of the set.'

'He is sorry for her!' cried Emma, distracted. 'Mr Martin does not dance. He does not know how.'

'I do not doubt it. So will you dance with me? It is a waltz. You cannot resist a waltz. They will be off in a moment.'

'I am tired.'

'Too tired. Then let me find you a chair, a glass of water.'

'I am too hot!'

'Too hot for a chair, a glass of water? Perhaps the terrace? Perhaps a walk on the terrace. It is a beautiful evening: the stars are nearly as beautiful as the stars on your breast.'

'It is too early for stars,' Emma recovered herself a little. But a flash of Harriet's silver and blue whirling past on Knightley's arm was too much for her. She gasped and turned away.

Mr Churchill's arm led her, took her out of sight of what she most feared to see. The terrace, through doors opening from the supper room, was cool, quiet, empty and one corner of it, to which Frank led her, secluded by a bower covered with flowering wisteria. A parapet running round the edge of the terrace, which then fell steeply to lawns below, made a seat which Frank immediately took.

Later, much later, when Emma tried to imagine why she

had followed Frank, against all her instincts and judgement, to this delicate corner of spring, this lover's place, she could only think it was her need to break her silent unhappiness with a confrontation, however painful, which caused her to do something so unladylike, so foolish, so wrong. Yet at the time, she merely thought of leaving the room in which Knightley danced – worse, waltzed – with Harriet.

'This scent reminds me of Jane,' Frank spoke in a low voice.

Emma did not hear the words for a moment; but joining company with Frank did not mean that she liked him any the better. 'How can you say that!'

'I can say that because I loved her.'

'Love like yours is not worth having; it is not love; it is self-indulgence; it is fancy.'

'Emma. Why are you so cruel? You used to understand.'

'I desire you to leave Highbury.' Emma stood in front of him. 'The Westons are good people. They will look after your son. They do not deserve to be given pain – they have done you no harm; they admire you; they believe in you!'

'What is it? Why do you speak like this? You see how I have changed; how I have reformed.'

'I do not believe it—'

'Do not believe it?'

'You are too evil – I know—'

'Know what? Know that I am passionate? That I can love more deeply than most men? Know that, although I can make a woman happy – oh how happy I made Jane for a while, you cannot deny me that! – Know also that my heart beats too fast, too hard—' He stood, his handsome face filled with intensity. 'I see a beautiful woman and, where a man with a colder heart can turn his back, walk away, talk calmly of the weather, the price of corn, his land, his politics, his money, everything in me rises to the beauty I see in front of me – I rise to it like a painter rises to art, a composer to music, a – oh Emma!' He took two steps forward.

Emma looked at him with horror. He was making love to her, Mrs Knightley, in the dusky light, under the pendulous wisteria flowers, on the Coles' terrace, during a dance given for the Sucklings. It was unimaginable. It was so unimaginable that she did not move away but stared, noticing his red lips, his dilated nostrils, the slightly lowered lids over his blue eyes.

He pounced forward suddenly; one arm round her waist, the other higher on the naked flesh at her neck; his breath on her cheek, his words pouring into her ear: 'I have always known you loved me; I could not have you before – whatever you think of me, I was Jane's then – ah, Jane, the best of me died with her – but now it is different. I see how you look at me, how your colour changes when I am near. You cannot disguise it from me, you cannot deny it – you love me! You need me! You are married, yes. Yes, you are married; but I have seen you with your husband, an old man; he has not awakened your love. No! No! He is good, you will tell me, kind, a gentleman. It is true but he cannot give you what I can – Oh, Emma, do not hold yourself from me. Come, let me kiss you! Let me show you how a young man makes love!'

Nothing in Emma's experience had taught her how to deal with such a situation, with Frank's clasping hands, his hot face, his breath so close, filled with tobacco and wine. Her instinctive desire to scream and wrench herself out of his arms was immediately followed by the realisation that she was only a short distance from the supper room whose doors stood open and beyond that lay the larger chamber where, judging by the music which still played gaily in the background – which had played throughout Frank's declaration – her husband still waltzed with Harriet Martin. But this must be finished very soon and then the whole company would flow into the supper room and many, heated by their exercise, would hasten into the fresh air, provided so thoughtfully for them by Mr Cole, in conjunction with the excellent weather. If only it had rained, thought Emma wildly, she would not have found herself in such a terrible situation!

'Mr Churchill—' she began in wavering tones. Quiet sensible words could be her only armour.

'No, Emma! That will not do! This coldness does not accord with meetings on river-banks, with flushed cheeks and panting bosom, with a hand snatched from mine— !'

'You mistake me – you have mistaken me – you fill me with—' she stopped, knowing Frank enough to understand that the word she was about to use – 'disgust' would only inflame him further. 'Mr Knightley will come out any moment. Mr Weston, too, your own father—'

'You are not so sensible as this – I know it – I must have a kiss—'

That burning breath on her face again – his lips against hers – 'Please – no!'

The noise of her heart, of his heart, of their panting, his pleading, her trembling words, had blocked Emma's ears to the sound of music. She did not hear it ending. As Frank placed his lips on hers, there was a noise that seemed as loud to her as a cavalry charge and Frank was sprung from her and in a second disappeared altogether from her view. Emma stood swaying dazedly.

'You are not hurt?' Mr Knightley was at her side, although not touching her.

'No. I—'

'He has gone over the parapet.' Knightley went to the stone ledge and looked over. 'He is a little wounded, I believe, but not mortally.' His tone was dispassionate. 'The grass is too soft.'

'He—'

'We shall say he fell—' Knightley spoke more quickly because a rush of guests, following the end of the dance, had come through on to the terrace, led by Mrs Tidmarsh, Mr Cole and the Eltons. 'Go inside, and I shall deal with Mr Churchill.'

'He is not dead?' asked Emma, hardly knowing what she said.

'Unfortunately not. Go now. Stop; let me arrange your hair.' He did so, his hands businesslike about her face; and yet she could feel they shook. Emma, murmuring she knew not what, passed by Mrs Tidmarsh and the others, just as Mr Knightley's strong voice called, loud enough for everyone to hear: 'May I be of assistance, Mr Churchill? I hope you are not hurt!'

Emma hesitated a moment but the response, and living response there certainly came, was too muffled for her or anyone else to make out. Opening her fan, she went quickly to the supper table and there found a place beside Mrs Weston, as a child may find shelter beside her mother from the terrors of the world.

'Well, my dear,' Mrs Weston patted her hand, 'you are heated for one who has come from outside. Let me advise a glass of wine and water.'

Emma took the glass and drank deeply. As her composure returned she waited for the news of Frank's fall to overwhelm the happiness of the evening.

38

A society totally unused to dramatic events in its midst soon loses the power of recognising such events when they do occur. It would have been thought impossible to all at Highbury that handsome, rich, well-bred Frank Churchill (doted on by Mr Weston and his wife) should pounce on Mrs Knightley with the intention of making love to her – by force, if persuasion failed, and within reach of the respectable company gathered at the Coles' – and that, furthermore, the calm, sensible Mr Knightley would be so incensed that he should throw Mr Churchill over the wall, to the danger of his life. It was impossible; it could not have happened. They were therefore compelled to believe the only slightly more likely possibility, that a young, active man had accidentally fallen off a parapet. This story, however, came with the imprimatur of Mr Knightley – a man respected for his absolute integrity. Mr Knightley, a gentleman-landowner, a magistrate, did not lie.

So, the general happiness of the Sucklings' Ball was not dispelled. Eating, drinking continued; and after supper, three more dances were performed with as much enthusiasm as before; water still sprayed from Mr Suckling's face; Miss Bates and Mrs Suckling struck up a most happy friendship in the card room; Mrs Elton told Harriet Martin of the two new rooms she planned for the Vicarage with wallpaper especially designed; Mr Martin behaved nobly and admired his wife dancing; Elizabeth Martin and the Reverend Dugobair Tidmarsh danced once, causing some confusion by the waywardness of Mr Tidmarsh's feet, and then spent the rest of the evening in earnest conversation – if conversation exists where one speaks and the other listens. All this continued as happily as if Mr Churchill, somewhat bruised and shaken, had not been escorted to his lodgings by Mrs Weston who wished to leave early to tend to her babies; as if Mrs Tidmarsh had not elected to accompany them, suffering from a headache. This was an accident and departures, though to be deplored, were not serious enough to quench the gaiety of the occasion, already well established.

Emma, who most wished to leave, knew she could not, and waited bravely, joining herself to Miss Bates and Mrs Suckling where her silence was unnoticed in the generous flow of words. Mr Knightley did not come near her till the end.

'Our carriage is here.' He bowed. 'Miss Bates. Mr Tidmarsh is already by the door.'

Oh, what paradings must be gone through before Emma could reach her room! The endless thanks, the journey back through the still soft night – the return to Hartfield where her father sat up yet and Mrs Goddard must be sent home in the carriage – the need to offer drinks – her only relief that Philomena was not in the drawing-room, having retired to her chamber. Her eye would have been too sharp!

At last, with weary steps, Emma mounted to her bedroom and there – any further action beyond her – she sat down on an armchair and waited for what must follow. A few moments more and Mr Knightley was with her; casting a brief glance at her, he went and stood silently by the window, his face turned away. Usually so controlled and deliberate in his manner, now his fingers pulled and twitched at the hangings.

At last Emma could bear it no longer. 'Speak! Speak! Say I am a fool!'

He turned, came into the room, peered at her, and then sat heavily on her little chair at the dressing-table. 'Say you are a fool? Ah. I would not say that.' He fell silent again.

'Please!'

'You say "please".' Now he spoke with more passion. 'What should I answer? I have known for many months now that you thought you loved him – I will not say that you truly loved him because I cannot believe so ill of you; I cannot despise you as I should have to do – He is young, charming, you are young, charming – you were drawn together before, you are drawn together now – it is natural—'

'But, Knightley—'

'Emma, now I must plead with you – I can bear everything but your lies – I know that you saw him last autumn – I hoped it would pass – you would forget – I thought perhaps London, a wider society, would make you see him for what he is—'

'Believe me, Frank—'

'Don't call him that!'

'My feelings for Mr Churchill—'

'Oh!' Mr Knightley put his head in his hands.

'My feelings are not what you believe—'

'You still will not understand. I know that you saw him several times last summer – I know that he held you under the willow, beside the river at Donwell—' he lifted his head and stared wildly, 'that he held you in his arms on my land, in view of my house, the house you do not wish to live in – I am not a fool, Emma, nor can I pretend to myself, that faculty has been left out of my make-up – I know you dread being alone with me at Donwell, because you cannot love me! You wish to, I have no doubt, I do not doubt you wish that your feelings were different for me – your love for him is not a comfortable love—'

'I do not love him!'

'I repeat – you were seen – it was reported – your manner ever since would have told me if Mr Martin had not—'

'Mr Martin?'

'I did not mean to say – but what does it matter? What does anything matter?' His head was in his hands. 'I am to blame. I should not have married you. I thought you loved me – and then I thought my love was enough for both of us—'

'How can I make you understand! I felt sorry for – him – in the beginning—'

'You could have told me—'

'I planned to – Oh how I wish I had!'

'Ah, wishes – wishes after the event—'

'He was desperate; he begged me not to tell anyone; he said he would drown himself in the river—'

'And you believed that? Emma—'

'Not exactly; but he was mad, tragic – I felt sorry for him – Every day I planned to tell you – but John's sadness came—'

'You blame my brother for your secrecy?'

'No – a little; I am only trying to explain how it happened—'

'You loved him; he held you in his arms then; he held you in his arms tonight—'

'Against my will! Please, you must understand, it is true that last year I did feel sorry for him but then I did not know what he was – now, now, he *disgusts* me!'

'Such passion? *Disgusts* – it is too much. Why should such a handsome gentleman disgust. It is too much. You must moderate a little if you are to inspire belief. Disgust, like hatred, can be a part of love.'

'No. No!' Emma stood, suddenly, and ran next door; the letter from Isabella – he could see then how disgust was not a part of some degenerate love. She thrust the letter at him. 'Read, read it. Then you will see how I could not love such a man – now I could not even feel sorry for him! Read!'

Mr Knightley read. The candlelight lit up his pale features, his frowning forehead, the grey in his thick hair, the lines beside his mouth. Emma, unable to sit down quietly, hung over him, wringing her hands, pulling at her hair. He read and put down the paper on her dressing-table. 'He is worse than I had imagined.'

'How could I love such a man!'

He looked at her desperate face. He looked long before he spoke. 'No, you could not.'

'You see! You see! He attacked me. I only did not scream because of the Westons, because of you. He forced himself on me. And by the bank, he grasped at me to save himself from slipping into the water. It was but a moment.'

'Can this be true? Can all these months of agony have been for nothing?' He was utterly bowed.

'Sit with me!' cried Emma.

He came; they sat together on the bed, arms round each other, exhausted; but a little spark of hope had been lit in Knightley's breast. However, before Emma could fan it into greater life, with tender looks and caresses, it was quenched again with further remembrance.

'But why, if this is true – if he was nothing to you but an object of pity – why did you keep it secret from me for all these months? This year when he nearly burnt Donwell you must have guessed I knew, protected him for your sake – Why, even now when you received this letter from your sister, did you not show it to me? I cannot pass over these facts, Emma, much as I might wish to. Only love would explain such secrecy.'

'I should have – I know – so often I have tried – but – we

have not always been in sympathy—' There, she had said it; she had admitted that all was not quite well between them. In her mind's eyes she saw the red of Frank's lips and then Harriet Martin's white bosom that dreadful evening of the dinner at Randalls.

'Not in sympathy,' he repeated her words but rather as if he accepted them than questioned them.

'Sometimes you have not seemed to want – to be close to me—'

'Oh, Emma! Can you not understand! I thought you loved someone else, that my presence was borne as a duty rather than a pleasure. I had too much pride to force myself on you when I was not welcome. If you knew how I long—!' he stopped.

Emma was confused; these passionate looks, these hints of self-discipline. Now she must say everything. 'But do you not – I thought – Harriet Martin – so beautiful, warm, a mother, so amenable, open—'

'Harriet Martin? Why do you talk of Harriet Martin? What is Harriet Martin doing between us?'

'I imagined you admired her – you sang – you danced—'

Knightley leant back a little so that he could better see the expression on Emma's face. 'You are not joking. You think that anyone who has an Emma Woodhouse as a wife could ever look at a Harriet Martin! Your modesty astounds me! It is only that, that stops me from feeling your words are an insult. How could you believe such a thing for one second – unless, unless—' his voice changed, 'it were an excuse for your own feelings for him—'

'No! No!' Emma held him, pressed her cheek close to his, 'You must never think that again!'

'And yet there is something more to be explained,' again Knightley pushed her away and his face was grave. 'Perhaps there are many more things. You found me unsympathetic?'

'Oh, let us forget—'

'No. No. We must not. I must ask you. This – lack of sympathy – did you feel it before – he – returned to Highbury? Was it in our marriage before then?'

Emma gazed at her hands, was silent.

'Tell me. You had always looked on me more as a father, brother—'

'Not any more!'

'But it was so, for sixteen years of your life. The change to lover was sudden for you; I had loved you for so long – I knew this; I was careful, aware of the disparity in our ages – I did not wish to frighten you – you were hardly more than a child—'

'I was not a child!' interrupted Emma.

'No. No. I feel now perhaps I was wrong – oh, my dear, I was afraid to show you the depths of my love for you, my urgent need – my dearest, dearest Emma!'

Now Emma must express her love for him and he must say everything he felt for her as often as they could both enjoy the hearing. The night was dark, the night was long. Expressions of love more heartfelt than any that had been spoken between them before kept them awake for many hours. It·was as if the nineteen months that they had already passed as man and wife, with all the joy, pain, turmoil and discovery, had only been a preparation for this long night of love.

39 ∫

Rain beat on the shrubberies of Hartfield, trickled down the shiny laurel leaves and ran off the grey slate tiles of the house. Emma woke to the sound, put out her hand in the expectation of finding that Mr Knightley had gone as he always had, and found instead her fingers held in a warm grasp. She smiled.

'Now I shall leave you. But you must not stir, I shall order breakfast to be brought up. Mr Woodhouse may believe that you over-exerted yourself dancing, although I will insist you are in perfect health.'

'I am in perfect health,' murmured Emma.

She lay, eyes half-closed, as Mr Knightley, washing and dressing, creaked from her room to his and back again. He stood at the door. 'And after we have both breakfasted to our satisfaction, we will consider how best to banish a certain scoundrel bearing the name of Mr Frank Churchill, from Highbury.'

'And also, how we best may break to papa our wish to take a holiday by the sea!'

'Exactly,' said Knightley closing the door, before opening it again to demand and receive one more kiss.

The breakfast tray duly appeared on Emma's bed; with it came a letter, addressed to Mrs Knightley in Mrs Tidmarsh's ornate and unmistakable hand.

This morning Emma was capable of sustaining any surprise but nevertheless she took the precaution of fortifying herself with eggs and porridge before opening the envelope.

Dear Mrs Knightley – I address you with more formality because you may wish it and wish that it had ever been so by the time you have laid down this letter. They say 'to understand all is to forgive all' – I prefer that to the French 'Pas expliquez pas regrettez'. It is because I want you to understand, you who have been so kind to me, my benefactress – you who I admire so much – that I pick up my pen, as I sit in Miss Bates's rooms and Frank waits impatiently – Does this not tell you something of the matter already? I wish you to understand, at least a little, my pride is involved, my affection for you – that affection too deep for you to see! But I do not seek or expect forgiveness. I have never wanted that from anyone – I must live with myself as I am.

I am going away with Frank Churchill in the full certainty of becoming his wife. But do not think I have changed my mind about him – or the view I presented to you of his nature – he is and always will be an amusing scoundrel, not quite a man – Perhaps his upbringing, the sternness of Mrs Churchill taught him one thing only – how to escape his responsibilities. Perhaps you will, with your recent experience of his unthinking impetuosity still vivid, think that too kind a judgement.

But I am a much stronger character than poor Frank – I am equal to him in my determination to get my own way – in me he will find no Jane Fairfax, a sad creature by all accounts. If he should leave me in Yorkshire – however big and desolate the house, I would not pine for him – I would rejoice in my freedom. Perhaps I would take in other foundlings like myself who have the shame of their birth increased by poverty and the humiliating knowledge that only unending hard work or lucky patronage can lead to a better life.

In Mr Tidmarsh, I found that patron; he married me when I was scarcely more than a child, taught me everything I knew, took me on his travels throughout Europe – but, oh, Emma! I cannot speak of it without offending you, you whose heart is as pure as a lily, as pure as mine was when he plucked me – let us merely say that he was not as I painted him to you – a loving old man – he was a harsh, cruel despot who has left his mark on both myself and his son. But enough of that. Dugobair is a good, true man, he will make Miss Martin a good, true husband. I can never be such; it is too late for me. I cannot live by my harp alone. I am tired; soon I will be old. I will never find another man who will take me on – or at least another man who I could bear to live with. You must understand that, although man and wife, my relationship with Frank will soon become, I trust – I shall work for it – more that of an older sister – a very tolerant older sister.

Dear Mrs Knightley – I revert again to that title – you must rejoice in having found one of the few gentleman in England, probably in Europe, who is good, handsome, tolerably rich (although you must watch his propensity to dispense with his land!) and adores you! Judge me, if you like, but compare our situations first. Since childhood you have had every kindness, every material comfort – indeed you have been placed on a pedestal by all who knew you. You may say you lacked the love of a mother, but I had neither mother nor father nor any being to give me anything beyond a miserable existence. Mr Tidmarsh brought me music – I owe him gratitude for that – he gave me the means for some independence, independence of spirit.

I will always be a free woman, an independent woman – my fate has made me that. Whatever I have, I have earned, and I have earned the right to Frank Churchill and Enscombe! You will have divined that love is not a great part of my feeling for him – I may not love him, although I enjoy his company more than you would like – but then he is incapable of true love. I hold him for a moment, captured, mesmerised, entangled in the strings of my harp – a moment that is enough to change my life! Think what it means for a foundling to become mistress of a great estate!

It is strange that I, like Jane Fairfax, my tender, tragic predecessor, will leave, as if abandoned, a musical instrument in dear Miss Bates' apartment (never underestimate the determination of that lady, my dear) – but unlike the first Mrs Churchill's ill-fated pianoforte, it will not stay there long. I shall make arrangements for it to be sent to Yorkshire as soon as I am settled – at first we will be abroad – Ah, Emma, Mrs Knightley, how do I return your hospitality! You must let your papa think ill of me, it will relieve his feelings. And yet perhaps I have opened your eyes a little to ideas beyond the confines of Highbury – that is not such a bad present to leave behind – Adieu! Farewell! I must go! – Frank pulls at my arm – the sun rises – Oh, Emma!—

When Knightley returned to the bedroom, he was surprised to find Emma still undressed. She picked up the letter and holding it out to him, spoke in a flat voice. 'Philomena has gone from Highbury with Frank Churchill. I cannot credit it; she has written her reasons; they are all mercenary. She will be very disappointed when she discovers the truth – Mr Churchill disinherited and as penniless as she.' Her voice changed, 'Oh, how could she! My friend!'

'Let me read.'

'Mr Tidmarsh assured me she had no interest in acquiring a husband or else I would have warned her more fully of Mr Churchill's bad character – and the punishment he had brought on himself must have come out in the course of our conversation.'

Mr Knightley read the letter; he put it down and sighed, 'Poor lady – she makes a sad case for herself. And now to be married to Frank Churchill, and Frank Churchill poor! I cannot think to be a teacher of the harp for the rest of her life would be a worse fate!'

'How could she go like that – under the cover of darkness, secretly – like runaways? They were both free; they had no need to behave like that!'

Mr Knightley sat on the bed. 'I must tell you, my dear, that, if Frank had not fled in the night, this morning I had decided to reveal his true character. He had masqueraded long enough. It were better the Westons were hurt now than suffer even more deeply later. Mr Churchill is one of those beings who bring nothing but misery, under the guise of good nature and charm. I was determined that he should leave Highbury and never return again. Even his son would be better without him; so I thought and so I still believe.'

'Oh, if you knew how I feared for the baby!' interrupted Emma.

'Indeed, my dear.' He held her hand before continuing. 'Mr Churchill would have guessed my intentions. He fled ahead of discovery.'

Emma pushed away the bedclothes as if to get up and then hesitated. 'I cannot feel sorry for her.'

Mr Knightley smiled. 'She is not asking for pity. Perhaps, indeed, she may be clever enough to steer Mr Churchill back to his uncle. It may not be too late for a reconciliation. Come, we cannot live others' lives for them. Until now, we have found it hard enough to manage our own. Today is a day for happiness!'

With such encouragement, with more affection, Mr Knightley diverted Emma's thoughts from the hurt of disloyalty so that they might enjoy the comforts of each other's company with all the perfection they had won the night before.

Side by side, they descended to the morning-room where together they must break news that must astonish, discompose and sadden all at Hartfield, Randalls, and the wider environment of Highbury and Donwell.

Not long ago, the task facing Emma – to own that her confidante and guest had abused her trust and snatched the gentleman who was still the scion of all hearts (at least those ignorant of his true nature) in Highbury – would have been beyond her. But the events of the last year had strengthened her. John Knightley's downfall had taught Emma about the possibility of misfortune – nearly tragedy – within her family circle which she had previously considered inviolate. She had learnt about the price of pride from Harriet's elevation and her own jealousy. She no longer felt omnipotent because she recognised she could only partly understand another and that her judgement would never be the whole truth. Above all, she had discovered the humility to give others permission to live outside her head.

This improvement in Emma's nature combined with Mr Knightley's love which, although stalwart as ever, no longer tried to protect her as a child, stood her in good stead during the difficult days that followed the elopement of Mr Churchill and Mrs Tidmarsh. She did not gloss the facts or evade them. She sympathised with the Westons – cast down with grief, although the abundance of small children needing attention allowed them little time for concentration on Mr Churchill's second concealed liaison. She accompanied Mr Tidmarsh to the Martins so that they should not consider the stepson tarred by the brush of the stepmother – nor did they, for Elizabeth Martin was so determined to be an erudite vicar's wife in London that nothing would have stopped her. Emma informed the Eltons of the news with a set face and only wished that the Sucklings had chosen any other time to visit for she could imagine how their gossip would spread about Bath and Bristol.

She was calm, she was gracious, and at the end of the week was rewarded by Mr Knightley saying, 'I think there is no need now for me to besmirch Mr Churchill's reputation as far as the truth. He has admitted his guilt by fleeing; I feel quite certain that he will not dare return and soon nobody will regret his absence.'

Emma was glad to acknowledge the truth of this. No news had been received from him, no news was wanted. And yet she did have regrets. Hesitantly, she opened her heart to Knightley as they sat on the white bench under the beech tree.

'I miss Philomena.'

'You miss Philomena!' Mr Knightley smiled in his astonishment.

'I do not want her back, of course I do not, after what she has done, but I miss her conversation, her liveliness, her education, the ideas she taught me to think about, the books—'

'The books are still here.'

'Unopened. I know. I have no concentration for them, no one to talk to about them – In truth, I find them quite dull—'

'Oh, Emma, give me your hand.' She did so. 'Do you think it is time we went to the seaside? Is that what you are leading to? You are afraid of becoming bored.'

'It is more serious than the seaside.'

'More serious than green waves and white birds. My dear, I am terrified!'

'No. No. It is what we have promised ourselves but I want it to happen now, before the apples are swelling on the trees. I cannot live at Hartfield any more because papa—' she took a breath, 'because papa, however dear to me, is a selfish old gentleman and uses my love for him as a weapon to keep me near him, his daughter for ever. I must take up my own life, make my own occupation, as others do. I understand now that Frank Churchill, Mrs Tidmarsh, even Harriet Martin, were all diversions from what should have been my real path. I am ashamed it has taken me so long to see it.'

'You should not feel ashamed. I have never blamed you.'

'But that is because you love me. My independence will lie in running Donwell, in opening up the great old house again, in caring for the gardens, in reading the books in the Donwell library. It is strange but it was as I started missing Philomena that I realised this. Tomorrow morning I want to go to Donwell Abbey with you!'

'You are autocratic!'

'Do not make fun of me. I wish to go with you and I wish to go on horseback.'

'Now I shall have to make fun of you for, as I know well, you have never learnt to ride.'

'I shall begin tomorrow,' said Emma earnestly, with the sort of beguiling look that would have melted a heart far harder than Knightley's.

'What if it should rain?'

'I shall still go.'

40 ∫

It did not rain. A brisk bright day saw Emma in a habit borrowed from Augusta Elton (smelling of mothballs since her Maple Grove days) setting out from Hartfield on a horse borrowed from Mr Weston, and led by Mr Knightley with James walking in attendance.

Mr Woodhouse, standing at the door with Miss Bates supporting him, seemed speechless with horror, although whether it was horror at his daughter's foolhardiness or his own at remaining outside for so long without hat or top coat, was not clear.

It is a tribute to the power of the human mind that it may shape and colour the inanimate according to mood and attitude. On the morning that Emma and Mr Knightley visited Donwell Abbey, Emma saw no dark corners, long tables, heavy panelling or unwanted ghosts. It was a warm, golden place, whose antiquity made it mellow and welcoming rather than overpowering. Her hand in Knightley's, she was struck by the perfectly extraordinary fact that she had never paced the stone corridors or walked up the oak staircase, with only Knightley at her side.

As a child, Donwell had been beyond her limits, as a married woman, it had been poisoned for her by the lurking presence of Frank and the too close threat of

Harriet Martin's supposed perfection. This visit was a new experience – they both felt that.

Nor did the excited arrival of Mrs Hodges, the house-keeper, who was woman enough to guess at once what this quiet inspection presaged, lessen Emma's confidence in the future she could now foretell for herself.

They moved into the gardens – as splendidly arrayed in pink and lilac and yellow and white as any bridal festoon. The trees were freshly green, the lawns smooth as new carpeting and only a fear of anticipation being the enemy to fulfilment, hindered Emma from sharing with Knightley an imagined picture of children – their children – at least four or five of them (two boys and three girls, she thought) – running merrily across the grass. She contented herself with a single sentence, 'It is a place for a family to live.'

In such perfect happiness, there remained one matter yet to be settled; its shadow could not be long or dark where there was so much decision, but nevertheless it must be broached. 'I believe we should tell papa of our plans, as soon as ever I have a glass of Madeira and water in my hand,' said Emma, placing an early rosebud in Mr Knightley's lapel, 'because I certainly will not be able to disguise for very long that my whole heart is turned towards Donwell.'

Mr Knightley being in uncomplicated agreement – his kindness to his father-in-law had none of the guilty fervour foisted on the daughter – there only remained the need for an appropriate moment. To Emma's chagrin, for at first she accused herself of cowardice, this did not present itself for some days; either there were callers or social occasions which could not be avoided – for the Sucklings' prolonged visit continued to be the excuse for many festivities – or her father was indisposed or, curiously, for no very good reason, unavailable, even to the extent of being absent from his habitual chair at the habitual times. When he was in the drawing-room, Miss Bates, as generously attentive as ever, made it impossible for Emma to conduct a private conversation.

After a full week had passed, Emma was both impatient and bewildered. 'I do believe papa is determined to avoid my company!' she cried to Knightley one night in their bedroom. 'I can hardly credit such a possibility but this night I saw him hide from me behind the door of the parlour and then scurry away when I had passed!'

Mr Knightley laughed. 'Perhaps he does not want to hear your news! Or perhaps he has a secret himself.'

'Papa, a secret! Fie, Mr Knightley. You must keep your imagination under more control!'

Eventually, Emma gave up calm rational waiting and determined on direct action combined with cunning. The next morning she saw Miss Bates lead out Mr Woodhouse for his daily walk to the shrubberies, and she immediately joined them.

'What a very fine day!' she cried, eyes bright. 'I cannot hang over my accounts another moment.'

'A very fine day – how true!' echoed Miss Bates, who, Emma noticed somewhat to her surprise, had her bonnet trimmed with a frill that was nearer pink than old-maidenly mauve.

'I think the wind a little cool – not quite trustworthy, indeed a most untrustworthy wind,' said Mr Woodhouse, glancing anxiously from one lady to the other. 'Perhaps I shall go inside—'

'No! No!' exclaimed both ladies at once and, taking an arm on either side, they set off down the gravel path.

Direct action having succeeded, it now only remained for Emma to put into practice cunning. 'Oh dear! she began. 'Oh, Miss Bates, I have forgotten a message for Sterne.'

The words were scarcely out of her mouth before Miss Bates had dropped Mr Woodhouse's arm – after giving it a most intimate and meaning squeeze, which Emma could

hardly avoid noticing – and had positively run back to the
house, leaving behind her a trail of, 'So pleased to help –
father and daughter – a fine day – an excellent day!'

She had not, Emma recollected, heard the message for
Cook but as it was a perfectly unnecessary instruction about
raspberry jelly, that was of no consequence at all. At last she
could break the news to her father!

'Dear papa – I have been trying to talk to you—'

'Oh! Oh!' His face was alarmed, pale, quivering.

Emma hardened her heart. 'Mr Knightley has been living
here with us as my husband for too long!'

'Oh! Oh!'

'Now, papa, we shall sit down on the white bench and I
shall tell you calmly—'

'The white bench, you say? My dear – the damp—'

'You are right, not the bench. We will walk.' Emma's
sense of urgency was increased by seeing, as they turned,
Miss Bates appear at a window, although she seemed to
be gesticulating towards her bosom, rather than making
any attempt to rejoin them. 'I have something to tell you.
My mind is made up. You shall have a room, two rooms,
three rooms – Donwell is quite big enough—' Carried away
by her brave telling, Emma did not at first notice that Mr
Woodhouse was also trying to speak.

'My dear – Emma – I, also—'

'So you will not be too upset if we close Hartfield and
remove to Donwell? Dearest papa, you have always desired
my happiness—'

'Oh, no. No. It would not do at all.' Mr Woodhouse shook
his head. 'Close Hartfield. Oh, no, no!'

'But papa!' Suddenly Emma was near tears, a child
again.

'My dear – you do not understand – there is no reason to
close Hartfield – I also have news for you – perhaps you will
not be surprised – Miss Bates feels sure you have suspected

these many months, although at my age, I would never have suspected – your dear mother – happiness – Oh!'

'Papa? Tell me, what are you trying to say?'

'Miss Bates has done me the honour of accepting my invitation to become the second Mrs Woodhouse.'

Emma, speechless, stared at her father who wore a glowing look of pride, modesty and a little shy pleasure at making an announcement which could cause his clever daughter so much amazement.

'I told Miss Bates you would be taken aback. I had been a little nervous, I must confess, of breaking it to you. But now you see why I need not move from Hartfield. I shall have a wife.'

Emma, still struck dumb, also saw why he had been avoiding her and could now understand all Miss Bates' recent cheerful humour and particularly the pink frill. She was seeing herself as a bride.

'I have written to Isabella already but the letter is not yet sent. She will be pleased, I believe, at seeing me happy.' Now the expression was a slightly contradictory mix of complacency and pleading.

'Yes, papa,' stumbled out Emma. 'Your happiness has always been our first thought.'

'And now you will not have to think so hard,' said Mr Woodhouse and this time complacency had definitely won the majority of his features.

Emma's amazement continued. Yet Mr Woodhouse was not in his dotage, however he might on occasion pretend to be, and Miss Bates was a respectable vicar's daughter, even though lack of financial backing had made her play a humbler role in society. But since John Knightley's downfall, money and position no longer meant so much to Emma that she could see them stand in the way of happiness. If she had been able to believe Miss Bates a selfish, scheming sort of woman, she would never have been able to approve of the matter, although it were beyond her power to halt it. But she knew Miss Bates was a good, true woman, properly attached to her father and his family and – whatever scheming she had employed (Emma remembered Mrs Tidmarsh's advice not to underestimate Miss Bates) – it had led to an outcome which would be of benefit to all, and most particularly to herself.

Mr Knightley, although nearly as thunderstruck as his wife, felt these benefits at once and added another. 'Since Miss Bates must be considered, despite a penchant for pink frills, past the age of bearing children, we may be sure that little Henry Knightley, although supplanted from Donwell, may inherit Hartfield. All in all I can only commend Mr Woodhouse and Miss Bates for acting with excellent good sense.'

There were now three marriages to be talked of in Highbury. One of course was presumed to have already taken place, although nothing was known of Frank Churchill and Mrs Tidmarsh beyond a brief note to Mr Weston in which he was presumed to have announced his intentions. From that day, Mr Weston, usually so fulsomely loquacious on the subject of his son, never raised his name in public again.

The second marriage was to be held in June, between the Reverend Dugobair Tidmarsh and Miss Elizabeth Martin. The awkwardness that might have risen over Mr Tidmarsh's unfortunate connection with such a disreputable lady as Philomena Tidmarsh was much diminished by his seeming utterly unaware of any difficulty. His only comment on her sudden departure, made to Mr Martin and overheard by Emma, was, 'Quem Jupiter vult perdere dementat prius.' But, since he did not translate, it made no one any the wiser. He was indeed radiant with happiness, impatient only for the marriage to be over so that he could take his bride back to London where she could light up the dark

corners of St Peter's. Already, it was established that Mrs Martin's wedding present would be an excellent pianoforte in just the same style as her own.

The third marriage, as was to be expected, caused far more comment than the other two. Ford's shop saw a daily gathering of scandalised ladies amongst whom the voices of Mrs Elton and the happy couple's dear friend, Mrs Goddard, were the loudest. But what cannot be altered must be accepted and soon there was a general prediction that a marriage made for reasons of comfort rather than any romantic attachment may be as likely to succeed when the participants are approaching the end of their lives than if they still have many years in front of them.

'To be sure, they will not have time to get tired of each other,' was Mrs Elton's generous comment, after she and Mr Elton had enjoyed a fine dinner at Hartfield, over which wedding arrangements had been discussed.

Emma's remaining anxiety was Miss Bates' desire to give Isabella pleasure by having all her children (or those that could walk) as attendants at the ceremony. Believing Isabella's disappointment would be much less than Miss Bates' if this did not take place, and determined to avoid a scene that could only be ridiculous, Emma encouraged Mr Woodhouse to arrange a wedding so quickly that Henry and John could not be retrieved from school and only Isabella and her husband might attend.

The marriage took place; Miss Bates said 'I do' three times and threw her bouquet in the direction of Mrs Goddard – a triumphant frivolity Emma had not been able to curb. Now there was nothing to stop Emma and Mr Knightley from beginning their new life at Donwell Abbey.

It was early summer; long months of nature's most benefi-cent weather lay ahead. Each new day found Emma more content, more grateful for her contentment.

The morning after Elizabeth Martin and the Reverend Dugobair Tidmarsh's marriage – following which an elegant reception had been held in Harriet Martin's even further extended dining-room – Emma looked at her husband across their own breakfast table. 'I have seldom seen such a joyful conjunction of two good people, about which I can only foretell happiness; yet – oh, Knightley! – for myself, I would rather climb a mountain in a hair shirt than progress again through the first year or two of marriage!'

Mr Knightley smiled and then looked grave. 'I would agree with your sentiment, exactly, my dear, were it not for one part of your declaration that I resolutely refute.'

'Oh!' – she held her toast outside her mouth, surprised at his tone.

'Who is this "Knightley" you address? He sounds to me like an old man due, indeed overdue, for retirement! Besides, I remember a promise—'

'Knightley? – A promise? I take your meaning—' her face too became grave, 'oh, George, dearest George!'

'Now I am in complete accordance with you.'

'Yet I could wish yours were a less royal name for I do not wish to be your courtier!'

'I wish you to be nothing less than who you are.'

'And who is that, may I inquire?' But the eyes were too bright, the face too inviting for Knightley to find the time to explain. With a shocking disregard for the servants, the toast rack and his cup of coffee, which went flying across the table, he dashed round and swept Emma into his arms with all the passion of the youngest and most ardent of lovers.